Understanding
Child Development
0–8 Years

3rd Edition

Jennie Lindon

Dedication
To my family – thank you for everything.

Orders: please contact Bookpoint Ltd, 130 Milton Park, Abingdon, Oxon OX14 4SB.
Telephone: (44) 01235 827720. Fax: (44) 01235 400454. Lines are open from 9.00–5.00,
Monday to Saturday, with a 24-hour message answering service. You can also order
through our website **www.hoddereducation.co.uk**

British Library Cataloguing in Publication Data
A catalogue record for this title is available from the British Library

ISBN: 978 1 4441 6718 4

This Edition Published 2012
Impression number   10 9 8 7 6 5 4 3 2 1
Year   2015, 2014, 2013, 2012

Hachette UK's policy is to use papers that are natural, renewable and
recyclable products and made from wood grown in sustainable forests.
The logging and manufacturing processes are expected to conform to the
environmental regulations of the country of origin.

Cover photo © pressmaster – Fotolia

Typeset by Pantek Media.
Printed in Italy for Hodder Education, An Hachette UK Company, 338 Euston Road,
London NW1 3BH.

Contents

Acknowledgements to the third edition

I am grateful to a large number of college tutors, early years managers, practitioners and advisory teams for their ideas and perspectives over many years. I appreciate the more recent contact with the growing networks for practitioners with Early Years Professional status. My thanks go to many colleagues on the informal early years network, for conversations that have explained and provided valuable follow-up ideas. Particular thanks to Peter Elfer (University of Surrey at Roehampton), Sally Featherstone (Opitus), Laura Henry (Childcare Consultancy), Penny Munn (University of Strathclyde), Iram Siraj-Blatchford (Institute of Education), Penny Tassoni (Early Years Consultant), and my fellow members of the 'What Matters To Children' team.

On the family front, my thanks to Tanith and Drew Lindon for permission to quote from the informal diaries that I kept of them as young children. I appreciated Drew's help with the section from page 50–51. My thanks also go to Lance Lindon for sharing insights from the occupational psychology area.

I also continue to learn a very great deal by watching children, listening to them and happily accepting an invitation to join them in play. They are the real judges of a sensible link between theory and practice.

Finally, I take the usual responsibility for this book, the ideas within it and any unintended errors. If you spot mistakes or misunderstandings, please let me know and I will correct them as soon as possible.

Every effort has been made to trace the copyright holders of material reproduced here. The authors and publishers would like to thank the following for permission to reproduce copyright photographs:

All photos © Andrew Callaghan, except:

Figures: 2.02 © Marka/SuperStock; 2.03 © Bettmann/Corbis; 2.04 © Ted Streshinsky/Corbis; 2.05 © The Archives of the British Psychoanalytic Society have granted us kind permission to reproduce this photograph; 3.05 © Kzenon/Fotolia. 7.02c, 7.04, 8.01, 10.04, 10.05 © Justin O'Hanlon.

A focus on early childhood

This opening chapter addresses some key issues around the need to understand children, how they generally develop and why a sound grasp of child development is so crucial. Theory and practice need to go hand in hand, but the term 'theory' does not have the same meaning for everyone.

The main sections in this chapter are:
- What, how and why in child development
- Reflective and knowledgeable practitioners.

What, how and why in child development

Young children are best supported by adults who really care about the well being of individual babies and children. That commitment comes alive when early years practitioners, and parents too, have a sound basis of child development knowledge, leading to accurate expectations. Of course, practitioners need plenty of ideas for what to do within a day, although those ideas need to be closely related to what currently interests children. There are many practical sections in the book but, overall, it is less of a book about 'what you can do' and much more about 'think about what you do'.

Why do practitioners need to know about theory?

Studies of children and their development have included not only what happens as babies and children grow, but also attempts to explain why and how development unfolds. The different broad theories of child development aim to show what is most important in that process.

Practitioners need a grasp of the range of theories that have been proposed to explain child development. Otherwise, it is easy to assume that one or two approaches they encounter make up the whole span. Current theories are communicated to parents through advice about parenting and childcare books. Theory shapes educational philosophy and practice for school. In different decades, a dominant theory can become part of the 'cultural wallpaper' and then basic assumptions are less likely to be challenged. By the start of the 21st century, the sociocultural, or social constructivist, view (page 49), has become prominent in early childhood studies and application to practice. There is much to value in this approach, but it is not the only way to explain child development or best approaches to good practice.

Different disciplines and understanding development

Ideas about child development have been influenced, directly or in a roundabout route, by several disciplines within the social and natural sciences: especially psychology, sociology, biology, medicine and philosophy.

Over several centuries, many advice books for parents were written by medical doctors, often from their experience as general practitioners or paediatricians. Only in more recent decades have developmental psychologists been acknowledged as the people to ask about children. The natural sciences have played a significant role, not least because some of the recognisable 'big' names were not developmental psychologists at the outset. Jean Piaget (page 33) was a zoologist with a passion for studying marine life and the philosophy of knowledge. Piaget wanted to find a link between the two disciplines and decided to further his ideas by studying the development of human children. His wife Valentine, another psychologist, made most of the early observations and the rest, as they say, is history. Piaget was working on his ideas through the 1920s and 30s in Switzerland. At the same time, Lev Vygotsky (page 37) was working in Russia. Vygotsky, a doctor, wanted to bring together biology and the fledgling science of psychology.

After the middle of the 20th century, boundaries between the disciplines became increasingly blurred. The 1960s' wave of 'new universities' in the UK took the radical step of bringing academic subjects together within 'schools of study'. This change created a large group of graduates (myself included) who regarded it as perfectly normal to talk regularly with people from other disciplines. My undergraduate degree was an early 'blend' subject, social psychology, and I worked alongside students of sociology, history, geography, economics, philosophy and a few biologists. The experience left me wanting to remain a psychologist, but open-minded about the source of potential good ideas.

Make the connection with... Social constructivism

Towards the end of the 20th century, social constructivism grew to dominate early childhood studies as the theory of choice. This theoretical position is a conscious blend of several different disciplines (page 49). But this melting-pot approach to ideas is relatively new in terms of the social history reflected in this chapter.

Psychology has strongly influenced early years in terms of the theoretical background to what is viewed as good practice. For a long time, sociocultural context was regarded as irrelevant in mainstream psychological research about children, as well as adults. More accurately, the particular sociocultural context of the Western hemisphere, especially Europe and the United States of America, was taken as the template for 'normal'. Developmental psychology traditionally focused more on individual children than the social context. There was a working assumption that what was observed, or posed in theory, was applicable to a 'universal child'. Some exploration was undertaken through cross-cultural psychology, a discipline that built bridges with anthropology.

Figure 1.1 Is there such a thing as a 'universal child'?

By the late 1960s it was recognised that an excessive proportion of psychological 'knowledge' was based on experiments involving rats, psychology undergraduates and members of the US armed forces, all of whom were under pressure to participate. Feminist reworking of psychology from the 1970s and 80s challenged a discipline what was had frequently operated as if male behaviour formed the template for what was considered to be normal. Social psychology formed a bridge to sociology, a subject traditionally more interested in social structures, with individuals in the background. Sociology has diversified and some sociologists developed a strong interest in family experience and the sociology of childhood.

The natural sciences continue to be important for how we understand young children. Sources from biology have informed exploration of sex differences in behaviour and some aspects of children's play. Biological psychology has developed as a separate discipline. Neuroscience and advances in computer technology have pushed the boundaries of research into brain development during childhood and through the adult years (page 62).

Holistic development or separate areas?

When you watch and listen to children it is very clear that they do not divide up their development. They move seamlessly from using their communication skills to question and speculate, using their physical skills to move from place to place and their thinking skills to work out how to assemble the materials they need to create a secret den. Children do not have a problem with holistic development: all aspects of their current skills work together with meaningful connections. Nor do children assign different values to the varied aspects of their learning. However, young girls and boys grasp very quickly if adults clearly value some skill areas or activities more than others.

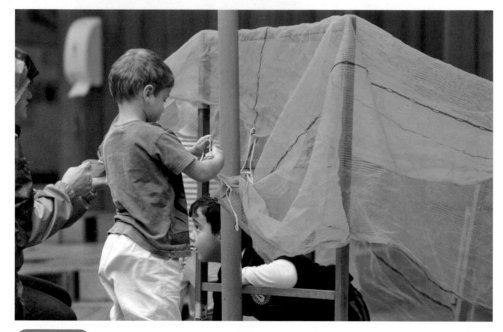

Figure 1.2 Children use their thinking skills to work out how to assemble a den

Anyone involved with children, for reasons of theory, research or practice, needs to keep a firm hold on holistic development. However, there will sometimes be a good reason to focus on one aspect of development at the moment.

- Researchers may narrow their focus to concentrate on one aspect of development in great detail. But useful applied research looks for the interconnections. Judy Dunn's work (page 166) was valuable because she challenged the assumption that it made sense to look at children's cognitive development without the vital emotional context.
- Practitioners sometimes need to concentrate on a particular aspect of a child's development; for instance, confidence in physical skills, because careful observation shows that the child needs focused help.

Early years guidance frameworks across the UK offer slightly different structures for areas of development. However, the consistent message is that the objective of describing the different areas is to ensure that no area is overlooked, nor deemed to be less important. The challenge for good practice, and the task of a reflective practitioner, is to ensure that adult understanding of development is not stuck in 'separate boxes'. An effective early years practitioner has to return frequently to an accurate picture of the whole child.

What does it mean?

Development: the sequence of physical and psychological changes experienced by human beings, which start with conception and continue throughout life.

A **holistic** or **whole-child** approach stresses the importance of thinking about and behaving towards children as entire individuals: all their different skills are important and support their whole development.

Growth: the physical changes over childhood and adolescence, both those visible from the outside and internal changes.

Learning: the process by which patterns of human behaviour are modified by experience.

To take a different example, a more holistic approach through health psychology has shown that children's physical well being cannot be separated from the rest of their development. Early psychological approaches to chronic illness treated children as if they were isolated individuals, reacting passively to their illness. However, a more rounded and less medical approach has shown the connections between mind and body, for children as well as for adults.

- A child's illness affects her emotional well being, but the impact is two-way. A depressed or frightened child copes less well with illness and medical intervention.
- Young children try to make sense of what is happening to them. In the absence of explanation and information, children may decide that their illness or need for surgery has been somehow caused by their 'bad' behaviour. Children use their cognitive skills to build a theory around the 'why' of a distressing experience. However, their limited knowledge of how the world works leaves them vulnerable to accepting blame for an event that was out of their control.
- Chronic illness or disability can affect family relationships and disrupt friendships, because children spend time in hospitals or ill at home. Children often need as much support for their social network as dealing with medical symptoms.

Figure 1.3 Physical skills also involve intellectual judgement

The balance between nature and nurture

A basic question asked about children is whether their development is determined by a pattern laid down before they were born, or whether children's reactions are the result of later experiences. This question sets the influence of nature (inborn reactions, heredity) in contrast with nurture (the impact of experience, their environment). The first answer is that child development is not as simple as 'So, is it nature or nurture?' Children's development is influenced by their genetic inheritance, including how young brains develop. But there is ample evidence that direct experiences work on that biological base, even before birth, and certainly from the earliest days of infancy.

What does it mean?

Nature: a term used to mean all the influences that are separate from the impact of experience.

Biological programming: the basic materials with which babies are born, including how their brains work and body chemistry.

Nurture: a term used to mean all the influences, other than genetics and biological programming. In this context 'nurture' is contrasted with 'nature'.

Experience: what happens to babies and children, either through their direct action, or how they are treated by other people and how social circumstances affect them through their carers' behaviour.

Environment: usually means the physical features of the location in which children are raised, but is sometimes used interchangeably with experience.

No sensible psychologist or biologist talks any more in blunt 'either or' terms about genetic and environmental factors, unless there is a well-supported causal explanation of a specific disability or chronic health condition. Patterns laid down through biological programming are only the beginning of the story of child development. Behaviour genetics is a relatively new area of research and studies have suggested that there is a genetic element in such varied areas as body shape, some aspects of cognitive problem solving, reading disability, extreme antisocial behaviour and variations in temperament. This approach explores genetics as a possible explanation and talks about probabilities but not certainties.

Computer imaging technology has allowed detailed study of the functioning of the brain. However, there is still a great deal we do not know about brain development, and a growing range of misinterpretations. For instance, responsible early years and school practice should be very alert to any differences in how boys and girls experience provision, or achieve against the current standards. However, many of the confident claims about sex differences in early brain development do not stand up to scrutiny. Lise Eliot (2009) concludes from a substantial review that any sex differences in brain functioning or structure are very small, and further studies often do not replicate the initial findings. However, Eliot points out that some small differences in development, such as girls starting to speak, on average, slightly earlier than boys, have an impact on daily experience. Persistent adult beliefs about 'typical' behaviour for boys or girls affect children's experiences, which are laid down in neural connections.

Figure 1.4 Is there such a thing as 'typical' behaviour for boys or girls?

Two periods in the lives of children seem to be especially influenced by biological programming: the first year of life and puberty. At both of these times, babies and then adolescents experience substantial physical changes that happen without conscious effort on their part. However, even these powerful internal forces can be further shaped by the environment.

Babies do not have to be taught to use their limbs, to crawl or walk; they naturally develop all the skills they possess. Yet malnutrition and severe restrictions on movement can limit babies' physical skills, as a result of ill health and lack of necessary practice. However, even serious deprivation does not have the same impact on all babies. Studies of very poor practice in understaffed residential nurseries in the 1940s and 50s produced distressing descriptions of babies in despair, who lay silent in their cots all day. Yet, other babies, less than a year old, were trying again and again to climb out of their cot and attract attention.

Around the world, young people experience puberty at some time between nine and sixteen years of age. The exact timing of the onset is largely caused by individual biological programming. But puberty can be delayed by a restricted diet and a great deal of physical exercise. The childlike appearance of some female gymnasts in the 1980s was created by extremely vigorous training programmes, which have since been described as abusive. In the first half of the 20th century, the average age of onset for puberty decreased in the Western hemisphere. The main reasons for this decrease seem to have been the result of a less physically active lifestyle for many children, combined with their consuming sufficient food for physical needs.

Reflective and knowledgeable practitioners

The last years of the 20th century and the first decade of the 21st century brought many changes to early years and school practice within the four nations that comprise the UK. Some developments and initiatives have been very welcome, not least the recognition that early childhood is so very important. However, UK society often still values very young children for what they will become and is inclined to be less interested in who they are at the moment. Ignorance about early child development, combined with significant pressures to provide economic value, has sometimes created a kind of educational bullying that risks derailing good practice with young children.

Being on the side of young children

Even experienced early years practitioners have sometimes been made to doubt the value of what they do and have felt a sense of headlong rush to move children at speed through crucial early skills and experiences. Early years practitioners need to find, sometimes rediscover, the sense of professional competence and knowledge that promotes the well being of children. The foundation for such confidence has to be knowledge about child development. What are realistic expectations for young children? Early years practitioners also need to gain the theoretical framework that supports such understanding.

The adults who are most helpful to children are willing and able to reflect on what they do. Practitioners (and parents too) need to see themselves as people who make choices and could therefore sometimes change how they react. In the professional sphere, this approach is called being a reflective practitioner and this description has a lot in common with the outlook of being a lifelong learner. This book addresses questions of 'What do we know about child development?' and 'What is the basis for our confidence about this knowledge?' Thoughtful practitioners are ready to consider 'How do I think about children?' and 'Are there alternative, maybe better perspectives?'

Practitioners who think they know everything are a hazard to children. When you are willing to reflect, you can learn, and that behaviour models a positive outlook for children. Finding scope for improvement is not necessarily a criticism of what has gone before; it can be much more about 'Let's try another approach here' and 'If I'm honest, I'd lost sight of …'. The many aspects to developing as a reflective practitioner are explored in Lindon (2012c).

Figure 1.5 Busy children will learn in many different ways

What does it mean?

Reflective practitioner: an outlook for early years, and other professionals, in which you are ready to think as well as to act and to explore the reasons behind practical ideas and approaches.

What is meant by 'theory'?

The word 'theory' is used in rather different ways and it is important to be clear about its meaning in the context in which it is used. In early years, playwork or school practice, the word is not always used in the more academic sense, which is discussed later in this section. For instance, within the early years profession, the term 'theory' is often used to mean the ideas behind what is proposed as good practice. Sometimes this reference to conceptual understanding is called a 'theoretical perspective'. You may also encounter the word 'theory' applied to what I would call descriptive information about child development. In that context, 'theory' refers to any idea that is not an activity to do with young children.

Different working definitions for 'theory' are not a problem, provided that it is clear which definition is applicable right now. In this book, I cover the more academic theories of child development in Chapters 2 and 3. Throughout the book different theoretical perspectives are covered that can inform, and sometimes improve, practice day by day with children. I do not apply the word 'theory' to descriptions of how children develop over the months and years. It is, however, a crucial area of knowledge, if practitioners are to operate with realistic expectations of babies and young children.

What does it mean?

Theory of child development: a set of ideas proposed to explain how children develop and sometimes also to predict what will happen under certain circumstances.

Theoretical perspective: a particular angle on making sense of events or experiences.

Key concept: an idea, arising from a theory or theoretical perspective, which can be used to shape practice, including aiding reflection.

Theory and academic practice

In the social sciences, a theory is a framework incorporating a set of ideas or principles that is used to guide the collection and interpretation of facts. Theories are sometimes developed from observations as the theorist strives to make sense of information that is already available. In a strict scientific definition, a theory should then generate clear-cut predictions that can be tested through research under controlled conditions. New information is gathered and interpreted so as to prove or disprove the theory.

What does it mean?

Theory: the word broadly means a set of ideas about experiences or events. 'Theory' and 'theorists' can take on different meanings in practice.

Research: this word broadly means finding out about experiences and events. Researchers use a variety of methods (see Chapter 4). Some research plans rest upon theory.

In reality, life is not that simple. Many theories within social science are not amenable to being proved one way or another, certainly not in the way meant by the physical sciences. Some limitations are properly placed by ethical considerations. But all theorists and researchers also operate within a time and place. The main theories covered in Chapters 2 and 3 only make full sense through their place on the social history timeline. Some research is easier to fund, and some theoretical concepts easier to promote, within one decade or cultural context than another. Despite claims to be supportive of evidence-based policy making, government sources of funding can be as tetchy about inconvenient results as commercial organisations.

Theorists are people too. The claims about objectivity and the reasoned consideration of information do not always hold true. It is very tempting to make sense of information in the light of your own theory, rather than recognise that somebody else's theoretical framework does an equally good, or even a better, job. Theory builders are creative thinkers and this process has a strong element of 'let's pretend'.

- *Let's pretend that the entire universe can be viewed as a kind of string.* There is a theory in physics which argues that physical matter consists of one-dimensional filaments that vibrate, a bit like guitar strings, to create particles. Nobody can see this 'string', but the concept has been widely used from the last two decades of the 20th century.
- *Let's pretend that all women experience penis envy.* This was the proposal of Sigmund Freud within his psychoanalytic theory that female personal development is shaped by the realisation, at about four years of age, that they do not have this appendage.

Young children grasp the boundary between pretend and reality. They step away from playing the game of 'Let's pretend I'm a helicopter and my arms are those whirly things' in order to have lunch. Creative adult thinkers, whose theory is now enmeshed with their professional career, can find stepping away more of a struggle. The nature of academic debate around rival theories can surprise outsiders with the playground level of exchanges, despite the long words and complex sentences. Media interest in research can be complicating factors, since the 'ifs, buts and maybes' of responsible studies do not make snappy headlines and short soundbites. All professionals involved with children, and adolescents too, share the responsibility to do at least a basic check, especially if the finding is likely to affect practice, or has already entered the arena of 'It's a well-known fact that …'.

Everyone does some theorising, a level of abstract thinking in order to make sense of the world and relationships. There seems to be a basic human need to bring some predictability out of an initially unfamiliar situation.

Young children try to work out what is happening and why. Partly they are fuelled by intellectual curiosity. However, children also feel more confident when there is tolerable certainty and reasonable predictability about daily life. It builds their sense of emotional security.

Children can work on the two broad patterns of theory building:

- Inductive reasoning: when you gather plenty of information and build your theory on that basis. Young children use this approach and there is increasing evidence (Gopnik, 2009) that babies do so too.

- Deductive reasoning: when you have a working theory and set up expectations on that basis. This pattern of theory building is more typical of adolescents; children will only manage it in familiar circumstances.

See if you can identify simple examples of theory building by children. What do familiar children do or say, even very young ones, which lead you to think that they have a working idea of how their world operates?

Theory, evidence and wisdom

Theories can guide us in making sense of what is happening to children and offer useful explanations of how children develop. Key theoretical concepts can lead to practical ideas that will help you to support children in their learning and puzzle out what they do not understand. You will soon realise that some theories take such diverse viewpoints that their respective supporters will never reach agreement. As practitioners who are useful to children, you need to keep an open mind and look for what you can take away from the different perspectives. Contrary to what enthusiastic theorists will sometimes claim, there is no evidence that any one group has a more complete understanding of young children in all their complexity.

In early years work, as in many practical professions, knowledge has been gained from two main sources:

1 *Evidence* is gathered from the systematic use of research methods, through which information is gathered and interpreted.

2 *Wisdom* is gained through insights that emerge through daily practice, what seems to work best and learning from colleagues, often but not always more experienced in years.

Figure 1.6 Wise practitioners offer an experience in ways that suit young children

Knowledge gleaned only from 'evidence' or from 'wisdom' can be of limited value on its own. When research knowledge is uninformed by the wisdom of practitioners, it can appear irrelevant to real dilemmas. However, well-planned research, when researchers take care to examine their assumptions, can test the 'everybody knows' statements about practice with children that otherwise continue unchallenged.

On the other hand, wisdom gained through experience, direct or from that of other people, needs to be responsive to research findings. Otherwise, practice can stagnate. Experienced practitioners need to share the wisdom they have gained. But their experience is most effective when they have reflected on the reasons for what they do and can share that process of thinking, as well as the details of practice.

Resources

- **Eliot, L.** (2009) *Pink brain, blue brain: how small differences grow into troublesome gaps and what we can do about it*. New York: Houghton Mifflin Harcourt. Access presentation at **http://fora.tv/2009/09/29/Lise_Eliot_Pink_Brain_Blue_Brain**
- **Gopnik, A.** (2009) *The philosophical baby: what children's minds tell us about truth, love and the meaning of life*. London: Bodley Head. Also a conversational feature on **www.edge.org/3rd_culture/gopnik09/gopnik09_index.html**
- **Lindon, J.** (2012c) *Reflective practice and early years professionalism* (2nd edn). London: Hodder Education.

Chapter 2

Explaining child development: considering nature and nurture

....

Few theorists or researchers would now try to argue for a stark choice between nature or nurture. However, the social history of explaining child development includes some theorists with firm inclinations weighted either towards biology or towards the impact of experience. This chapter considers two broad schools of approach to explaining, and sometimes describing, development throughout childhood. The discussion covers some key aspects of what the theoretical approach says, but also includes implications that continue to apply to practice with children. All the theories and theorists described in this chapter, and in Chapter 3, continue to exert an influence on current practice with children.

The main sections in this chapter are:
- Biological maturation theories
- Environmental learning theories.

Biological maturation theories

Some theories focus especially on the impact of biological and maturational processes on human development. The focus of all biological theories is that the patterns of development that everyone shares and our individual differences are based in:
- The instructions laid down in the genes (an inherited pattern) and control exerted by hormones
- The patterns of maturation triggered by messages from the brain, including human body chemistry
- Inevitable patterns that arise from biological constitution and basic human drives.

Theorists who ground their ideas in biology do not usually claim that the environment has no part to play. They argue that genetic programming and the internal workings of the brain are a powerful influence and should not be discounted. Biological maturation theories were largely out of favour by the mid-20th century, but there is now renewed interest in the biological basis to development and behaviour patterns.

A process of maturation

Arnold Gesell and his colleagues, working in the USA during the 1920s and 30s, established a maturational approach to child development, which still exerts influence today. Gesell (1954) believed that the sequence of development for babies and children was controlled by a process of maturation, which means the emergence of physical characteristics, shared by all members of a species and triggered by the information in the genes. He believed that the environment has a supportive role, but that the push towards change was internal to the child.

Gesell and his team studied babies and children in great detail and their descriptions were very specific to particular ages. Their research work was extended into developmental tests for assessing babies and children. The ideas of 'milestones' and 'developmental norms' largely emerged from Gesell's work. The maturational approach, as developed by Gesell, influenced advice books for parents throughout the 1940s and 50s. Some writers were very specific about what 'your child should be doing' at given ages. A related idea that passed into advice for parents was that babies and children would achieve the different developmental stages and skills when they were ready and that certain kinds of behaviour, such as two-year-olds' tantrums, were 'phases' that would pass.

What does it mean?

Maturational theory: the approach that there is a developmental sequence of changes, controlled by instructions in the genetic code that is shared by all children.

Developmental norms: statements about what any child is likely to be able to do or understand within a given age range, usually with the proviso that special needs have not exerted an impact on a child's potential.

Developmental milestones: a term often used for what are seen as the more important achievements for children in different areas of their development.

The maturational approach to child development stimulated a tremendous interest in the detail of what children did. The focus on 'normal' development was a contrast with the psychoanalytical approach, also prominent at this time, which highlighted so much that could apparently go wrong. The maturational approach reassured parents that they were not personally responsible for every 'hiccup' in their child's development. This removal of blame could be a relief.

On the other hand, if development unfolded whatever adults did, the straightforward maturational approach did not generate practical ideas of how parents could help, beyond sitting out an apparent phase like tantrums. Unreflective application of the ideas can still lead to rather sweeping statements about 'all' children of a given age. To stay with the example of tantrums, it is accurate that many two-year-olds, and young children who are slightly older, swiftly run out of their ability to cope with frustration. However, the behaviour of the grown-up involved may have precipitated, or at least failed to prevent, the emotional and physical meltdown. There can be more than one individual having a tantrum in a fraught situation and not everyone is two years of age (see Lindon, 2012e).

Sound knowledge of child development

A rigid approach to developmental norms failed to allow for much variety between individual children, and some resulting materials were very specific about what should happen at a given age. Additionally, for many decades the maturational approach to 'normal' child development was strongly based in a Western and Eurocentric context. The idea of a 'universal child' has been roundly criticised since the 1980s, at the same time as far greater awareness has grown of variations in child rearing, both within and between cultures. An additional concern is that children with disabilities could seem to be invisible in terms of normal development. It is disheartening and very unhelpful if children are defined largely by their failure to reach developmental milestones on time. A more inclusive approach has required that information about patterns of development can be extended to include details of finer steps along the way.

Undoubtedly, there can still be problems if early years practitioners use information about child development in an inflexible way. However, my professional stance remains that good practice with young children is impossible without a sound knowledge to inform realistic expectations for children within a broad age range. This professional need was met for many years in the UK by Mary Sheridan's booklets on development (1960, 1977). The original publications are still reliable for much of the description; but in a more diverse society, they increasingly looked monocultural because of specific assumptions around aspects such as dress and eating utensils. The material was updated by Meggitt and Sutherland (2000) and, in a different way, is covered in Lindon (2012e).

Figure 2.1 First steps are an exciting development

In your own practice how do you work towards a suitable balance between a sound basis of knowledge about child development and acknowledging individual patterns and differences?

- How do you refresh your knowledge and check that your developmental expectations of young children are reliable?

- How do you decide whether to be concerned about a child, that their development is delayed in one or more areas?

- On what basis do you come to the conclusion that individual children are doing well for their age? It cannot just be in terms of comparison with other children you know well. If, for instance, many of the children in your provision have limited communication skills, then a 'normally' conversational three-year-old may appear outstanding.

- In what ways do you ensure that you notice the slower progress of a child whose disability continues to affect their pattern of development, although perhaps not in all aspects of their learning?

Of course, it is important to be flexible about using broad developmental expectations. Children vary in the age at which they accomplish all the different skills of their development. It is certainly not possible to make absolute statements along the lines of 'At 14 months of age all toddlers will be able to ...'. However, part of early years professionalism is the ability to recognise those children who are doing well for their age and are ready to be stretched, to enjoy a well-judged challenge within their everyday experiences. But early years practitioners should also be aware, in a constructive way, of those children who are struggling and need some extra help. You need a sound basis to answer 'When should we worry?' It is possible to build a flexible use of knowledge of child development without 'signing up' to rigid maturational theory.

Make the connection with... Realistic expectations

The Effective Provision of Pre-school Education (EPPE) project (page 58) identified sound knowledge of child development as one of the key markers for quality in early years provision, linked with their research of the best outcomes in terms of children's learning.

You need reliable information to make sense of how best to relate to children and to hold realistic expectations. The problems that can arise from unrealistic expectations are raised in other sections of this book, for example early literacy (page 152) and equality practice (page 237).

A biological basis for human behaviour

The development of attachment

Biologically, humans are part of the mammal family of creatures. A strand of theory and study has looked for connections between human behaviour and that of our closest animal relatives. Konrad Lorenz, a zoologist working in Austria from the 1930s, observed animal behaviour and was the founder of the discipline of ethology. Lorenz showed that there were crucial periods in the early days of mammals, and some birds, when attachment had to take place between infant and mother. Some patterns of animal behaviour seemed to be innate: animals were born with these tendencies; they did not learn the behaviour through experience.

In the later part of his career, Lorenz applied his ideas to human behaviour. John Bowlby, working in the UK from the 1940s, used the studies to explain the early attachment behaviour of human infants. Bowlby believed that the development of attachment specifically between baby and mother was an innately driven set of behaviours that protected infants at a vulnerable time.

A biological basis for play

There has also been interest in the possible biological origins of children's play. Young mammals all show apparently spontaneous, playful behaviour with their peers. You will observe such activity if you watch young lambs in the fields, or watch nature television programmes about mammals within the cat family, such as lion or tiger cubs. Young mammals, besides human children, use props in their play: logs for jumping, materials that can be dragged by limb or jaw and sticks held by young mammals from the ape or monkey family.

The biological explanation for playful behaviour is that it has a survival function for young mammals. They practise physical skills that will be useful for adult life. The playful exchanges between youngsters build social connections that strengthen troupe life for mammals that live in large extended groups. Immature mammals copy the actions of their elders, learning some skills that are crucial for obtaining food and self-care. Playful behaviour is common in young mammals raised in social groups and only extreme social deprivation seems to prevent that development; this is true for young humans as well as for young monkeys. The conclusion drawn is that playful and exploratory behaviour is part of the mammal, and therefore, human biological programming for life. Play is not instinctive, that is to say the behaviour is not automatically triggered, but young mammals seem to be strongly predisposed to play.

Pause for reflection

See if you can engage children in an exploration about 'Is it only children who play?' Three-year-olds may manage a conversation, but this question is far more likely to make sense to four- or five-year-olds. You could start with 'I was wondering ...' and explore the following:

- Have the children made observations of their own pets or animals within their extended family?

- Children living in, or who visit, rural areas may have watched lambs or calves in the fields.

- In partnership with parents, you could weave in learning about play through good nature and animal documentary programmes on the television.

- What do children think? Are the animals playing? What games or play items do they seem to like? Do only children and animals play, or do adults play?

The psychoanalytic approach

Many early years practitioners are aware of the ideas of Jean Piaget and Lev Vygotsky, because from the late 20th century ideas from their theories have been woven into childcare textbooks. (These theorists are discussed in Chapter 3.) Piaget and Vygotsky developed their theories over the 1920s and 30s, but neither theory gained much attention outside their immediate circle for about 30 years. The first half of the 20th century was dominated by the psychoanalytic theory of Sigmund Freud (discussed in this section) and the behaviourism of researchers like B. F. Skinner (discussed from page 25). Neither of these theorists made detailed observations of real children, such as those gathered by Piaget or Vygotsky. As Alison Gopnik et al. comment about the original theories, 'Freud largely relied on inferences from the behaviour of neurotic adults and Skinner on inferences from the behaviour of only slightly less neurotic rats' (2001: 19). However, both schools of thought have diversified significantly since their infancy and both have exerted an impact on early years practice.

Sigmund Freud

Freud worked largely in Vienna, Austria from the 1890s, developing a clinical practice in neuropsychology. He worked from case studies and adult patients, and also, it would now appear, from his own personal traumas. Freud became convinced that energy from the libido, an unconscious sexual drive, was the force behind most human behaviour. His emphasis on the biological motivation places him with this grouping of theories. But his emphasis on the emotional life of children and adults led to the very different psychoanalytic tradition, starting in the late 19th and early 20th centuries. The

Figure 2.2 Sigmund Freud (1856–1939)

theory was also linked with Freud's development of a form of therapy called psychoanalysis. This approach to therapy has diversified since that time and the general therapeutic approach is sometimes called psychodynamic.

Freud developed a theory of stages in children's development in which the libido exerted most impact in the part of a child's body that was sensitive at that age. Freud proposed five psychosexual stages: oral, anal, phallic, latency and genital. Freud believed that, at each stage, children needed sufficient stimulation for the area of their body in which key sensations were focused. He proposed that over- or under-stimulation led individuals to become fixated, by which he meant that they were stuck at that particular developmental stage, continuing to struggle in adult life with that unresolved emotional conflict. This theory claimed that the basics of adult personality were determined by the time a child reached five years of age.

Psychoanalytic theory moved on from biological drives to emphasise that behaviour was shaped by unconscious thoughts and feelings, as well as conscious processes. Some material in the unconscious can only rise to full awareness if people are prepared to explore the possibility, either in personal introspection, or through therapy. A further development in Freud's theory was that anxiety gives rise to conflict, which children and later adults manage through a range of defence mechanisms. These forms of self-protection work at the unconscious level. Freud regarded them as psychologically healthy, unless they led to a serious distortion of reality. The concept of defence mechanisms has entered much of ordinary conversation; for example, Freud's explanation of suppression, when an unhappy experience or uncomfortable dilemma is pushed to the back of your mind for a while. Another defence strategy is that of projection: dealing with anxiety or inability to cope by claiming another person feels in this way.

Psychoanalytic theory has a wealth of ideas but very few are open to objective challenge (to be honest), like a fair number of interesting, psychological concepts. However, some ideas, such as the idea of infantile sexuality, are presented in such a circular way that any observation can be fitted to the theoretical concept. Some applications of the defence mechanism of denial, for instance of childhood abuse, have extended to the claim that the very fact of denying something traumatic happened is evidence that it must have occurred. The application of Freudian ideas to child development has sometimes led to a depressing view of childhood and family life as an inevitable minefield of problems. Some stages, for instance adolescence, have been presented as being considerably more fraught than is the experience of many families. There is also the potential problem of a self-fulfilling prophecy when parents, or other adults, approach adolescents in the firm expectation of being presented with trouble.

The striking contribution of psychoanalytic theory was to highlight unconscious feelings and thoughts; that everything is not described by what we observe on the surface. This powerful focus led Freud and his fellow theorists to be in continuous argument with the behaviourists. The importance of feelings, recognising the emotional life of children and of their parents, was in striking contrast to the fierce training approaches to childcare of behaviourists such as John Watson. Benjamin Spock was very influenced by Freud and his advice books for parents brought the practical applications of psychoanalytic theory into ordinary homes from the 1940s.

Some readers may well feel that Freud and his ideas are ancient history. But psychoanalytic theory has exerted a significant influence on Western thought, as much for the breakaway groups as for the original ideas. By the second decade of the 20th century, there were fierce arguments between different individuals within the original group. Some theorists left on a permanent basis, to develop their own distinct approach. Many of the disagreements were about Freud's strong emphasis on the sexual drive as the main explanation of development. Ideas evolved along separate paths and considerable attention came to be focused on the impact of experience and social context for child development.

Alfred Adler

Adler was a doctor who explored psychopathology, working closely with Freud in Vienna until 1911, when he left Freud's circle to develop what he called individual psychology. Adler and his followers emphasised the struggle against feelings of inferiority and increasingly explored children's life within their family, especially the impact of birth order on the experiences of childhood. Adler believed children's behaviour, and later that of adults, was shaped by their interpretations of what happened in social interactions. Children developed a belief system about themselves and their sense of self-worth, which in turn influenced children's abilities to relate to other people in a sense of shared social interest.

Figure 2.3 Alfred Adler (1870–1937)

Alfred Adler and another Austrian doctor, Rudolf Dreikurs, developed the first child guidance clinics in Vienna. These were all closed by the Austrian government in 1934 and Dreikurs emigrated to the United States of America in 1937. Alfred Adler had been visiting the USA regularly since the 1920s. Rudolf Dreikurs developed Adler's ideas into a practical approach to guiding children's behaviour that has been influential in some parenting programmes. Dreikurs and his colleagues also applied their insights to the school classroom. A key idea has been that adults can guide children's outlook and behaviour in a more positive manner, once they recognise the purpose behind the child's behaviour. Dreikurs developed concepts to bring together emotions and behaviour, the importance of encouragement and using consequences rather than punishment (Lindon, 2012d).

Erik Erikson

Erikson was born in Germany and became interested in psychoanalysis in the late 1920s after meeting Anna Freud, who had joined her father in the psychoanalytic movement. In 1933 Erikson emigrated to the United States of America and by the late 1930s he began to study cultural influences on child development, especially the experiences of children from different American Indian groups. Consequently, Erikson developed his theory that all societies develop a social response to deal with similar problems within personality development, yet the exact solutions differ. By 1950, he had finalised his view of psychosocial development: a sequence of stages that were strongly influenced by the society in which children were raised.

Figure 2.4 Erik Erikson (1902–1994)

Erikson viewed behaviour as fuelled by a series of basic tasks, or dilemmas, that children face at different ages. Erikson made sense of development through how children resolved these tasks, sometimes presented as crises. He proposed that in the first year, babies face the dilemma of basic trust versus mistrust: of the predictability of the world, of babies' ability to affect events and the behaviour of key people around them. By the time young children reach two and three years of age, their dilemma has become a balance between the desire for autonomy versus shame and doubt. Toddlers' increased mobility enables them to act more independently. Yet this development is balanced against the reaction of others to toddlers' preferred actions and the need to learn some self-control. Erikson argued that by the age of four and up to five years, children's main task was to resolve initiative versus guilt. Young children's physical and intellectual abilities allow them to be creative. However, this activity has to be balanced with learning limits, from a growing sense of conscience and boundaries set by adults.

In Erikson's theory, children's behaviour will be shaped by how they balance the competing possibilities of each dilemma and reach some degree of resolution. Balance is a key issue since young children need, for instance, some level of wariness. Total and undiscriminating trust would not be a psychologically healthy outlook. Erikson also diverged from original Freudian theory by taking a view of developmental change that stretched into young adulthood, rather than being essentially complete by five years of age. Erikson thought that middle childhood was the time for dealing with a dilemma between industry (or competence) and inferiority. Adolescence was the period when young people explored and re-examined their personal identity in a dilemma of identity versus role confusion.

Psychoanalytic theory in England

The original psychoanalytic movement remained strong in Austria until Freud escaped from the Nazi occupation in 1938 with his youngest daughter, Anna, and they settled in London. Anna Freud was irritated to find that Melanie Klein, with her rather different theoretical interpretation, was already well established. Anna Freud had to use funds from the USA to set up her nursery and she established the Hampstead Child Therapy Clinic. In 1984, two years after her death, the Anna Freud Centre was established and continues to support children and their families.

Melanie Klein, who was also an Austrian psychoanalyst, had moved to London in 1926. She had diverged from traditional Freudian theory to focus almost exclusively on the very early years of the mother–child relationship, as the forum for powerful infant emotional impulses. The psychoanalytic ideas of Melanie Klein and John Bowlby (see page 83) directly affected national policy and nursery practice, especially around the time of the Second World War and the years following it (Riley, 1993). The ideas of both Anna Freud and Melanie Klein influenced the development of play therapy in the UK. Once again, later theoretical positions have evolved and many play therapists do not subscribe to any version of Freudian theory.

Susan Isaacs

Susan Isaacs worked in England from the 1920s and was initially influenced by the ideas of Melanie Klein. A common thread between Klein and Freud was that they both believed the unconscious life of children, including the emotional conflicts underpinning the development of identity, was revealed through the themes and symbols of children's play, especially imaginary play. Susan Isaacs parted company with this psychoanalytic tradition once she concluded that children's play had a broader developmental function than reflecting emotional turmoil.

Figure 2.5 Susan Isaacs (1885–1948)

Susan Isaacs is significant because her ideas have affected early years theory and practice. She exerted a direct influence during the 1930s under the name Ursula Wise, when she answered readers' questions on the problem page of *Nursery World*. She ran the Malting House School in Cambridge, which for five years offered an education to about 20 children, aged from three to ten years. Her approach offered great scope for active exploration and learning based on children's consuming interests. Isaacs made very detailed observations of what children did at the school and she became as interested in studying children's thinking processes as their emotional life. Her books are thought-provoking and contain much that is relevant to early 21st-century practitioners (Drummond, 2000; Graham, 2009).

Susan Isaacs envisaged play as an emotional release but also that it had an equally important educational function. Susan Isaacs drew on a range of theoretical sources, including the ideas of Jean Piaget, with whom she did not always agree (page 68). She appears to be the original source for the concept that children's play was their work and her writings reflect a deep respect for their ability to drive and organise their own learning.

Figure 2.6 Children take their play very seriously

Take another **perspective**

The psychoanalytic approach has supported very detailed observations of babies and children, not only with their families, but also in out-of-home care, such as day nurseries. This tradition has promoted the importance of personal relationships and the need for a key person approach in group care (page 89).

In my professional career as a psychologist, I have never felt so convinced by a theory that I have wanted to 'sign up' with that school of thought and abandon all others. I take issue with some of the ideas within psychoanalytic theory, but I also challenge some concepts from other theoretical standpoints.

You do not have to agree with all the theoretical concepts behind the observational research from a psychoanalytic base. You can look at the applications and the power of an approach that puts young children and their personal experience at the centre of how to judge good practice over early childhood.

Environmental learning theories

Most theorists who have a strong focus on the impact of the environment and learning through experience do not deny the impact of biological factors. It is a matter of balance, of believing that the major causes of developmental change are located in the child's environment. An alternative perspective is that understanding the impact of experience provides far more scope for effective action to support children's development.

Learning theory developed as the major competitor to psychoanalytic theory in the first quarter of the 20th century. Learning theorists focus on what children, or adults, learn through experience and the consequences of their behaviour. So this approach is sometimes called behaviourism. In basic terms, behaviour is understood to change, following patterns of reward and punishment. The extreme behaviourist stance, which few theorists now take, was that newborn babies start with biological reflexes, but everything else is then learned through direct experience.

Learning through conditioning

The principles of learning theory were first explored in work with animals and three names are most associated with this aspect of behaviourist theory:

1 *Ivan Pavlov* was a Russian doctor whose research into the digestion of animals led him, by the late 1890s, to formulate his laws of the conditioned reflex. By the 1930s Pavlov worked to apply his ideas to explain human psychiatric problems. Pavlov's theoretical concepts describe a process called classical conditioning.

2 *John Watson* was a psychologist working in the USA from the early part of the 20th century. By the 1920s and 30s, Watson's theory of behaviourism dominated psychology. He asserted that human behaviour should, like any animal behaviour, be studied under exacting conditions in an experimental laboratory. Watson resigned his post as a professor in 1920 after adverse publicity about his divorce. He then promoted his ideas through books, including emotion-free childcare advice for parents. His firm ideas still echo in claims that babies are spoiled if you pick them up when they cry.

3 *B. F. Skinner* (always known in this form; his first names were Burrhus Frederic) was a psychologist working in the USA from the 1930s. Skinner was strongly influenced by the ideas of Pavlov and of Watson, but he judged that classical conditioning was a limited explanation.

The simple, rather mechanical-sounding explanations of the early work based on dogs, rats and pigeons do not make much sense when applied to humans. Much like the psychoanalytic tradition, the diversification of ideas in the following decades has led behaviourists a long distance from the first theoretical perspective. However, you need to understand the basics, in order to make sense of how learning theory then developed.

Classical conditioning occurs when a new signal or stimulus brings out an existing behavioural response. One example would be that, if you stroke a young baby gently on the cheek, she will automatically turn and begin to suck. She does not have to learn to turn and suck. It is an automatic reflex with which babies are born; and it is a very useful one if you are trying to get a distracted baby to feed. Classical conditioning involves an involuntary response; the response is not an active choice, but is an inbuilt physical reaction.

In classical conditioning terms, the touch on the baby's cheek is the unconditioned stimulus and the turning and sucking are the unconditioned response. The term 'unconditioned' means that the baby does not have to learn either of these reactions. Now, other events, or 'stimuli', can become associated with the unconditioned stimulus of touch. For instance, perhaps the mother talks gently as she picks the baby up for a feed, or the baby seems to recognise the mother's familiar smell and starts to turn and try to suck without the touch on the cheek. The sounds of the mother's words or her body smell have become a conditioned stimulus and the sucking is now a conditioned response to learned patterns. The baby's behaviour has changed as the result of experience.

Pause for reflection

- Classical conditioning is an oversimplified process to use when attempting to explain the complexity of human learning. But you probably get closest to this pattern when feelings and senses are involved. People and places can become associated in the most basic, and non-rational, way with both pleasant and unpleasant events. These reactions are personal and can last a long time.

- My stomach still churns in reaction to a distinctive aroma of institutional cooking. The smell brings back an unhappy memory of being forced to eat a 'disgusting' school lunch at the age of five. On the other hand, the smell of coal dust has positive associations for me. It triggers happy memories of playing in my grandparents' garden in a Welsh mining village.

- Think for a while and you will almost certainly come up with similar personal examples of an association, when your reaction was not deliberate in any way.

B. F. Skinner explored a second type of learning through direct experience, which was called instrumental or operant conditioning. The second term became more usual. This process involves linking a new response to an existing stimulus. In contrast, classical conditioning links an existing response to a new stimulus. The change is achieved through the principles of reinforcement. Any behaviour (response) that is reinforced is likely to be repeated in the same or similar situation in which the reinforcement (stimulus) previously happened. In contrast to classical conditioning, operant conditioning involves a deliberate action as a response to events.

Through these processes, Skinner trained laboratory birds and animals to perform complex actions, including getting pigeons to play a kind of table tennis. He applied the ideas to human learning processes to propose the efficiency of programmed learning by teaching machines; this occurred long before the introduction of computer software. Using these programmes, children or adults could learn at their own pace and were rewarded for correct responses.

Make the connection with... **Step-by-step learning**

There have been practical applications of the behaviourist approach in carefully structured learning programmes for children, including those for children with physical or learning disabilities. It is possible to use the ideas without the queasy lack of emotion proposed by Skinner or Watson, for whom feelings were an inconvenient, disruptive factor in the process.

A focus on the step-by-step learning has been valuable in illuminating all the finer developments that are very important to notice, teach and reward when children's development may be slower than or different from that of their peers. An example would be the practical ideas behind the Portage system, a home-visiting programme for young children and their families, originally developed in Portage, USA, during the early 1970s. For more information see **www.portage.org.uk**.

Take another **perspective**

It is intriguing to note that the logical ideas of B. F. Skinner depended partly on chance and human error. When I was studying experimental psychology as an undergraduate, I was told the following account of how Skinner discovered that reinforcement did not have to happen every time in order to change behaviour.

Apparently, one night his equipment went haywire, or possibly a hapless research assistant failed to check that it was functioning. The next morning the pigeons were performing bizarre movements for no apparent reason. Investigation showed that the equipment had been delivering the reward food pellets in a much more random way, and not how Skinner had required the machine to be programmed. The pigeons were now repeating actions they happened to be making when the food arrived. It did not matter that this movement was not rewarded every time; it worked often enough to satisfy a pigeon. The concept of partial reinforcement was born.

Social learning theory

Early behaviourist theory depended on research with animals, but soon the ideas were applied to explain and predict human behaviour, including that of children. There are two basic propositions in behaviourist learning theory:

1 Behaviour is strengthened by reinforcement.

2 Behaviour that is reinforced on a partial schedule is stronger, more resistant to stopping altogether, than behaviour that has been reinforced every time.

However, explanations of children's learning do not work well if they depend entirely on classical and operant conditioning and the kind of rewards that are attractive to dogs or rats. Throughout the 1960s, Albert Bandura, a psychologist working in the USA, developed his theory of social learning.

Bandura noticed that a powerful predictor of children's behaviour was what they could directly observe other children's or adults' behaviour. He added the significance of personal feelings of reinforcement and the link between thinking and observational learning. The more sophisticated approach of social learning theory provides explanations with greater flexibility. These theoretical concepts make more sense for the daily life of children, as opposed to pigeons, even ones who can play table tennis.

In his social learning approach Bandura added two more key propositions about the process of learning:

3 Children learn new behaviours mainly through the process of modelling: adults show through their own behaviour how they would prefer children to behave. This proposition leaves open the real possibility that children also imitate adult behaviour that those grown-ups did not intend to be copied.

4 Children do not only learn actual behaviours that can be observed. They also learn ideas, expectations and develop internal standards about what to do, or not.

Figure 2.7 Children persevere with what they find rewarding

The basic explanation of behaviourism remains that reinforcement increases the likelihood that the behaviour of children or adults will be repeated. Behaviour may be strengthened by positive or negative reinforcement:

- *Positive reinforcement* is the addition to the situation, of something pleasant. Reinforcement could be tangible rewards, such as sweets or a prize. But, with children, it is just as likely to be a smile, or hug and words of praise. When

UNDERSTANDING CHILD DEVELOPMENT 0–8 YEARS

positive reinforcement is present after an action, it increases the likelihood of that action happening in the future.

- *Negative reinforcement* is the removal of something unpleasant or unwanted from the situation. For instance, perhaps a child does not want to go to bed. She whines and finds excuses to stretch out the bedtime routine. Her parent persists for a while in saying, 'Hurry up!' and shouting, 'Get upstairs, it's bedtime.' But the parent soon gives up and lets the child settle on the sofa. The child's strategy will be strengthened because it has worked: the unwanted going to bed has been postponed.
- *Partial reinforcement* is a pattern in which behaviour is not reinforced, positively or negatively, every single time. Ordinary life for children tends to follow this pattern, since even adults who try to be consistent do not achieve total consistency. Learning on the basis of partial reinforcement is stronger than behaviour learned with continuous reinforcement. Individuals persist longer with an established pattern of behaviour, when partial reinforcement ceases. Experience has informed them that reinforcement does not occur every time, so it is worth persevering; maybe the gaps between rewards have just become longer.

Reinforcement strengthens a pattern of behaviour, thereby increasing its likelihood. On the other hand, punishment may weaken the pattern.

- *Punishment* is the removal of something pleasant from the situation, such as refusal of sweets, cancelling treats or privileges. But punishment can also be the addition of something unpleasant, such as verbal criticism and nagging, making children do disliked chores, insisting on silence or physical punishment such as hitting. In human interactions, punishment is used with the intention of stopping a given behaviour. However, the results are unpredictable. Children, and adults too, may simply become secretive and ensure they are not observed.
- *Extinction* is the term that describes the complete removal of a pattern of behaviour; it no longer occurs.

It is important to grasp that in behaviourist theory the term 'punishment' is not the same as 'negative reinforcement'. (I stress this point because I have encountered too many instances in childcare and early childhood studies books where authors have wrongly stated that negative reinforcement is the addition of something negative.) In behaviourist theory, reinforcement always increases the likelihood of a given behaviour and that applies whether the experience is of positive or negative reinforcement.

Intrinsic reinforcement

Albert Bandura emphasised that feelings shape behaviour through internally experienced rewards, such as a sense of personal satisfaction and pride in managing something. These feelings are unlikely to emerge spontaneously and familiar carers have an important role to play. Adults not only share their own delight in what children manage but also, through their own adult behaviour, can encourage children to relish a sense of personal achievement and work for that as a goal, not just tangible rewards. Indeed, an overemphasis on rewarding children for specific 'good' behaviour can persuade them that they are only working towards the tangible reward. The risk is that a sense of internal satisfaction is not created and that children do not learn to guide and regulate their own choices in behaviour (Lindon, 2012d).

Thinking and observational learning

Bandura further extended his version of learning theory to cover how children are not passive observers, or unthinking imitators, and began to refer to his approach as social cognitive theory. Bandura's ideas are a reminder that many theories of direct relevance to work with children are a blend of different approaches. Albert Bandura's theoretical approach brings together thinking and behaving and has more in common with the family of cognitive developmental theories than with behaviourism. Bandura proposed that children develop abstract ideas from observational learning: working out what is admired or disliked behaviour, developing attitudes and a sense of their own worth.

Make the connection with… Enduring personality traits

Albert Bandura believed that human learning does not always require the kind of direct and visible reinforcement described in operant conditioning.

His ideas were influenced by a 1928 study by American psychologists Hugh Hartshorne and Mark May. They created an experimental situation in which children between the ages of ten and thirteen years had the choice to yield to the possibility of cheating and stealing, or to be honest and considerate of their peers. The study showed that the children were not consistently honest or dishonest, so challenging the idea that honesty would be a fixed trait of character by this age. The best predictor for the children's choice of behaviour was the actions of the other children around them. Some commentators on this study have also noted that children may have sophisticated explanations for why they made a less than 'honest' choice.

Bandura developed his ideas that children learn through observation of others, familiar adults and other children: they look for a model to imitate. During the period when he was working, Bandura was also able to note that children observed others through the medium of television.

Bandura proposed that the extent to which children learn through observation of others does not depend only on what there is to observe around them. The end result will also be affected by:
- The exact focus of children's attention
- What they are able to remember
- What children can physically copy, given their skills at the time
- What they are motivated to imitate. Children are far less likely to copy an adult whom they dislike, unless it is in mockery.

If you watch children, you will be struck by the extent to which they copy others; the motivation to imitate seems strong. In family life especially, the wish to copy is fuelled also by the strong attachments made by many children to their parents. When young children spend time in out-of-home care, they will form a close personal relationship with their carer; indeed they need to be enabled to get emotionally close. So early years practitioners and, in a group setting, a child's key person, in particular, will be a focus for imitation. Responsible adults reflect on how they set a good example that they will be pleased to have children copy.

Figure 2.8 Children learn through watching each other

What does it mean?

Behaviourism or learning theory: a set of theoretical propositions that focus on the impact of experience in shaping behaviour.

Social learning theory: a development of behaviourism, which recognises that human behaviour is further shaped by feelings, direct observation and thinking about experiences.

Modelling: learning through observation and then direct imitation of another person. This term is also used to mean behaving in a deliberate way so as to provide actions or words to imitate.

Resources

- **Drummond, M.** (2000) 'Susan Isaacs: pioneering work in understanding children's lives', in Hilton, M. and Hirsch, P. *Practical visionaries: women, education and social progress 1790–1930*. London: Longman.
- **Gesell, A.** (1954) *The first five years of life.* London: Methuen.
- **Gopnik, A., Meltzoff, A., Kuhl, P.** (2001) *How babies think: the science of childhood*. London: Phoenix.
- **Graham, P.** (2009) *A biography of Susan Isaacs: a life freeing children's minds.* London: Karnac Books. (I accessed some chapters online with a search of Jean Piaget + Susan Isaacs.)
- **Lindon, J.** (2012d) *Understanding children's behaviour: play, development and learning* (2nd edn). London: Hodder Education.
- **Lindon, J.** (2012e) *What does it mean to be one? A practical guide to child development in the Early Years Foundation Stage*. London: Practical Pre-School Books. A set of four books, for each year of early childhood, so also *What does it mean to be two? (three?, four?)*.
- **Meggitt, C. and Sutherland, G.** (2000) *Child development: an illustrated guide – birth to 8 years*. London: Heinemann.
- **Riley, D.** (1993) *War in the nursery: theories of the child and mother.* London: Virago.
- **Sheridan, M.** (1960) *Children's developmental progress from birth to five years: the Stycar sequences.* Windsor: National Foundation for Educational Research.
- **Sheridan, M.** (1977) *Spontaneous play in early childhood: from birth to six years.* Windsor: National Foundation for Educational Research.

Explaining child development: from cognitive developmental to sociocultural perspectives

The cognitive developmental family of theories focuses on how children think and make sense of their world. Theorists place considerable emphasis on children's experiences with play materials, the evidence of their senses and how they build knowledge from the experience. As this theoretical approach developed, there has been an increasing emphasis by some theorists on social relationships with adults, or between children. Development of social constructivist theory has gone further to incorporate a sociocultural framework and a strong emphasis on the context, as well as personal experience of children.

The main sections in this chapter are:
- Cognitive developmental theories
- Sociocultural theories.

Cognitive developmental theories

Jean Piaget and Lev Vygotsky are both significant names in the development of this family of theories. However, in terms of the social history timeline, the spread of their ideas was geographically relatively limited, until Piaget's ideas were translated into English from French and Vygotsky's from the original Russian.

Piaget and stage theory

The ideas of Jean Piaget have exerted a very strong influence on early years philosophy and practice in the UK. Piaget initially developed his theories from observations made by Valentine Piaget of their own three children from babyhood. This resource was extended to include children of his research team at Geneva, in Switzerland, from the late 1920s onwards. The team undertook a series of experimental studies designed to test Piaget's propositions about what children understood at different ages. His detailed theory is now seen as one foundation to the constructivist approach. However, Piaget had common ground with some of the biological theories. He proposed a 'genetic epistemology': a timetable established by nature for the four stages of child development.

Piaget developed his theory of developmental stages from observing that children of an equivalent age made similar mistakes and appeared to develop very similar concepts to explain how the world worked. The essence of his stage theory of development was that the process of learning was not just 'more of the same', not simply a quantitative build-up of information. In contrast, Piaget argued that, once young children's thinking had been provoked to move to a qualitatively different stage, there could be no return. At various stages during childhood and adolescence, children started to think in a significantly different way about their world.

Make the connection with... Other theories

Jean Piaget proposed that children were not just small grown-ups, but that they learned in a qualitatively different way from adults. He described children as active participants in their own learning, constructing their own understanding and furthering their own knowledge.

Piagetian theory has had such a strong influence on UK early years practice, and also education in school, that it is easy to overlook that his ideas were very radical at the time. Piaget's image of the child as a little scientist was in stark contrast with other perspectives in Europe and the USA during the same period.

Over the first half of the 20th century, the prevailing educational belief was that children were essentially empty vessels that needed to be filled up with adult-given knowledge. The main theoretical positions on offer were the behaviourist approach of John Watson, or the Freudian approach of emotional turmoil. Piaget's alternative view that even young children were active learners and thinkers was a major breath of fresh air and the reason that people such as Susan Isaacs went to visit Piaget in Geneva.

Adaptation through schemes/schemas

Piaget explained that young children construct their understanding of the world through their use of schemes or schemas. I use the word schema, since this term is familiar in the UK because of the work of Chris Athey (1990).

A schema is more than a mental category; it is a word used to explain ideas in action and the grouping of a set of actions linked with an idea. During the first two years of life, which Piaget called the sensorimotor stage, the prevailing schemas are very physical. Babies and toddlers use their physical skills to explore and all their senses provide vital channels of information. Piaget proposed that for a baby, an object was essentially the same as its feel or taste. So an adult observer can refer to a baby's holding or sucking schemas. Piaget proposed that, from about 18–24 months of age, toddlers develop schemas that go beyond physical sensation and have an intellectual content linked with the actions. He interpreted observations of very young exploratory behaviour as evidence that the children had made cognitive connections, supported by the physical exploration within their current schema(s).

Schemas support active development because they change in response to experience. Piaget proposed three processes of adaptation to explain how young children learned:

1 *Assimilation*: objects, events and experiences are drawn into and made a part of an existing schema. For instance, a baby incorporates a new rattle into her grasping and shaking schema. In this way, existing schemas can become more varied, but the essential nature of this schema does not change.

2 *Accommodation*: children encounter experiences that will not fit an existing schema. Piaget theorised that a new schema is then created through the means of physical experimentation, from thinking out loud through spoken language, or through silent thought for older children. Children's schemas (and our own adult ones) are reorganised and, if necessary, changed through this process of accommodation.

3 *Equilibration*: in order to explain why children make this effort, Piaget proposed that they have a powerful desire to make sense of their world. It feels uncomfortable to persist with inconsistency and the imbalance of a schema that does not work. Through equilibration, children make the significant leaps of childhood learning, as they abandon schemas that cannot cope with the new information and understanding of the world.

Piaget's stage theory of child development rested on three very significant equilibration points within childhood. At each time, Piaget claimed, schemas undergo a major reorganisation and children shift to a qualitatively different phase in their development.

- When children are aged about 18 to 24 months, the dominant sensorimotor schemas change to incorporate the first use of symbols: an object standing for something else and the symbolism of the use of spoken language. This major change brings children out of Piaget's first developmental stage, the sensorimotor, and into his second, called the pre-operational stage.
- Children aged between two and six years of age extend their use of symbolism and explore a wide range of abstract concepts and mental ways of organising and understanding the world. Piaget described their thinking as egocentric. He meant that young children could only make sense of the world from their own perspective and were unable to take alternative perspectives into account. It is important to realise that Piaget meant that children were self-centred in a cognitive way; he did not imply they were 'selfish'.
- Piaget proposed that between the age of five and seven years children made the shift into a whole new level of thinking, that of operations. These are the mental activities such as categorising, use of number and early scientific concepts such as conservation: that an amount remains constant regardless of how it appears. This new level of understanding took children into the

concrete operational stage, a period that Piaget believed lasted up to about the age of 12 years.

- By the brink of adolescence, children had gained such a broad and thorough understanding of ideas in action, their concrete operations, that they were able to deal with increasingly complex ideas in their head and move into the stage of formal operations.

What does it mean?

Stage theory: an explanatory approach that proposes there are distinct stages of development through which all children pass in the same sequence.

Schemas: repeated patterns of behaviour that characterise how children explore and understand their world at a given time.

Adaptation: Piaget's theory of how children's schemas change in response to experiences: through assimilation, accommodation and the drive for equilibration.

Deficit or incompetence model: an approach that focuses more on what children cannot yet do, rather than on their current level of competence.

Challenges to the stage theory

Few theorists now hold uncompromisingly to original Piagetian theory, but the ideas have been the source of much creative research and rethinking. In fact, some divergence of opinion was clear from the 1920s. Lev Vygotsky (page 37) questioned some of Piaget's assumptions and took a different route in Russia. But Susan Isaacs in England was also doubtful about Piaget's evidence for pre-operational thought.

Figure 3.1 Adults need to understand a child's learning journey, for instance towards literacy

The practical problem is that Jean Piaget defined young children, particularly those aged from two to six years, mainly in terms of what they could not yet do. This view of young children has been called a deficit or incompetence model. In her observations during her time as head of the Malting House School, Susan Isaacs drew upon much the same research as Piaget, but reached different conclusions about children's ability. Isaacs took more of a bottom-up than a top-down perspective. She offered positive descriptions of cognitive competence in young children: what they could do and how, rather than what they could not yet do (Drummond, 2000; Graham, 2009).

By the 1970s other researchers, notably Margaret Donaldson (1978) in Scotland, were challenging the validity of Piaget's conclusions by exploring the impact on his experimental methods of apparently minor changes in the wording of questions or layout of materials (page 68). In subsequent decades there was a steady move away from the more solitary learners, who featured in Piaget's theoretical perspective, towards how children learn within their social and cultural context.

Take another **perspective**

Piaget's ideas have exerted a significant influence on UK early years and school practice. Revisiting his ideas, as well as challenging some of the assumptions, has in turn generated important implications for practice.

- Piaget's insistence that children constructed their own understanding and were active learners led him to emphasise that adults should create environments in which children could discover for themselves. This approach has sometimes been interpreted within early years practice that 'learning through play' means a strict non-interventionist role for adults. Margaret Donaldson challenged this approach with her ideas of children's enjoyment of the role of novice (page 182). An important good practice debate continues over the role of adults in play and the nature of child-initiated learning.

- Piaget's ideas about early mathematical concepts had the positive effect of highlighting the importance of active, hands-on learning, but his conclusions tended to underestimate what children understood about number. Practical research studies have explored how much children understand of early mathematical concepts and the means to support young learning (Caddell, 1998a; Maclellan, Munn and Quinn, 2003).

The influence of Lev Vygotsky

Lev Vygotsky worked in Russia through the 1920s and 30s. He was one of the first people to disagree with Piaget's theory of child development. However, Vygotsky's premature death meant that he could only respond to Piaget's early publications. It is important to realise that much of what is presented now as a Vygotskian model of play and learning is the result of continued reworking of his ideas, especially in the 1980s and 90s.

Unlike Piaget, who had a very long academic career, Vygotsky had only a decade of generating ideas before he died at the age of 38 from tuberculosis. The Stalinist purges took place in Russia; developmental psychology was banned and most of Vygotsky's research team were sent to prison. His work was inaccessible outside Russia, until the political climate changed and his working papers were translated into English (1962 and 1978). These publications provide Vygotsky's discussion of theoretical concepts, relatively informal experiments and his practical suggestions for how children learn.

Vygotsky placed far greater emphasis than Piaget on the social context in which children explored and learned. Vygotsky also viewed language as a vital social tool. He did not believe that children operated as the 'lone scientist' of Piaget's view; and Vygotsky described learning far more as a process within social interaction. If Piaget is described as the pioneer of an approach of individual constructivism, then Vygotsky is seen as the founder of the social constructivist approach. This perspective is also the reason why Lev Vygotsky is sometimes placed with the sociocultural family of theories.

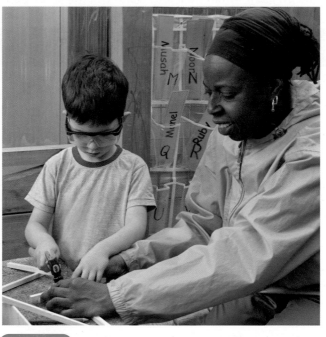

Figure 3.2 Children welcome well-judged help

Vygotsky felt that early language, during the years when children speak out loud to themselves in play, should not be dismissed as immature or egocentric, since it was an instrument of thought. The whole feel of Vygotsky's approach is much more a competence model: young children already have skills and add to these through experience. Vygotsky felt play was significant, but did not see it as the only way that children learned. Interestingly, he warned against the drawbacks if adults intellectualise play and overlook the significance of the emotional content for the children themselves.

Vygotsky used his concept of *the zone of proximal development* to explain how children's learning could be supported (page 174). The term 'proximal' is the English translation of a Russian word meaning 'nearby'. Vygotsky felt that play could create positive conditions for learning within the zone and he was interested in how adults could best help children to learn. But Vygotsky also proposed that children helped each other within the zone, through social and play interactions.

What does it mean?

The zone of proximal development: the area of potential learning for an individual child at a given time.

Jerome Bruner

Jerome Bruner is an American psychologist, who has mainly worked in the USA but led a large UK research project at Oxford in the 1970s. Bruner developed Piaget's ideas but was also influential in bringing Vygotsky's ideas to the English-speaking academic world. Bruner was asked to write a foreword to the English translation of Vygotsky's collected research papers and was bowled over by the fresh approach. Bruner began to look at ways to develop the ideas and the gaps in application that Vygotsky had never had the opportunity to explore.

Jerome Bruner disagreed with Piaget's view that children's development should be left to unfold without intervention. Bruner believed that development could be accelerated in a positive way, when adults took a more active role in children's learning. Bruner was especially concerned that children whose circumstances provided poor intellectual stimulation would be seriously disadvantaged without the input of an active role for early years practitioners and school teachers.

Piaget stressed the importance of children's physical environment in stimulating a child to learn. However, Bruner saw language as an important medium for adults to stimulate children to think and understand beyond their current grasp. He was in favour of a child-centred environment and learning through discovery, but believed that adults should actively anticipate difficulties and help children directly.

Bruner (1990) further developed Vygotsky's theoretical perspective into the concept of the spiral curriculum, of how children learn through discovery, with the direct help of adults, and by returning again and again to the same materials or ideas. Bruner proposed that children were able to extend their understanding over a period of years, because later learning could build on what they had learned previously, and through sensitive help from adults. Jerome Bruner's concept of learning as cyclical is shared by writers such as Lillian Katz (see also page 102) in that children need to revisit ideas and experiences. The practical implication is that supportive adults need to provide a flexible learning environment, in which children can easily access and use resources, exploring connections that make sense for them now.

What does it mean?

The spiral curriculum: the idea that children will revisit play resources and experiences over the years, but then use the opportunity in a different way because their cognitive development has progressed.

Scaffolding: supportive technique used by adults to offer verbal or non-verbal guidance to children who are in the process of gaining a new skill or understanding.

Jerome Bruner felt that young children learn most easily through the medium of their play. Familiar play materials could remain of interest to children, as the months and years passed, but older children used the same, or similar, materials in qualitatively different ways. Bruner developed the concept of scaffolding to explain how adults could use their greater experience appropriately to help children to understand and to think. He used the visual parallel of scaffolding on a building site to explain how observant adults can provide temporary guidance to a child, who is in the process of gaining a new skill or understanding. Once the child feels competent, this particular bit of scaffolding support can be removed.

Pause for reflection

An example of the spiral curriculum in action is how a rich array of building bricks, or wooden blocks, is a creative source of learning for all children.

- Babies like bricks to hold, look at and drop. But as they become toddlers, the same children relish bricks as a simple build-up and knock-down resource.

- Three- and four-year-olds use a good store of bricks as the construction material for buildings. But they also use bricks to create boundary lines that are essential for other games, to make enclosures for toy animals or cars. They use blocks for stepping along or over, or for delicate balancing games. Different sizes and shapes may serve as props in their pretend play.

- Children aged five, six and older may still enjoy building impressive structures with bricks. But they may also use them deliberately as the raw materials for counting, weighing and relative weight, exploring mathematical concepts that now make sense to the children.

At any point in these years of exploration and learning, the supportive adult input could work within the zone of proximal development (see also page 174), with adult skills of scaffolding. What might be appropriate kinds of support?

You could build up current and past observations of children you know and explore the building blocks example. If you would like to focus on blocks, contact Community Playthings for their free DVD, *Foundations: the value of unit block play* at www.communityplaything.co.uk.

- Other possibilities are to gather observations of the different ways in which children use the potential of dressing-up clothes: from the very simple hat-on-head or scarf-over-the-face game of toddlers through to the complex pretend play of the older children.

- Combine your observations with those of colleagues or fellow students, who work with children of a different age, or who knew these individual children when they were younger.

Figure 3.3 Blocks have endless possibilities

Sociocultural theories

The discipline of developmental psychology spent decades studying children, as if it were irrelevant where and how they lived, or even the context in which they were observed or asked questions for research purposes. Cross-cultural psychology developed throughout the 1960s largely in order to test whether propositions, for instance from Piaget's ideas, applied outside the Western hemisphere. The discipline moved closer to anthropology, with an interest in documenting ways of raising children, searching for common themes, as well as contrasts. The socio-cultural approach developed through the last decades of the 20th century and has aimed to place children in context, without losing their individuality.

Systems theory
Systems theorists argue that every system, whether biological, economic or psychological, has wholeness and an order to how it works. The whole consists of the parts and their interrelationship. So, change in one part of the system will

affect other parts; it is not possible to separate them. Arnold Sameroff applied the theory to understand family dynamics: family life is created by the relationships between parents, children and any other close relatives. The experiences of individuals within any family are influenced by the way this family operates. Sameroff takes the analogy of music: you cannot possibly appreciate a melody if you only listen to a series of single notes. The unique tune is created by how those musical notes are set together, whether they merge in harmony or clash.

What does it mean?

Systems theory: an approach emphasising an interaction between the whole and the parts in any system. Applied to families, systems theory argues that family life cannot be understood by focusing only on individual family members.

The other defining feature of a system is that it adapts to change in the same way that Piaget described for children's cognitive development (page 35). Families can be resistant to change, some more than others, and, if possible, they will absorb some new feature into family life without major readjustments: Piaget's idea of assimilation. But sometimes, family life becomes very stressful, unless particular readjustments are made that shift how the family runs: Piaget's idea of accommodation. Such change is challenging but may be painful and resisted by families who have a strong vested interest in the current situation.

The systems theory approach to looking at family life has practical implications, for instance that:
- Families are seen as self-balancing systems: they establish a way of coping that for them defines normal family life. Young children assume that every family operates like their own, until social interaction provides a contrast.
- All families act so as to achieve a balance in their relationships and family communication patterns help to maintain this balance. Changing the balance, or having change thrust upon a family, can be stressful.
- If equilibrium seems precarious, family members exert effort to restore it. Sometimes, equilibrium may be maintained largely because one family member or a sub-group imposes their will on others in the family.

Alfred Adler (page 21) made the point that each child is, in effect, born into a 'different' family because they face a different configuration of people and existing roles than either an older, or a subsequent child. Children are themselves active family members, responding and reacting to the family system. They make alliances with, or feel resentment towards, individual parents, siblings or other relatives in the close family. Of course, families do not operate in a social vacuum. Adults are affected by the ways in which the surrounding community judges their actions. Cultural traditions may create expectations that are a source of conflict within families and yet may be a strong source of support for others.

The development of family-orientated therapy, rather than therapeutic intervention focused solely on the child, was a recognition that family dynamics can be key in bringing about positive change for some children.

Family members help to maintain the balance overtly and covertly. For example, parents may resist help with the problem, or series of troubles, they regularly present about their child. It may be very important that general difficulties in the family can be directly attributed to the disruptive behaviour of a son or daughter.

Under these circumstances, it can be disconcerting to have the problem resolved. Tanya Byron (2005) described the challenge faced by some couples once their young child had accepted a bedtime routine. The adults then faced each other for long evenings, unpunctuated by the patter of feet and cries of protest.

- Think about how this dynamic could show itself in early years provision. Is it easier to talk about 'behaviour problems' from children than unrealistic expectations from adults?

Systems theory applies to any social group, so the ideas are just as relevant to the social interaction and roles within a working team.

- Reflect on how the dynamics of your own team or study group operate. What kind of roles do individuals take on, or have thrust upon them? What changes occur if someone is absent or a new person joins the group?

- Take your time when considering these concepts. It can be unsettling to apply the ideas to oneself rather than other people.

An ecological approach

Urie Bronfenbrenner, a psychologist based in the USA, travelled to observe children in other countries and developed his theory to take account of childhood in a given time and place. He saw his approach as a way to study the ecology of human development and the theory is sometimes know as the ecological systems theory. From the 1970s Bronfenbrenner worked to describe the impact of children's environment, without downplaying the uniqueness of individual children.

The ecological approach is a reminder that children do not develop in isolation. Bronfenbrenner's approach (1979) offered a balance to theories that continued to focus on individual children, at most in the context of their immediate family. One advantage of the ecological approach is the attempt to grapple with parts of the social system that indirectly affect children. Children are influenced by the details of culture or faith, of current economic policy or the demands of adult employment, as they trickle down through the layers and into personal relationships.

Bronfenbrenner developed a model that is usually presented visually as a series of concentric circles. However, the concepts are also represented like a set of Russian dolls: the type where each doll nests within another. Such a resource can be taken apart until all the dolls are revealed, down to the very smallest one.

- The innermost circle of the microsystem encompasses children's direct, daily experience with family, peers and friends. It also includes settings of which the child has direct experience: early years setting, schools or places of worship. Children's socialisation occurs within this circle.
- Bronfenbrenner calls the next layer the exosystem. This circle, or doll in the set, includes the social system that affects children. The impact may be their own direct experience but can also be filtered through their family. Important aspects can be the neighbourhood, local social networks including their parents' friends and the world of work, which affects children through parents' experiences of job pressure or unemployment.
- The outer layer is the macrosystem. This circle includes broad social structures: education, economic systems and cultural values. Economic policy may result in relative wealth or poverty in the child's family. The ethnic identity of child and family gains meaning from the predominant cultural values of the society.

Make the connection with... **Childhood happens in a time as well as place**

Bronfenbrenner recognises the impact of time as well as place. In some discussion of his theory, he talks of the chronosystem: broad social changes that affect the nature of childhood over the years.

You can consider the following questions in a 'What if ...', or 'I wonder ...' context. But, depending on your own age, create the opportunity to talk with a fellow adult who experienced their childhood in a different decade from you.

- Consider the significant changes for a child growing up in the UK during the early 21st century, in contrast with a 1970s or 1950s childhood.

- For example, discuss familiarity with computers, video or television.

- What was the likelihood that children in other decades attended some kind of early years setting and what difference might that have made to their life and that of their parents?

- What about the weight of traffic on the road, or the likelihood in earlier decades that the family would own a car?

What else could be realistically seen as broad social changes that affect childhood over time?

Bronfenbrenner acknowledges that the richness of his ecological model, reflecting the genuine complexity of ordinary life, makes it hard to design research that could test the detail of how one part of the system impacts on another or causal links. It seems a price worth paying for such a thoughtful approach and the model is amenable to a research method led more by the narrative approach (page 61). The effects of the environment are complex and the most likely influences are of interactions, rather than linear patterns of cause and effect. In later reworking of the theory, Bronfenbrenner worked to redress what he felt had become an imbalance away from the impact of children's individuality.

Pause for reflection

There is good reason to be concerned about rising levels of clinical obesity in childhood and the health consequences of a more sedentary lifestyle for many children now. But what is to be done?

Use Bronfenbrenner's ideas to identify the strands of this practical problem.

- For example, what are the role and responsibility of parents and later of the children themselves?

- What about responsibility for the content of nursery or school meals and the fact that some schools generate funds from selling crisps and fizzy drinks?

- Companies who sell snack food and advertisers who promote the goods say that it is inappropriate for government to control sales or restrict advertising. What do you think?

- Discuss your ideas with colleagues and build up a model of what you judge to be the strands of cause and effect in this area of practical social concern.

Social construction of childhood

During the 1990s Berry Mayall and other sociologists in the UK became interested in how social structures and dominant social values shaped the way in which childhood was viewed and the daily experiences of children. Berry Mayall was involved in several large-scale studies of children in the UK and she brought together insights from psychology and sociology into an area of study that is now described as the sociology of childhood.

What does it mean?

Sociology of childhood: a branch of sociology that has focused on children and childhood in the context of social groups and society as a whole.

Social construction of childhood: the idea that there is neither an absolute nor a universal image of a child and childhood. The image is created by social attitudes grounded in time and place.

A key concept is that of social construction of childhood: that childhood experience is neither universal in the details, nor fixed within a single society over time. Childhood may exist as a permanent social category in society, as distinct from adulthood, but social circumstances determine children's experiences and the boundaries to their daily life. Current attitudes and social values within any society shape the prevailing childhood and ways of talking about children. For example:

- Are children important in themselves or only for what they may become?
- Economic pressures, for an entire society or families who are under the greatest stress, exert an influence on how children are viewed. How important are their needs, if these are seen to conflict with adult priorities?
- Is it universally unacceptable for children to work? What if children's economic labour is crucial to family survival?
- Is children's involvement in household chores part of a family or community philosophy about ways to raise competent children?
- To what extent are children seen as legitimate targets for commercial interests, as young consumers or purchasers?

How should children be raised?

Christina Hardyment (1995) is a social historian who has described the changing views in Europe of how children should be treated, from 1750 up to the end of the 20th century. Her examples of advice given to parents are a timely reminder that opinion has changed dramatically and continues to circle. Hardyment shows that experts can disagree, even within the same decade, and adds the useful reminder that families do not necessarily follow the prevailing advice of their era. Even popular advice manuals cannot tell us what all parents actually did with their children during that decade.

Advice varies within an era; for instance the 1940s and 50s are often presented as the era of firm routines, uncompromising discipline and minimal interest in play. Yet the following extract comes from the 1950 edition of *Care of children from one to five*:

> Many of the troubles of management which arise in childhood are due to the persistent refusal of grownups to regard a child as a proper human being. Some persist in calling the child 'it', others talk about him to his face as if he were not there … Say 'naughty' as little as possible. It is not naughty to shout and romp, to fidget about, to be 'always on the go'. Mischief is only a sign that the child needs more to do. It may be exasperating for the grownups but it's perfectly natural to him. Forcing a child to be quiet or inactive will only cause his pent-up energy to overflow into bad behaviour, tantrums and irritability. (Gibbens, 1950: 121–2)

John Gibbens (a medical doctor) first wrote his childcare manual in 1936 and it was so popular that it was reprinted many times. (I have the fourth edition on my shelf because my mother consulted that very book to raise my brother and me.) John Gibbens's views have much to offer current debates in early years practice about making sense of children's behaviour and the problems that follow if young children are expected to do a great deal of 'sitting nicely'.

Social role and status

Berry Mayall (1994, 2002) has argued that, in the UK, children are often assigned minority social status: that their views are frequently judged as less important than adult priorities. The development of children's rights and consultation with children have been a practical way to address this inequality. Studies have explored the importance of children's own views of their daily experience, how they view their social world, or experiences at school, or when ill in hospital.

The sociological concept of role is that adults, as well as children, have different parts to their life, in which they have a qualitatively different social position and relationship. For example, you may be a daughter or son, but also have a long-standing family role as sister or brother. You may have a more recent role as a parent and be a colleague, or a manager, to another set of people. You may have experienced the temporary role of patient when in contact with medical services. The sociological approach to childhood looks especially at the roles for children, for instance as a school pupil. Mayall describes what she calls the 'scholarization' of childhood, by which she means the way in which the school experience has come to dominate family life. Children and young people spend many hours in school, but parents are also told how to use family time, especially with homework given in British primary schools.

Figure 3.4 Children need to make strong bonds with their parents

Make the connection with... **Power relations**

Consider Berry Mayall's ideas about the 'scholarization' of childhood. To what extent are children and the years of childhood defined in terms of the educational experience of school?

- My particular annoyance is the way that under-fives are regularly called 'pre-schoolers', rather than babies, three-year-olds or simply 'young children'. I draw the parallel and say, do we call adolescents pre-workers? Are people in their 50s or early 60s regularly called pre-retirees? Why is it only young children whose identity is defined by the next 'stage'? And what does that communicate about the relative importance of early childhood?

- Most discussion around the transition into primary school is about how families and early years settings can prepare the children for school, with a lot of 'getting them ready for ...'. Hilary Fabian (2002) is unusual in calling a whole section of her book 'Preparing schools for children'.

- Look also at the discussion about early years provision and partnership with parents in Chapter 10.

Figure 3.5 Family experience tells children what is valued

> ## What does it mean?
>
> **Role or social role**: a description of the social position of being in a particular relationship with other people and social institutions such as the family, school or paid work.

The sociocultural perspective

The theoretical stance of social constructivism is very strong now within early childhood studies in the UK and has developed into a sociocultural model. The approach has drawn from theorists in early developmental psychology, such as Lev Vygotsky, but there are also important sources within sociology, cross-cultural studies and philosophy.

The sociocultural approach draws on the traditions of cross-cultural psychology and anthropology, aiming to avoid the evaluative comparisons that were sometimes part of earlier academic traditions. Certainly, cross-cultural psychologists and anthropologists did not all previously describe non-Western cultures in a demeaning way. But reports sometimes gave a feel of the 'interesting' or 'exotic', as contrasted with the more 'normal' Western template. Academic discussion of social constructivism or sociocultural theory uses terms like 'postmodern', 'poststructural' and 'discourse'. This section explains the origins of the approach and provides definitions for these specialist terms.

Postmodernism

This concept comes from a radical rethink in sociology. The argument is that sociology as a discipline started with the analysis of modern society. 'Modern' is defined as the changes brought about by the industrial revolution. Sociological analysis was in terms that make sense from an industrial type of society: that social class was significant, family was an important social structure and adults gained their personal identity from work.

Sociologists proposed that from the 1970s onwards the whole social situation changed. The nature of society in the Western world had altered, so an alternative way of analysing society was required: the postmodern approach.

- One of the changes, it is argued, is that personal identity cannot be summed up accurately in large groupings. Social change is widespread, so identity is much more fluid. One person could have a multiplicity of identities and make active choices to take on an identity, for example by changing their accent or style of dress.
- There was a reaction in sociology against the grand narratives and a move towards the individual narrative as a perspective to be respected, even valued more than broader social concepts. There is a sense of pluralism: that a range of personal narratives will offer a full and meaningful explanation.
- There was also a reaction against what were seen as the big myths: that science was objective and would be a source of progress and well being. This perspective also drew from the philosophical position of existentialism (page 51).

Poststructuralism

The poststructuralists overlap with the postmodernists. The movement was a reaction against the previous dominance in sociology of structuralist principles and theories such as Marxism. There are two broad ways to think and talk about society: action (through personal decisions and perceptions) and structure (institutions that became autonomous, for example religion).

- The key idea of structuralism was that these social structures were like the puppet master and more powerful than individual actions. People could only wield power through the structures, as puppets on the strings.
- The structural approach to analysis was challenged, with the claim that the exercise of power is more a matter of interpersonal relations. Some people are in a better position to wield power and work the puppet strings. It is possible to gain power, especially with greater fluidity of personal identity, which provides a link with the postmodernist analysis.

So, this form of sociological analysis was called poststructural. The new approach placed a great emphasis on language and held that use of words can be seen as a barometer for the power relations.

- Forms of analysis from linguistics, including semiotics, proposed that words can be fluid and are separate from concepts. The same words have an infinite possibility of meanings and are always open to interpretation.

- It is possible then to analyse spoken and written words to reveal the meaning and power relations behind the words. For example, use of language within the medical profession, such as calling people 'patients' and 'cases', reflects the balance of power.

Patterns of language, linked with ideas, are particular to a given sociocultural group and can be analysed as a whole, as discourse, and can be challenged. An example is how the social model of disability was used to confront the words and linked concepts of the medical model (page 225). Another relevant example would be the discourse that underlies promotion of hitting children as a form of discipline. In order to understand the key concepts in the early childhood studies of academic discourse, we also need the strand of philosophy.

Deconstruction

By the 20th century, philosophers in France and Germany, but not in the UK, had developed a philosophical position called existentialism. A central theme of this philosophical approach is that meaning cannot be found unless you recognise that humans are engaged in the world. Their experience of objects and events provides them with meaning. The assumption is that humans seek to understand anything because they are involved with it. So there will always be a particular point of view and complete objectivity is impossible, even in the pure sciences such as physics and chemistry, let alone the social sciences.

The existential position values concrete and personal experience more highly than the general and abstract. So existentialism stresses that, in the search for understanding, it is more important to be involved than to be detached. The impossibility of scientific objectivity is not therefore a problem. In fact, the traditional scientific values and methods – a positivist approach – were dismissed as misguided and irrelevant to valid inquiry.

The existential tradition led to further explorations of how meaning was always embedded in context. Jacques Derrida was influential in promoting the process of deconstruction, that of stripping bare an event or a piece of writing in order to reveal the structure of assumptions and finally reach what is unique about it. You could release social meaning by analysing discourses.

Discourse

So, the term discourse means much more than the words alone. For example, the word 'stress' is grounded in a context of meaning and varies along many more dimensions than the word 'nerves', which was common in the mid-20th century. Discourse is a collection of ideas, practice and of power relations in society. If you analyse scientific discourse, you are able to define the explanations and power relations that are mediated through language. Because language itself constructs people's ideas, the process of deconstruction, it is argued, releases meaning and illuminates context. The analysis also proposes that you have to have the word for a concept, in order to bring about any change.

- Gather examples of how the way in which people talk about an experience, or an area of practice, could shape and may restrict possibilities. Look at the discussion about partnership with parents on page 222 and consider how words and outlook can create very different meanings for this phrase.

- Some discourses incorporate rigid and mutually exclusive opposites: if you are A, then you cannot be B. You may be able to think of some ways of talking, and arguing, that are underpinned by this pattern.

- A predominant discourse can be challenged. For instance, in the USA some young adults challenge the discourse around ethnic group identity that says you can be either 'black' or 'white' and nothing in between. A new approach to identity has arisen, in which some young men and women claim an ethnic group identity that blends different sources.

Applications for childhood

Discourse is a key concept for the sociology of childhood and the social constructivist approach. This idea rests within a theoretical framework that children are born into a pre-existing society, in which the dominant culture(s) have shaped attitudes about values and priorities. The prevailing pattern of discourse determines from childhood what we regard as natural, normal, obviously the right choice, or priority. Discourse is manifested through verbal and non-verbal behaviour. The choice of words shapes thought and the details of how people talk about an issue or area of practice communicate a great deal about attitudes, priorities and values.

Young children construct meaning from their experiences and learn spoken language to express their ideas and feelings. However, they learn the meanings and values that dominate their sociocultural group and deal with the clash of values between groups to which they belong.

What does it mean?

Sociocultural theories: approaches to explanation of adult and child experience through social interaction and the context provided by a social and cultural group.

Social constructivism: a focus on how children, or others, make meaning of experience, with full attention paid to the context of experiences.

Figure 3.6 Children's experiences are shaped by what adults provide

The social constructivist position argues that few young children learn the same things at the same time. Therefore, support for early learning cannot proceed, as if all children pass through the same experiences in sequence. Children construct their own view of reality from personal experiences and use this outlook to deal with new information. So, in this theoretical position, adults' most important task is to understand individual children's understanding and strategies for learning. The approach therefore stresses the context in which children learn and that practitioners need to seek ways to make learning meaningful for each child.

The social constructivist movement in the UK has been influential in encouraging an adult role as enabler or facilitator of children's learning. A more active directing role is seen as potentially disruptive of early development because of the importance of children's own concepts. The power of the approach is in stressing the pointlessness of adults' pushing on with their own plans for children's learning, when there are no links to children's current understanding.

The theoretical ideas have been applied in research through the concept of pedagogy: that of the whole approach of adults whose aim is to support children's learning. The word 'pedagogy' describes the craft of teaching and the interactive process between adult teacher, child learner and the learning environment. So the term does not mean the same as 'curriculum', although a particular approach through a specific curriculum could be part of pedagogy. The term is not restricted to early years practitioners, nor to early years settings and can be applied to parents with their own children, as home-based pedagogy.

International links have furthered the sociocultural base of this broad theoretical perspective. Alternative cultural traditions are used to give context to the experiences of childhood, family life and early years or schools services. There have been especially strong links between the UK and the early years approach in New Zealand and Australia and the particular approach of the centres in the Reggio Emilia region of northern Italy.

> ## What does it mean?
>
> **Pedagogy**: the actions and outlook of practitioners in direct interaction with children and their learning environment, which can be seen to include family and community.

Resources

- **Athey, C.** (1990) *Extending thought in young children: a parent–teacher partnership.* London: Paul Chapman.
- **Bronfenbrenner, U.** (1979) *The ecology of human development.* Cambridge MA: Harvard University Press.
- **Bruner, J.** (1990) *Acts of meaning.* Cambridge MA: Harvard University Press.
- **Byron, T.** (2005) *The house of tiny tearaways.* London: BBC Worldwide Ltd.
- **Caddell, D.** (1998a) *Numeracy in the early years: what the research tells us.* Dundee: Learning and Teaching Scotland.
- **Caddell, D.** (1998b) *Numeracy counts.* Dundee: Learning and Teaching Scotland.
- **Donaldson, M.** (1978) *Children's minds.* London: Fontana.
- **Drummond, M.** (2000) 'Susan Isaacs: pioneering work in understanding children's lives', in Hilton, M. and Hirsch, P. *Practical visionaries: women, education and social progress 1790–1930.* London: Longman.
- **Fabian, H.** (2002) *Children starting school.* London: David Fulton.
- **Graham, P.** (2009) *A biography of Susan Isaacs: a life freeing children's minds.* London: Karnac Books. (I accessed some chapters online with a search of Jean Piaget + Susan Isaacs.)
- **Gibbens, J.** (1950) *Care of children from one to five* (4th edn). London: J&A Churchill Ltd.
- **Hardyment, C.** (1995) *Perfect parents: baby care advice past and present.* Oxford: Oxford Paperbacks.
- **Konner, M.** (1991) *Childhood.* London: Little Brown and Co.
- **Mayall, B.** (ed.) (1994) *Children's childhoods: observed and experienced.* London: Falmer Press.
- **Mayall, B.** (2002) *Towards a sociology for childhood: thinking from children's lives.* Buckingham: Open University Press.
- **Vygotsky, L.** (1962) *Thought and language.* Cambridge MA: MIT Press.
- **Vygotsky, L.** (1978) *Mind in society: the development of higher psychological processes.* Cambridge MA: Harvard University Press.

Research as a source of information and ideas

Research has extended our understanding of how the different parts of children's development relate together: of the whole child that we see day by day. Studies, recent and not so recent, have supported greater awareness of how events support or block children's psychological and physical health. However, research teams do not have all the answers, any more than do experienced practitioners.

The main sections of this chapter are:
- Different ways to study children
- Planning and interpretation in research
- Linking research with practice.

Different ways to study children

In the early decades of research into child development, methods were largely experimental and researchers strove to meet scientific standards of objectivity. Interesting ideas still emerged through open-ended observation, two significant examples being the descriptive materials offered by both Jean Piaget and Lev Vygotsky. However, both these influential figures also tested their ideas through more controlled, experimental methods in the psychological laboratory.

Standards for research

H. Rudolph Schaffer (1998) identified five qualities of well-organised research, undertaken in the traditional, experimental model. He proposed that studies should be:

1 *Empirical*: the conclusions of the research are based on direct observation, not on hunch or some variation of 'Everybody knows that ...'.

2 *Systematic*: the data are collected according to a clear plan, explained in the research report. Methods are not altered by an individual whim.

3 *Controlled:* good research is designed so that explanations or patterns of cause and effect can be deduced as reliably as possible.

4 *Quantitative:* results can be measured accurately and reliable statistics presented.

5 *Public:* details of methods and findings should be open to scrutiny. It must be possible to compare studies and make supported generalisations.

Social scientific research was first established within a tradition of numerical measurement and statistical analysis. Quantitative analysis was seen as the sound basis for concluding that one group was different from another and to track patterns of cause and effect. The descriptive case study tradition belonged more to therapy, where information was gathered in detail from individual experiences or sequences of events.

It is important to understand the traditions described by Schaffer, because such studies have contributed to our understanding of children. A proportion of research about children and childhood is still undertaken through carefully designed experiments, for example the work of Alison Gopnik (2001, 2009) and her colleagues. However, throughout the last decades of the 20th century, some researchers within the social sciences, including those who studied child development, challenged the value of objectivity and quantitative methods.

What does it mean?

Quantitative: analysis of the results of an experiment or observation in terms of numbers, percentages or further statistical analysis. There are mathematical rules for use of different statistical methods.

Qualitative: analysis of observational material in terms of descriptive themes or patterns.

It is not a stark either–or choice; some studies combine both methods.

The development of more subjective methods, including participant observation and narratives, was part of the social constructivist movement (page 49). Supporters rejected the illusion of objectivity in the scientific method, also known as positivism, arguing that social phenomena do not have meaning independently of social actions. Social constructivists present a subjective approach that is not only equally valid, but also more meaningful than detachment through objectivity. There is an emphasis on qualitative, descriptive information, with the fair argument that much that is of interest in child development does not reduce to quantitative analysis and statistics.

Careful research conducted within a constructivist framework still addresses quality. Glenda MacNaughton et al. (2001) propose similar standards to those outlined by Schaffer, although they choose different terms. For example, they stress that research should, among other qualities, be:
- *Ethical:* research should be based on the informed consent of those involved and do no harm.
- *Transparent:* a standard that is similar to Schaffer's 'public' point, in that any research report should enable other people to follow decisions about how the research evolved, what they call the 'research trail'.

- *Contextualised:* there are clearly stated descriptions of the philosophical, theoretical or policy context in which the research was planned and undertaken.
- *Equitable:* research should acknowledge the bias, interests and concerns of researchers.

In a nutshell, it should be possible for someone who is not part of the original research team to understand the aims of any piece of work. It is important to be able to follow what was done and have a sound basis for accepting or disputing the interpretations drawn from the materials that have been collected. A reliable researcher or team should be honest about the limitations of their results for conclusions and any practical applications.

Different research methods

A considerable amount of research has been undertaken with children and their families, and many different approaches have been used. All of the various methods have some built-in drawbacks, as well as advantages.

Experimental methods

Some studies are planned under controlled conditions, perhaps in a psychological laboratory, which would be an ordinary room possibly with a one-way mirror and with the facilities to record exchanges when appropriate. The room may be set up with play materials; a researcher may go through a set of activities and questions, or parents may be asked to interact with their babies. Experimental designs are an attempt to control some of the many factors in the variety of children's ordinary lives. In the traditional method, there are an experimental group and a control group; only the former has a specific experience and the control group is supposed to be the comparison.

The classic experimental method works best when researchers are interested in specific explorations that can be studied in a small-scale way. It is still the case that other random factors can be at work, not least when you are studying the reactions of babies or young children. The whole experimental control group method is a researcher's nightmare when dealing with real children and families outside the laboratory. It is impossible to control all possible sources of variation and good research has to recognise any difficulties.

For example, researchers who are interested in the impact of different types of early years provision do not have, nor should they have, the right to direct families to use particular kinds of provision, according to how it suits the research design. Research teams have to assess whether the families that opt for the childminding service are noticeably different at the outset from the group that has chosen the day nursery option. The big question then is to determine the extent to which any significant differences between the children in development can be explained by their early years provision and what is better explained by family details, like mother's educational level or family's social class.

The Effective Provision of Pre-School Education (EPPE) (**http://eppe.ioe.ac.uk/**) research team wished to compare children who had some type of early years group experience prior to reception class in England with children who had stayed at home. However, in the late 1990s it proved to be a serious challenge to find children who had experienced no early years setting at all. The research report is clear that this 'home' group was very different in sociocultural background, including proportionately more children from minority ethnic groups and children with disabilities, from the main sample. The comparisons made in the report, and the conclusions about the beneficial effect of good-quality early years provision, depend upon use of a complicated statistical model.

Using a mix of methods

Many of the studies of children and families involve a mix of methods, perhaps observations but also interviews and different types of psychological or educational assessment. For example, the original EPPE research included the assessment of many children and gathering information about the provision they attended. However, a smaller study involved direct observation of some children and their early years practitioners (Siraj-Blatchford et al., 2002). The characteristics of children's home learning environment were judged by what parents said they did, in response to a set of questions. The study largely focused on group provision, but offered some information from telephone interviews of a sample of childminders.

In a longitudinal design, the same children are studied over a period of time. The EPPE research has continued to study the same group of children over their primary school years, becoming the Effective Pre-School and Primary Education project. The study has now followed those children into adolescence, with their secondary school experience. In the USA, the National Institute for Child Health and Human Development is tracking more than 1,300 children over ten towns and cities (**www.nichd.nih.gov**).

In contrast, a cross-sectional research design enables study of different ages, without waiting for the same children to grow up. For example, research into children's moral development has studied how children in different age groups are able to reason about a moral dilemma. In that type of study, children are asked similar questions, or given similar challenging experiences, in order to explore whether younger and older children approach the same situation in different ways.

Cross-cultural or cross-context designs include children from more than one social class, culture or country. A meaningful cross-cultural study can be hard to plan: it may make no sense to ask the same questions in a different setting. Socio-cultural studies tend to step aside from direct comparisons. Researchers may look in detail at child rearing patterns, or the approach to early years education in different cultures. They aim to understand the ideas in place and perhaps to consider what can be learned for another sociocultural context.

Consider each of the different approaches described in this section. What are the advantages and disadvantages of each method?

- For example, longitudinal studies can gather a great deal of information, but the fact that they are carried out over long time spans means that society has changed since the studies began. So how far can the lessons of this research be applied now?

- It is possible that in a cross-sectional design, something has happened that has affected many or most children. Perhaps what is observed of seven-year-olds is only explained partly by their age. Some of the difference should be attributed to a significant educational change that has affected them, but not the group of 11-year-olds in the same study.

- A small study or narrative approach may provide meaningful descriptions, but how much can the study be generalised to other children or settings?

You could return to this reflective activity when you have completed this chapter.

Naturalistic observation

From the 1970s and 80s more researchers aimed to observe events and behaviour that occurred as naturally as possible. Studies were undertaken in settings that were part of children's daily life: nurseries, schools or their own home. There was concern that the desire for experimental control could remove most of the variation of genuine interest. For instance:

- Jerome Bruner led a major research study based in Oxford throughout the 1970s, which developed a target child method of observation. Similar studies gathered observational data on children or adults and then analysed the information by categories, such as types of play or adult behaviours. Judy Dunn focused on naturalistic observation of children in their own home, in communication with parents and siblings.

- Some observational studies moved away from a quantitative approach altogether and used qualitative methods: identifying themes and supporting this interpretation by examples of events and conversations. Such an approach adopts a more narrative method: the aim is effectively to tell the story of a child's experiences or that of a group.

- Researchers still aim to make sense of what they observe: to analyse and reach well-supported conclusions. An example is the work of Peter Elfer and Dorothy Selleck for the Early Childhood Unit, described in the Everyday Stories resource (**www.everydaystories.org.uk**).

Figure 4.1 How do children choose to use a resource?

The aim of observers in this type of research is to remain uninvolved, to the extent that they do not make a significant difference to the events that unfold in front of them. However, good-quality research always recognises that the behaviour of children, and perhaps even more so that of adults, can be different because of the presence of an observer. One way to resolve this issue is to spend time becoming a familiar, and ultimately almost ignored, presence. Even if you make notes from the outset, a practical step is to abandon the first day's observation.

Take another **perspective**

There is a limit to how much you can become part of the background as an observer. Researchers are people too and many are unwilling to reject children who are persistent in wanting a chat, and even more so when children are upset.

- Joyce Robertson made the written observations, while James Robertson held the camera for their influential 1950s films about separation (page 74). In the film of a young boy staying in a residential nursery, you can see clearly one point where Joyce Robertson cannot stop herself from hugging the boy as he leans against her in total distress.

- Peter Elfer has written (in articles about his research during 2003–4 for *Nursery World*) of his unwillingness (very reasonable in my view) to be rude and try to ignore a young child who was demonstrably pleased to see him, as a familiar visitor in the nursery.

Some narrative studies are undertaken by a participant observer: someone who is also directly involved in the setting and is not trying to step to one side. Vivian Gussin Paley (1984, 1988) offers one example of the reflective reporting approach in her accounts of a year in nursery school. Her studies focus as much on what she learned as on the consuming interests of the children over those months. Action research is often undertaken by practitioners who remain part of daily life in a nursery, while documenting a change. An example is Penny Holland's (2003) observations of the removal of a ban on weapons play in the early years centre where she worked (see page 208).

Some researchers have made detailed longitudinal observations of individual children, sometimes with whom they have a personal relationship – a pattern which you could say started with Jean Piaget and the observations of his young children. Robin Campbell (1999) described in detail how Alice, his granddaughter, learned her early literacy skills. Campbell draws practical conclusions and applications from the narrative of Alice's learning journey. Cath Arnold (1999) described the development of Georgia, who attended Pen Green centre where Arnold was part of the team. In Arnold's (2003) account of Harry, it became clear that, as well as being an experienced practitioner, she was also grandmother to both children.

What does it mean?

Participant observer: a development of the observational method, in which the person observing may remain active in what happens: playing or talking with a child, although ideally not over-influencing what happens.

Narrative approach: a variation of observation, in which there is an attempt to document the detail and flow of events as they happen, often from the perspective of individual children.

Action research: studies in which researchers, who may also be part of the working team, document change as it evolves.

Some practical researchers have involved children more directly in the gathering of information. Margaret Carr (2001) pioneered the approach of the children's learning stories: a narrative flow that aims to follow the cutting edge of children's learning through their self-chosen play and current interests. Carr developed this approach to child-centred documentation in New Zealand and it has been adopted to an extent in the UK. Consultation projects have explored research methods that work effectively to bring children into the process. The Mosaic approach, developed by Alison Clark and Valerie Wignall (Clark and Moss, 2001), involved young children as researchers, enabling them to express their views, use cameras to take photos and to lead the researcher on a nursery tour.

Computer imaging and neuroscience

Until computer imaging technology was developed, it was only possible to study human brain function as the result of surgery, autopsy and trying to generalise from animal studies. There are now options to study brain activity of live, healthy humans of different ages. Such studies have significantly extended our understanding of the impact of experience on young children.

The EEG (electroencephalogram) is the main technique used by neuroscientists to study babies and young children, when there is no medical reason for looking at their brain function. The EEG records brain waves and leads to a computer-generated picture of what is happening in different locations within the brain. Detailed EEG recordings are studied, together with video recordings of babies and young children engaged in various experiences and activities. It has then been possible to draw some conclusions about the amount and location of brain activity in the different parts of a child's brain.

Babies and young children wear a cap lined with special sponges. This geodesic net enables the EEG to monitor brain waves, without the slight scratching of the skull that is necessary to attach electrodes. The electrodes sense the natural electrical changes at the scalp that are triggered when groups of neurons are activated in the brain.

The complexity of the methods used in study of the human brain can challenge the understanding of anyone who is not a neuroscientist. Fortunately, reports have emerged that are understandable for readers outside that profession (Shore, 1997; Healy, 2004; Tayler, 2007; Howard-Jones, undated, *circa* 2008).

Planning and interpretation in research

Carefully conducted research can open our eyes to what children can do or how we can best support them. But the lessons of research, and the concepts generated by studies, must be seasoned with wisdom. Questions need to be asked of any kind of research, for example, 'What leads you to say that?', 'Does this apply to everyone?' and my favourite question, 'So what?', a query that does not have to sound as confrontational as it looks on paper.

Unfortunately, you also sometimes need an additional question, 'Are there vested interests here?' when research implications are being communicated to you by a third party. For example, some commercial enterprises have been keen to seize aspects of the brain research as supporting a particular product or certain type of teaching method. In autumn 2009 the educational division of Disney, producers of the Baby Einstein DVDs, offered refunds after the threat of legal action from parents in the USA on the grounds of misrepresentation.

Ethics and values

Research in social sciences, including psychology, has become more respectful of the people involved in observations and experiments who are not the researchers. It is symbolic that my own professional organisation, the British Psychological Society, required from the 1990s that articles for its house journal no longer used the impersonal term 'subjects'. People have to be described as children, students, parents, and so on. This shift in words was evidence of a change in attitude and power relations; do you remember 'discourse' from page 51?

The ethics committees of professional organisations or universities are far more concerned than, say, in the 1960s or 70s that anyone involved in research is able to give their informed consent. People need an honest description of the study which they are being invited to join or are being asked to allow their child to join. Information can only be withheld if there is a good and safe reason to do so. Then participants in a study must be given an information debriefing after the work is complete.

> ### What does it mean?
>
> **Informed consent**: people have enough information to be able to agree or decline to participate in a research study, interview, questionnaire or any other method. Parents give consent on behalf of young children.
>
> **Debriefing**: people are given results, or a full explanation of their participation after a study is finished.

In past decades, researchers were very concerned about ethics and values, but the priorities were different. What really mattered were the scientific standards of objectivity, appropriate statistics and not cheating on the data. For example, in 1920 John Watson, the founder of behaviourism (page 25), and Rosalie Rayner published a series of experiments with a nine-month-old baby known as Albert B (sometimes referred to as 'Little Albert'). Watson and Rayner used the techniques of classical conditioning to make the baby scared of a white rat. Albert was happy to play with a series of animals, until the researchers hit a steel bar with a hammer right behind the baby as he reached for the rat. Albert very soon associated his fright at this racket with the rat and began to panic as soon as it appeared. Watson and Rayner reported that Albert's fear then spread to other white fuzzy objects, including a rabbit, dog, a fur coat and a Santa Claus mask. They used the study to argue that fears are learned through direct experiences and so could also be removed.

Watson and Rayner were challenged by their contemporaries because their conclusions rested on a sample of one baby; they had no control group and were inconsistent in their reporting of procedures and results. Current readers are more likely to be shocked by the description of a desperate baby: crying and trying to escape the white rat and presumably also from the researchers, who in the grainy photograph appear to wear a very scary Santa Claus mask (Cole and

Cole, 2000: 26). Watson and Rayner claimed that learned fears could be removed by similar procedures. In the original report, which you can access on the internet (**http://psychclassics.yorku.ca/Watson/emotion.htm**), Watson and Rayner say that Albert left the hospital, where he spent his baby months, just as they were about to attempt to reverse his fears.

Make the connection with... **Children's fears**

The ethics of the study with Little Albert are unacceptable, but the point about learned fears is valid. Young children, and adults to an extent, often make sense of a situation that induces fear by linking key elements.

I am not the only parent (sample of my two-year-old son's hospital experience in 1983) who has had to support a very young child through extreme wariness of anyone in a white coat, resulting from a single frightening, although not painful, procedure done by only one person.

Interpretation and generalisation

Any research study has to tackle the major issue of interpretation: what sense can be reliably made of the findings and what conclusions can be drawn? Then, how far is it justified to generalise those conclusions beyond the precise time, place and individuals involved in this study?

Some of the interpretation issues are about decisions made when a study is set up. For example, suppose a research team chose to observe children in their nursery during the hours of 'free play', but not during tidy-up time or lunchtime. They cannot then conclude that the most valuable early mathematical activities occur through the medium of play activities. The research plan has specifically excluded the possibility (a real one, in my view) that tidying up, or laying the table, provides a meaningful context for children to use and extend their understanding of mathematical concepts such as number or size and shape.

Figure 4.2 Children do not only learn from play activities

Researchers need to be ready to check their assumptions. One local study of night waking in early childhood (personal communication at a conference) had to re-organise when the team realised that some parents in the 'no problems' group were woken up most nights. However, these parents had not sought help at the sleep clinic, where the team found the 'problems' group.

Assumptions also need to be challenged at the interpretation stage of a study. Some observational research in the 1970s and 80s focused on adult behaviour, often in an attempt to distinguish the interactional styles of teachers from nursery nurses. Some studies had an unchecked assumption that any differences between the groups must indicate the more beneficial style of teachers. None of the studies that I encountered at the time of my review (Laishley, 1984; I then worked under a different surname) had started by defining clearly what was appropriate practitioner behaviour to support young children. Then it would have been possible to plan observations to determine who was behaving in this way and whether differences could be explained by professional qualification.

Cause, effect and the control group

The experimental method is supposed to ensure objectivity. However, researchers are people and commitment to a particular theory can sometimes close minds to other possible interpretations.

Sara Smilansky explored what she called socio-dramatic play as part of her challenge to Piaget's conviction that those children who were younger than six or seven years of age could not handle abstract ideas. She stressed that sophisticated levels of thinking could be observed in socio-dramatic play, and that such play was therefore important to promote in early childhood, especially for children from socially disadvantaged families. Smilansky developed a method called play tutoring and set up research to demonstrate her theoretical proposition. Children in the play tutoring group, in comparison with a control group, increased their level of socio-dramatic play and showed an improvement in their social and intellectual skills. Smilansky presented the findings as an endorsement of the power of play tutoring and the essential nature of socio-dramatic play for children's learning.

In the 1980s, Peter Smith and his team undertook research to check Smilansky's claims (Smith, 1994). They contrasted three groups of nursery children: one group received play tutoring; a second group had a more general skills training session but with the same amount of adult attention; and a third group had nothing additional to their normal nursery session. Children who received either of the two extra sessions showed equivalent improvements in intellectual and language development. Generous adult attention and friendly communication were the key input; there was nothing special about play tutoring, as such.

Make the connection with... *Cause and effect*

It is often complicated to tease out genuine causal relationships. In 2009 there was significant media coverage of a report from Simon Moore (2009) and his colleagues at the University of Cardiff. The headlines were along the lines that eating sweets and chocolate led to violent behaviour.

The Cardiff team's interest was provoked from earlier research showing that violent adolescents with impulsive behaviour also had very unhealthy diets. The report analysed data from the British Cohort Study, which has followed 17,500 individuals born in 1970. They looked at the sub-group who had been convicted of a violent offence by 34 years of age. They found that 69 per cent of this group had eaten sweets and chocolates on a daily basis at the age of ten years. Of the group without any criminal conviction for violence, only 42 per cent had eaten sweets every day.

The explanation is not that daily sweet consumption causes violence. That claim would not stand up, if only because 31 per cent of the convicted group had not eaten daily sweets. The report suggests that the unrestricted access to sweets is part of a childhood in which the children were not enabled to learn impulse control: that you cannot have what you want straightaway. There are other possibilities of interpretation, but given the historical data they can be no more than considered guesses.

Are the conclusions valid?

Jean Piaget's cognitive developmental stage theory (page 33) exerted significant influence on views of child development. However, even at the time of his research some researchers challenged the conclusions that he drew from his interviews and experiments with young children. Susan Isaacs had contact with Jean Piaget in Geneva and in the late 1920s he visited the Malting House School in Cambridge, of which Isaacs was the head. Two examples of research, reported in Cole and Cole (2000: 351), highlight care about conclusions.

Figure 4.3 So how exactly does a bike work?

Jean Piaget drew support for his pre-operational stage from interviews he held with young children about how bicycles work. During the interview a bicycle was propped against a chair, so the child could see it. An interview with Grim, aged five and a half, shows the kind of response that made Piaget say that children of this age operated with pre-causal reasoning. The interview began in the following way.

Piaget asks, 'How does the bicycle move along?' Grim replies, 'With the brakes on top of the bike.' The interview continues with:

P: What is the brake for?

G: To make it go because you push.

P: What do you push with?

G: With your feet.

P: What does that do?

G: It makes it go.

P: How?

G: With the brakes.

Susan Isaacs was sceptical of the evidence, apparently provided by interviews with children like Grim. Cole and Cole quote from Isaacs's observation of Dan (aged five years and nine months) in Malting House:

At that moment, Dan happened to be sitting on a tricycle in the garden, back-pedalling. I went to him and said, 'The tricycle is not moving forward, is it?' 'Of course not, when I'm back-pedalling,' he said. 'Well,' I asked, 'how does it go forward when it does?' 'Oh well,' he replied, 'your feet press the pedals, that turns the crank round, and the cranks turn that round' (pointing to the cog wheel), 'and that makes the chain go round, and the chain turns the hub round, and then the wheels go round – and there you are!'

Of course, you cannot take Susan Isaacs's observation of Dan and say it proves all five-year-olds understand how bicycles operate. But Isaacs did not generalise from Dan to the knowledge of all his peers. She put a fair challenge to Piaget's claim that five-year-olds, in general, are unable to make causal links about the workings of a familiar item, in this case a bicycle. Philip Graham (2009: 164) takes up the story to describe that Piaget took Isaacs's criticisms seriously and discussed the details in his research papers. Piaget's counter-argument was that the Malting House children were above average intelligence and ability and that Dan was operating more like a six- or seven-year-old child, so the findings did not present a real problem for Piaget's theory.

Children try to make sense of a situation

Several decades later, Margaret Donaldson and her team in Edinburgh challenged Piaget's interpretation of young children's replies as 'wrong' and evidence of immature thinking. Margaret Donaldson had started her career in developmental psychology when behaviourism was very strong in the UK. She spent several months in 1957 working with Piaget in Geneva. Donaldson was impressed with his methods and the scope of his theory, but was unconvinced that Piaget was correct in the detail. During the 1960s and 70s, Donaldson set up a nursery in the Psychology department at Edinburgh and began research with the children who attended. During the same period she had strong links with Jerome Bruner in the USA, who was working to identify the educational implications of his theoretical concepts (page 39).

Margaret Donaldson and her team were interested in early language and thinking and they seriously considered how Piaget's classic experiments might look to children: the sense they might have made of the situation. Her team worked from the assumption that what children said to researchers made sense to those children. It was not inevitably 'wrong' and was often as 'right' as they could make it, given the oddities of the research situation and the questions that adults had asked them. Philip Graham (2009) describes how Nathan Isaacs, who also spent time in the Malting House School, came to similar conclusions: adults' questions to children needed to connect with their level of understanding, or else their replies could be misinterpreted in the context of adult knowledge.

Make the connection with... **Daily practice**

The work of Margaret Donaldson and her team reminds us that any adult can easily decide that their perspective is the only, or most sensible, one. Piaget proposed that young children were egocentric: unable to take the perspective of other people. But often this term could be applied to adults. As a reflective practitioner, you will consider play and other daily situations in which you are closely involved with children.

- Take a moment to reflect … Are there routines or less-than-easy situations in which it is tempting to believe that the children's perspective is much the same as yours: of course they know or understand …?

- In conversations, especially if you are keen to help children learn an idea, you need to watch and listen. If children look confused, perhaps from their point of view the adult has asked odd questions. It is the adult talking nonsense and not the child in their efforts to reply (see also page 180).

- Responsible practitioners are ready to consider what sort of answer a child is giving to a question, rather than simply deciding it is the wrong answer.

- That steady stare sometimes means that a four-year-old brain is working overtime: trying to work out what it is you want to know. What are your intentions in asking this rather incomprehensible question?

Margaret Donaldson (1978) and her team ran many of Piaget's experiments with minor changes. They made an important shift in interpretation with their key assumption that young children did not 'switch off' their thinking skills just because they were in an experiment. Despite adult intentions to control the setting for research purposes, of course children bring in social expectations about how adults behave and what they usually want when they ask questions.

For instance, the team experimented with Piaget's three mountains scenario. In the original method, children sat by a model of three mountains and the researcher placed a doll at different locations. Children had then to say, or show from a selection of photos, what the doll could see. Young children usually said or showed the doll as having their own visual perspective.

- Donaldson's team first gave three- to five-year-olds some experience of a layout, in which a toy figure can see another figure from some positions but not others. Then they introduced the three mountains layout. Children could mostly say correctly when the first figure can see the second and when the latter is hidden from view.
- They tried several variations on a blocked view experiment and reported that children made more sense of the situation when it was explained as 'hiding'. A naughty boy might be hiding from a policeman or a mouse from a cat. Given a believable scenario, the children were far more able to 'look through the eyes' of one of the figures in the setting.

The team also varied the conservation experiments that Piaget used to support his view that children younger than about five years could not understand that number remained constant, even if objects were moved into a different pattern.

- The Edinburgh group found that children were far more likely to say that two rows consisting of the same number of toys were still the same when a soft toy, Naughty Teddy, had pushed one row up tighter, than when the adult researcher had brought about the same change.
- One possible explanation is based on children's sophisticated social understanding of relations between children and adults and how the latter usually behave. It is very possible that when an adult makes a change and then asks a question about whether it's still the same, children are misdirected into thinking that something must have happened. Otherwise, why would an adult ask that kind of question?

It is important to know that, even with Naughty Teddy messing up the rows, some children still concluded that a more stretched-out row made 'more' in terms of number.

Linking research with practice

Research, following any method, does not offer a clear-cut answer to all the practical questions that are relevant to people who spend their days with children. H. Rudolf Schaffer (1998) describes how practitioners, and policy makers, usually want straightforward answers about what to do, or what is not recommended. However, research studies, and responsible interpretation, rarely provide answers without a strong seasoning of 'it all depends'.

Make the connection with... **Different priorities**

Charles Desforges (2004) neatly summed up the potential research–practice gulf when he asked whether 'Researchers have got lost in thought whilst practitioners have gone missing in action'. Desforges raised key issues about the need to link, what I have called evidence and wisdom (page 12).

Here, I will add my own opinion based on a great deal of reading and attendance at conferences and seminars. Problems arise not because researchers follow a theoretical position based on positivism or constructivism. Academically inclined speakers enthused by the narrative approach, and the power of sociocultural theory, are as likely as their more traditionally scientific colleagues to fail to connect with early years practitioners.

Part of the problem is, I suggest, an enthusiasm for using specialist terminology such as 'discourse' (page 51) that is unfamiliar to outsiders, despite the insightful perspective from social constructivism about the power relations created by choices about language.

Research in a time and place

In his review of how research could, or could not, inform practice, H. Rudolf Schaffer (1998) describes how the ideal of carefully planned and controlled research can rarely be met, because of the complexity of most social issues of any interest. However, the social priorities of the era often determine the questions that shape a research plan, the interpretation of findings, even whether the team can get funding in the first place, not to mention whether an unwelcome report gets minimal coverage. Schaffer points out how studies of children and the effects of divorce were first undertaken when social attitudes towards divorce were hostile. The research plans focused on finding negative effects.

A similar pattern was followed in the early research into day care. The experience was believed to be harmful, so the job of research was to quantify those inevitable negative effects. If any readers are thinking that bias is a problem of the past, this is not true. There is a genuine risk now when considering day care in the UK that opinion has swung in the opposite direction. Political priorities have defined childcare as the block to getting mothers back into the workforce and to reducing child poverty. In some quarters, there is confident repetition that research proves time spent in any early years setting delivers measurable benefits for children's development, when the accurate picture is more complex. Research showing that very young children may be harmed by long hours in day care, especially when the provision is of doubtful quality, has sometimes been dismissed. Even more unacceptable is the fact that the researchers have sometimes been simply attacked in print as antagonistic towards women (Belsky and Steinberg, 1978; Belsky, 2001).

Prevailing social values can determine what is studied. Alison Gopnik et al. (2001) describe how, for decades, most developmental psychology in the USA was uninterested in babies and very young children. Partly this omission seemed to arise because babies and very young children tend not to cooperate in controlled experiments. But it was also relevant that young children were seen as women's work and therefore irrelevant to almost exclusively male academic departments.

Over the last quarter of the 20th century, it was largely unacceptable to study male–female differences and certainly to allow that there could be a biological explanation for differences, at least as important as the power of socialisation. Even at the beginning of the 21st century, Simon Baron-Cohen (2003) describes his extreme caution about presenting his ideas that adult male and female brains work differently: not better or worse, just in a different way, on average. There is definitely room for caution, given some of the sweeping myths about sex differences in brain development. Lise Eliot (2009) takes care to explain the ways in which small differences in early childhood appear to be accentuated by differential treatment of the sexes, until some significant differences can be tracked by middle childhood and beyond.

Short- and long-term consequences

Policy makers wish for research to deliver swift and clear-cut answers. However, effective interventions sometimes work over a much longer time span than is convenient for political life, especially in an atmosphere dominated by short-term measurable outcomes.

During the 1970s, many programmes in the USA and then in the UK were designed to improve the achievements of children from socially disadvantaged backgrounds through early educational intervention. These projects were assessed by differences in measures of intelligence (IQ tests) between children who had attended special programmes, or had been in the control group. A boost for IQ in the intervention group did not last longer than the early years of school and the gap between the two groups typically closed. This apparent 'wash-out' of the IQ difference dashed hopes that children's early educational experience could counteract social deprivation. These findings spread a significant level of gloom over practical early years research during the late 1970s and early 80s. (If your career does not stretch back that far, please believe me; people became very depressed!)

However, some of the best-organised and well-funded American projects continued to follow children through their schooling and they found a long-term impact of the early experience. The successful programmes, such as the High/Scope Ypsilanti programme, had a clear structure for children's learning, an active role for children in the day and significant parent involvement in the details of the children's experience. Children from such programmes showed greater competence in school and stayed in education. They were less likely to be assigned to remedial classes, or to be kept down a year: a common option in the USA when children are struggling. By early adulthood the young people had higher aspirations for employment; the girls were less likely to have become pregnant in adolescence and both sexes were less likely to get into trouble with the law.

The high-quality early childhood programmes seemed to have created a positive outlook in the children. They viewed school as a useful experience and themselves as people who could achieve and overcome difficulties. However, just as important is the fact that parents had been closely engaged, which meant that they fully supported their children and took a positive approach to schooling. The IQ difference faded; positive attitudes lasted, along with a drive to persevere and succeed. The longitudinal EPPE research in England is showing that a good-quality early years setting can contribute to closing the gap between children from socially more, and less, advantaged backgrounds.

Make the connection with… **What does a term mean?**

Parent involvement was a factor in the long-term positive impact of the well-funded early childhood programmes in the USA. However, it is not accurate to assume that any project that describes an element called parent involvement is necessarily referring to very similar developments within the service.

Desforges and Abouchaar (2003) and Harris and Goodall (2007) describe the great difficulty in comparing research when studies refer to 'involving parents', but actually mean very different approaches by the same term. The overall conclusion was that the only kind of parent involvement that had a significant impact on children's achievement was when parents were closely engaged in their children's learning.

The effective initiatives in primary school were aimed directly at acknowledging and encouraging what Desforges and Abouchaar summed up as 'at-home good parenting'. There could be sound reasons for offering other kinds of involvement for parents in the life of an early years or school setting. But there was no basis for assuming that this kind of involvement would have any impact on children's development or academic achievements.

Does research affect practice?

Some research over previous decades has demonstrably affected practice and a few examples are given here. You will find further examples in other chapters. Greater ease of access to information via the internet seems likely to increase the links, especially since good-quality summaries and updates from organisations such as the Early Childhood Unit (page 247) always give a website address.

Maternal deprivation theory

John Bowlby (1965) documented the genuine distress of children who were separated from their families through the evacuation of children from UK cities during the Second World War. The evacuees, and children he studied in residential orphanages, had often been separated from their family and even siblings were sometimes divided. However, Bowlby's psychoanalytical basis led him to interpret the impact of separation on children as maternal deprivation: the temporary or permanent loss to a child of a mother's care and attention. His practical conclusions were that, unless children had the exclusive attention of their mother, especially for the first three years in childhood, then children would be permanently emotionally damaged.

John Bowlby's approach was convenient when the war ended and the government wanted to persuade those women who were mothers to go back into the home, out of the jobs they had occupied for the war effort, and close down the day nurseries (Riley, 1993). The maternal deprivation theory continued to be very influential and shaped views about employment of women who were also mothers and the lower age limits for children to enter nursery class or school. Fresh approaches to attachment have led to a rethink, including the legacy of John Bowlby (page 83).

Children in hospital

The research of James Robertson and Joyce Robertson (1989) brought about significant changes in hospital practice for children and their families. Up to the 1950s and 60s, it was medical practice to treat children in hospital as if they were any other patient: small bodies that were ill, but cried a lot at the outset. Medical opinion was that children had short memories, so there could be no lasting ill-effects, even when parents were made unwelcome, because they allegedly upset their children.

James and Joyce Robertson made two films: *A two year old goes to hospital* in 1953 and *Going to hospital with mother* in 1958. The documentaries show the genuine distress felt by children on separation from their family, combined with the strange situation of a hospital stay. The children's distress was interpreted by the Robertsons in terms of separation from their mother, in line with John Bowlby's maternal deprivation theory. The view now would be that children had been separated from a network of family relationships. A shift away now from the exclusive focus on the mother–child relationship does not reduce the ground-breaking nature of their observational research.

James Robertson, in particular, was very active in using their material to try to change hospital practice, but it took time and a considerable amount of pressure. They managed by 1959 to get government guidance to recommend that medical practice recognise the full emotional and social needs of sick children. However, many medical teams continued to resist any change. The turning point came in the 1960s, when excerpts of the films were shown on television. A group of mothers in Battersea, south London, formed Mother Care for Children in Hospital (now Action for Sick Children). This organisation put sustained pressure on medical teams to acknowledge the distress of children and to enable easy family contact to maintain key relationships.

Challenging assumptions in practice

From the 1990s onwards some researchers became committed to bringing the children's point of view. As you will appreciate from the discussion about Susan Isaacs (page 23), in some ways there was a rediscovery of the value and power of approaching any situation from the children's perspectives.

Consultative action research projects have found ways to enable even young children to express opinions and preferences. Judy Miller (1996) describes how children could think about possible purchases for their nursery, even though they did not yet fully understand the abstract ideas of money. Wendy Titman (1992, 1994) describes ways of enabling primary school-age children to express their views and informed insight about their own school grounds. See also the discussion from page 208 about rethinking the ban on what adults judged to be war and weapons play.

Research can be wrong; experts can be mistaken

It is not only practitioners, or policy makers, who would like a straightforward answer to a straightforward question. The media of newspapers, magazines and television want information and even the quality end of the media can struggle with the 'buts', 'maybes' and lack of a neat cause-and-effect pattern. The legal system has looked towards expert witnesses to provide definite answers in cases of child protection. Early years practitioners need to be aware that 'experts' can be egocentric, unable to see alternatives to their own theory, and are sometimes proved wrong.

Unexplained infant deaths

During the 1970s and 80s, parents in the UK were told that laying babies on their back put them at risk of choking and that the safest position was on their stomachs or their side. This very firm advice was based on research with premature babies, which was then, with no further justification, generalised to the care of full-term babies. By the 1990s, statistical tracking showed a rise in unexplained infant death, often called cot death. Further research identified the stomach sleeping position as a risk factor in what became called Sudden Infant Death Syndrome (SIDS). The advice to parents was reversed and the level of unexplained infant deaths dropped significantly.

Careful tracking of the level of unexplained infant deaths, before and after the reversal of advice, showed that behaviour change by parents had reduced the level of unexplained infant deaths. This episode is a sober warning about the risks of generalising from small-scale research findings. But the link between sleeping position and infant death is not an absolute cause and effect. Many parents who followed the 1980s instruction did not face the tragedy of losing their baby. Sleeping position was a significant risk factor, but research continues to look at other factors, such as smoking in the family home and genetic vulnerability.

The back sleeping position seems so 'obvious' to practitioners who have trained since the 1990s that I have heard doubts expressed that parents were ever told to put their babies to sleep on their stomach. (To this reservation, I must reply in true pantomime style, 'Oh yes they were!')

I raised my babies in the early 1980s and could not reconcile this instruction with information that young babies could suffocate if given a pillow. I put my son and then my daughter to sleep on their side – alternating left and right each time – until they were agile enough to change their own sleeping position.

What causes autism?

In the 1970s, expert opinion agreed that the pattern of child behaviour we now call autistic spectrum disorder was caused by emotionally cold and unresponsive mothers, who were offensively called 'refrigerator mothers'. The mother-blaming theory sat comfortably with the strong post-Freudian influence in much of psychiatry and a male-dominated profession. This theoretical perspective caused considerable distress within families and it is most likely to have delayed the more constructive approaches that are now available to support parents.

Research can be confusing; experts may not agree

The idea of hyperactivity in children gained a hold in the late 1970s and early 80s. Even at that time, some researchers expressed doubts about a significant syndrome and alarm about normal childhood exuberance being inconvenient to adults, who might press for solution through medication. There remains considerable disagreement about the definition and causes of Attention Deficit Hyperactivity Disorder. If practitioners, or parents for that matter, only encounter one strand of the available research or application into practice, they can be forgiven for believing that what they have heard or read is the whole story.

Advice on a healthy diet has become progressively more confusing as small-scale research projects seem to suggest that a particular food is beneficial or that another food has risks to health. An important issue for early years practitioners, and parents, is that advice suitable for a healthy adult diet cannot simply be transferred to diets for infants and young children. Children's food has to fuel their growing, as well as maintain health. But children also appear to have different nutritional requirements from adults because their bodies work differently.

Figure 4.4 A healthy diet is very important for children's growth

Make the connection with... **What did the research actually say?**

Sometimes it is useful to discover what was actually done in a research study. One piece of folk wisdom was 'Research has shown' that left to their own devices, children will choose a balanced diet over the days, even if their choices are unbalanced within each day. This advice became close to letting children eat whatever they liked.

During the 1970s I passed on this misleading information as an inexperienced child psychologist, until experience as a parent in the 1980s made me question it. I found a description of the original research in the 1983 first edition of Christina Hardyment's (1995) *Social history of childcare advice*. It is now possible to read the original research report on the internet:

(www.pubmedcentral.nih.gov/picrender.fcgi?artid=537465&blobtype=pdf)

Clara Davis undertook a study in the USA in 1938 about 'self-selected feeding'. The research studied babies of six to eleven months of age, who were starting on solid foods, and followed them for six years. These children were in a residential home and some were in poor health at the outset. They were given a wide array of food from which to select their meals. But all the choices were good-quality, freshly cooked food. It was true that some children ate nothing but bananas for one meal, or were very enthusiastic about potatoes one day. Their food intake and health were monitored carefully and they were healthy, energetic children. However, the children's choices did not include crisps and fizzy drinks, nor did they snack between meals.

I think this study does offer practical implications for parents and practitioners. But what do you think should be the link to practice now?

Figure 4.5 Early childhood should be a happy time for young children

Evidence-based policy and practice

The perspective of social history, as well as an understanding of the nature of research, is now especially important with the growth of evidence-based policy and practice. It is a laudable aim that good practice, for early years or other practical professional fields, should rest on good-quality research. However, the environment in which research is undertaken is a very different world from practice, let alone government policy making.

Substantial research projects, such as EPPE, have worked to address assumptions that could undermine the validity of their conclusions. A clear statement of values, as well as methods, is needed for evidence-based practice. Recommendations for what is provided to children need to be grounded in information that is open to challenge. The EPPE research made a strong point about what leads to quality in early years group provision. However, public statements by ministers tend to imply that any early years provision will improve children's outcomes.

It is easy for misinterpretation of research, or over-enthusiastic application of ideas, to become self-perpetuating. For as long as enough people keep saying that something is a proven fact, it becomes less likely that anyone will ask, 'Proven by whom?' or 'Can you give me the reference?' Paul Howard-Jones (2008) offers a summary from a seminar series that brought together experts from both neuroscience and education. They were concerned about the 'neuromyths' that have gained credence on the basis of repeated misinformation. The report challenges, in particular, the tenuous research basis of many programmes that claim to promote brain-based learning and some of the application of individual learning styles. Some of the basic ideas can be sound, such as the importance of enabling children to be physically active. However, the claims about precise consequences for brain functioning or right- and left-brain learning do not stand up to scrutiny in terms of any underlying neuroscience.

The concept of evidence-based policy has gained ground. Yet, as David Bridges (2009) points out, the relationship between the nature of research and the demands of policy decision making is far from straightforward. The Labour government (up to 2010) developed an unprecedented interest in commissioning educational research and literature reviews. Some of this funded research was very useful for early years practice. However, official acceptance of findings was influenced by whether a report offered support for a policy to which a governmental department was already committed, for example over the contentious issues of when and how to teach children to read and write.

What does it mean?

Evidence-based practice: an approach that values making clear links between information gained through research and actual practice. The term is often also used to mean good daily practice, in which practitioners are able to put into words the rationale for their choices.

Evidence-based policy: an approach in which policy directions are influenced, or supported and justified, by research on relevant topics.

Take another **perspective**

You will have noticed that the references in this chapter have ranged over many decades. Research from many years ago can still resonate throughout later decades in terms of what the study allegedly proved or said. However, I think also that it is unwise to draw some arbitrary time boundary and decline to learn from any studies 'older' than that point.

We also need respect for social history to avoid the blithe assumption of 'we know it all now'. Past mistakes seem easy to identify, with the luxury of hindsight. It is tempting to pronounce, 'How could they…?' or 'Surely it was obvious that …?' Current misinterpretations or serious misapprehensions will take time to be revealed. It is deeply unwise to think that now (whenever 'now' is) we cannot possibly be halfway up a new dead-end, or desperately in need of somebody to say, 'Hold on. What makes us so certain that …?'

Resources

- **Arnold, C.** (1999) *Child development and learning 2–5 years: Georgia's story.* London: Paul Chapman.
- **Arnold, C.** (2003) *Observing Harry: child development and learning 0–5.* Maidenhead: Open University Press.
- **Baron-Cohen, S.** (2003) *The essential difference: men, women and the extreme male brain.* London: Allen Lane.
- **Belsky, J., Steinberg, L.** (1978) 'The effects of day care – a critical review', *Child development*, Vol 49, 929–49.

- **Belsky, J.** (2001) 'Emanuel Miller Lecture – Developmental risks (still) associated with early child care', *Journal of Child Psychology and Psychiatry,* Vol 42 , no 7, 845–59. **http://cep.lse.ac.uk/seminarpapers/23-02-07-BEL.pdf**
- **Bowlby, J.** (1965) *Child care and the growth of love.* Harmondsworth: Penguin.
- **Bridges, D.** (2009) '"Evidence-based policy": What evidence? What basis? Whose policy?', *Teaching and Learning Research Briefing,* February, no. 74. London: Teaching and Learning Research Programme. **www.tlrp.org/pub/documents/Bridges RB74 Final.pdf**
- **Campbell, R.** (1999) *Literacy from home to school: reading with Alice.* Stoke-on-Trent: Trentham Books.
- **Carr, M.** (2001) *Assessment in early childhood settings.* London: Paul Chapman Publishing.
- **Clark, A., Moss, P.** (2001) *Listening to young children: the Mosaic approach.* London: National Children's Bureau.
- **Cole, M., Cole, S.** (2000) *The development of children.* Worth Publishers: New York.
- **Desforges, C.** (2004) 'Talking point', *National Educational Research Forum Bulletin,* Issue 1, Summer. **www.eep.ac.uk/nerf/bulletin/index.html**
- **Desforges, C., Abouchaar, A.** (2003) *The Impact of Parental Involvement, Parental Support and Family Education on Pupil Achievement and Adjustment: a Literature Review.* London: Department for Education and Skills. **www.education. gov.uk/publications/standard/publicationdetail/page1/RR433**
- **Donaldson, M.** (1978) *Children's minds.* London: Fontana.
- **Early Childhood Unit**, *Everyday Stories* (Descriptive observations from the research undertaken of under-threes in day nurseries during the mid-1990s by Elfer, P., and Selleck, D.). **www.everydaystories.org.uk**
- **Eliot, L.** (2009) *Pink brain, blue brain: how small differences grow into troublesome gaps and what we can do about it.* New York: Houghton Mifflin Harcourt. Access presentation at **http://fora.tv/2009/09/29/Lise_Eliot_Pink_Brain_ Blue_Brain**
- **EPPE**, *Effective Provision of Pre-School Education Project,* **http://eppe.ioe.ac.uk/** The project is following the children through primary and into secondary school and you can access research papers on this site.
- **Graham, P.** (2009) *A biography of Susan Isaacs: a life freeing children's minds.* London: Karnac Books. (I accessed some chapters online with a search of Jean Piaget + Susan Isaacs.)
- **Gopnik, A., Meltzoff, A., Kuhl, P.** (2001) *How babies think: the science of childhood.* London: Phoenix.
- **Hardyment, C.** (1995) *Perfect parents: baby care advice past and present.* Oxford: Oxford Paperbacks.
- **Harris, A., Goodall, J.** (2007) *Engaging parents in raising achievement – do parents know they matter?* Brief No DCSF – RBW004, London: Department for Children Schools and Families. **www.education.gov.uk/publications/standard/ publicationdetail/page1/DCSF-RW004**

- **Healy, J.** (2004) *Your child's growing mind: brain development and learning from birth to adolescence.* New York: Broadway Books.
- **Holland, P.** (2003) *We don't play with guns here: war, weapons and superhero play in the early years.* Maidenhead: Open University Press.
- **Howard-Jones, P.** (undated, *circa* 2008) *Neuroscience and Education: Issues and Opportunities.* London: Teaching and Learning Research Programme. **www.tlrp.org/pub/commentaries.html**
- **Laishley, J.** (1984) *Taking responsibility for young children: Who? Where? When' – a consideration of issue, evidence and implications Discussion Paper 1 for the National Nursery Examination Board.* London: NNEB.
- **MacNaughton, G., Rolfe, S., Siraj-Blatchford, I.** (2001) *Doing early childhood research: international perspectives on theory and practice.* Buckingham: Open University Press.
- **Miller, J.** (1996) *Never too young: how young children can take responsibility and make decisions.* London: Save the Children.
- **Moore, S.C., Carter, L.M., van Goozen, S.H.M.** (2009) 'Confectionary consumption in childhood and adult violence', *British Journal of Psychiatry*, no. 195, 366–7. You can find a summary on **www.rcpsych.ac.uk/pressparliament/ pressreleases2009/confectionaryconsumption.aspx**
- **National Institute for Child Health and Human Development**, **www.nichd.nih.gov**, accessed on 24 August 2011.
- **Paley, V.** (1984) *Boys and girls: superheroes in the doll corner.* Chicago: University of Chicago Press.
- **Paley, V.** (1988) *Bad guys don't have birthdays: fantasy play at four.* Chicago: University of Chicago Press.
- **Riley, D.** (1993) *War in the nursery: theories of the child and mother.* London: Virago.
- **Robertson, J., Robertson, J.** (1989) *Separation and the very young.* London: Free Association Books.
- **Schaffer, H.** (1998) *Making decisions about children: psychological questions and answers.* Oxford: Blackwell Publishing.
- **Shore, R.** (1997) *Rethinking the brain: new insights into early development.* New York: Families and Work Institute.
- **Siraj-Blatchford, I., Sylva, K., Muttock, S., Gilden, R., Bell, D.** (2002) *Researching Effective Pedagogy in Early Years: Brief No. 356.* **www.education.gov. uk/publications/standard/publicationDetail/Page1/RB356**
- **Smith, P.** (1994) 'Play and the uses of play', in Moyles, J. (ed.), *The excellence of play.* Buckingham: Open University Press.
- **Tayler, C.** (2007) 'The brain, development and learning in early childhood', in Centre for Educational Research and Innovation, *Understanding the Brain: the Birth of a Learning Science*, Part II, 161–183. **www.oecd.org/ dataoecd/39/53/40554190.pdf**
- **Titman, W.** (1992) *Play, playtime and playgrounds.* Winchester: Learning Through Landscapes/WWF UK.

Chapter 5

Social and emotional development: the foundation

The importance of social and emotional development is strongly emphasised in early years guidance across the four nations of the UK. Every key document stresses that emotional security and warm relationships underpin healthy early development. The necessity of supporting the emotional development of young children cannot be in doubt. But it is too easy to skim over what may appear to be a fuzzy area and to focus in daily practice on apparently higher priorities, such as a misplaced rush towards literacy. This chapter covers significant concepts to ground a crucial concern with children's feelings and emotional well being.

The main sections of this chapter are:
- The importance of attachment
- Emotional literacy
- Dispositions: where feeling meets thinking.

The importance of attachment

Attachment is a central idea in any discussion of children's social development. Ideas and perspectives have varied since the mid-20th century. However, the consistent theme emerging is that early experience matters.

What is meant by attachment?

Attachment is a bond of affection between two people, in which a sense of personal security and commitment is bound up within that relationship. Secure attachment within very early childhood seems to be a crucial building block for healthy development. Attachment is a set of internal feelings, so you cannot directly observe it. But you can see the presence or absence of attachment behaviours. For example, young children may greet their parent with enthusiasm after even a short separation and may cling tightly, especially in times of stress or uncertainty. Attachment, like any relationship, is a process and not a single event.
- A first bond can be formed in the period immediately after birth providing that the mother and father are able to have this very early contact with the child. The close relationship of affection starts from the very early days. For this reason, special baby units encourage parents to spend time with and hold premature or sick babies, who cannot yet leave hospital.

- The early days are not a one-off, use-it-or-lose-it bonding opportunity, a concept that was dominant in the 1970s and early 80s. Attachment strengthens during the early months of a baby's life through time spent together in play, communication and through the personal routines of physical care.

What does it mean?

Attachment: feelings of emotional closeness and commitment between children and significant people in their daily life.

Attachment behaviour(s): a pattern of action, and reaction from a baby or child that leads an observer to judge the extent to which the child is emotionally attached to an adult.

Mothers are important and …

From the mid-1940s to mid-70s the prevailing view on children's social development was that of John Bowlby, supported by Mary Ainsworth and Donald Winnicott. Bowlby studied a group of juvenile delinquents, finding that many of them had experienced disruption in their early family attachments. He also documented the emotional distress of children who were evacuated from English cities during the Second World War, usually without their mother.

Bowlby explained the adolescents' antisocial behaviour and the children's emotional distress by the separation from their mother, although it would have been more accurate to say that many children had been separated from their family. However, Bowlby's maternal deprivation hypothesis was consistent with key ideas in the psychoanalytic theory of that time: mothers were seen as the most crucial ingredient in young children's early life. In theoretical discussion, fathers or siblings scarcely rated a mention, except possibly as rivals for a mother's attention.

Bowlby's practical conclusions were that mothers needed to be highly available to their young children and that disruption of that crucial attachment put children at emotional risk. His views shaped research, policies and practical advice to families in the UK over several decades. Certainly in the mid-1970s and early 80s, it was not unusual to hear blunt statements that a claimed rise in what we would now call antisocial behaviour in children or young people was clearly caused by all those mothers who had insisted on going out to work.

From the beginning, some psychologists had challenged parts of Bowlby's theory. Additionally, as Clarke and Clarke (1998) and also Barbara Tizard (2009) documented, John Bowlby had significantly rethought his own position by the mid-1950s. He concluded that he had overstated the negative consequences if mothers were not continuously with their young children. From the 1970s onwards, the stream of criticism became a tidal wave. Research reviews, for example Michael Rutter (1972), challenged the interpretation of the data underlying the basic theory. The social movement of feminism meant that beliefs about 'normal family life' were also challenged. A greater awareness of cultural diversity undermined the highly Eurocentric view that mothers were exclusively responsible for childcare.

Research as well as daily observation shows that many young children demonstrate a strong attachment to their mother. But there is consistent evidence that infants and very young children also develop strong attachments to others within their family, often to their father but also to siblings and other relatives. The key factor seems to be, not surprisingly, that other family members spend time to get to know the young child and to build an emotional rapport. There is no evidence in these situations that very young children are confused, or that family attachments to figures other than the mother were 'second best'. On the contrary, children seem well able to distinguish the objects of their attachment and to anticipate and enjoy different care and playing styles.

Early experience does matter

Barbara Tizard (1986) offered a valuable rethink on Bowlby's views and influence. He could be fairly challenged on some details, but he was right about the pressing emotional needs of young children and the serious consequences when close attachments were disrupted. Tizard pointed out the immense importance of the research of James Robertson and Joyce Robertson (page 74) in changing hospital practice, despite their greater focus in discussion on children's separation from their mother, rather than from their entire family and home.

Tizard suggested that the focus on rebutting Bowlby's overemphasis on the role of the mother had led people to overlook the vital implications of his analysis of mothering. Young children need emotional support, unconditional love and a strong adult commitment to taking good care of babies and children. Nearly a quarter of a century after Barbara Tizard wrote that review, the needs of children have not changed. Good early years practice has to focus on what familiar adults should do, in order to nurture babies and young children. Some of this nurturing will be met by children's own mothers, some by their fathers and other close family members and some by other familiar adults, to whom parents have entrusted their children.

Figure 5.1 The needs of young children have not changed: they need support, love and a strong adult commitment

Make the connection with… **Children without family support**

Some of the 1970s critiques of Bowlby were optimistic about the ability of children to recover fully from even very harsh early experiences. By the 1980s, John Bowlby himself, strongly influenced by Michael Rutter's research, had concluded that negative consequences from maternal separation were not irreversible. Certainly, we do not need to return to the Freudian view that later patterns are utterly fixed by five years of age. However, the experiences of early childhood do matter, because they shape how children, and later adolescents, make sense of, and therefore react to, their social world.

Early experiences of disruption and distress will leave their mark and a great deal depends on what happens afterwards. Some children experience serial disruption of relationships and continued unpredictability in their daily life.

Consider making contact with your local residential or fostering service. Of course, you will not ask about the confidential experiences of individual children or adolescents. However, fellow professionals who work directly with looked-after children, in fostering or residential care, will be able to give a sense of how much hard work can be needed when early experiences have been harsh and disruptive.

Figure 5.2 Emotionally secure children are caring towards each other

There is a limit to the resilience of children, when adults let them down or disappear from their life. In her 1986 review, Barbara Tizard drew on her research over the 1970s into the experiences of children in residential care and the negative consequences of a high turnover of caretakers. In one study Tizard

SOCIAL AND EMOTIONAL DEVELOPMENT: THE FOUNDATION

reported that, between the age of four months and four and a half years, the sample of children had experienced an average of 50 caretakers in their residential home. The continued disruption of attachment seemed to disturb the ability of some of the children to make relationships later in childhood.

Michael Rutter (1999) and his team have undertaken a longitudinal study of Romanian children, adopted from the impersonal orphanages of their birth country into UK families. The research has documented significant improvement in the serious cognitive delays of the children at adoption. However, the degree of 'cognitive catch-up' was better for those children who had left the orphanages by six months of age. Children who left between 12 and 18 months of age had experienced serious emotional deprivation and physical harm through malnutrition. The team assessed that the psychological deprivation had led to developmental consequences that are harder to alleviate, even when children are adopted into a loving family. Some children growing up in the UK experience a high level of abuse and neglect. Camila Batmanghelidjh (2006) has documented the stories of children and adolescents who attend her Kids' Company in London and the toxic effect of being forever let down by adults and having to raise themselves, sometimes also younger siblings.

Young brains and early experience

Children can be resilient through minor troubles and, fortunately, they do not require parents and other carers to be perfect in every way. However, there are limits; young children are affected by harsh treatment and unpredictable daily lives. Research about early brain development (Gerhardt, 2004; Healy, 2004; Tayler, 2007) supports concerns long expressed by early years professionals who are involved with children. Repeated experience of emotional harshness (it does not have to be physical as well) and unpredictable adult behaviour (not the odd 'off day') creates elevated levels of cortisol in young brains. This chemical is present in saliva and so changes can be measured with a simple test.

Cortisol is a steroid hormone secreted by the adrenal gland and, like all hormones, it circulates through the body via the bloodstream. Cortisol reaches the brain, where it regulates response to stress. Human brains need cortisol but too great a level of the hormone blocks children's ability to learn in positive ways. But, equally important, their brains make other connections that show through their behaviour, including anxious or aggressive actions. The young children have become 'hardwired for trouble' and are swift to interpret the actions of others as a potential threat.

In contrast, babies and young children who have experienced warm and consistent nurturing have lower levels of cortisol than those babies whose daily lives have been highly stressful or traumatic. The other significant difference is that when the nurtured infants experience stress, the natural elevation of cortisol reduces more rapidly. Their experience is telling them that this is just a blip, not further proof that adults cannot be trusted.

Strong emotional states create chemical changes in the brain. So, neither anxious parents nor early years practitioners help very young children by putting them on a treadmill of 'stimulating' intellectual activities. Such frenetic activity, however well intentioned, is far more likely to backfire.

Young learning unfolds best of all when positive emotions experienced by young children facilitate chemical secretions in the brain that help the messages to cross the synapses. These substances, called neurotransmitters, help learning when children feel rested, able to make their own choices and are feeling emotionally secure. In contrast, feelings of exhaustion, anxiety and pressure can make it impossible for the neurons in the child's brain to send or receive the necessary signals.

The emotional environment is largely created for young children through the behaviour of the adults: what they do, what they say and the powerful messages of their body language. What are the practical applications of this finding to your own practice?

Developing close relationships within childcare

The research and theory on attachment and separation are a complicated, and often emotive, area. However, it is clear that out-of-home early years provision must be organised so as to enable children to form attachments, and that these should not be disrupted without warning. Social pressures have changed from the time when John Bowlby developed his ideas about attachment, but children have not changed. They still become distressed if important attachments are disrupted and serious attention to this reality has implications for policy, as summarised by John Oates (2007).

What matters for quality care?

Research reviews have generated very similar key issues that focus on the importance of close, affectionate relationships to ensure quality in out-of-home care for young children.

- Margaret Henry (1996) focused on the importance of responsiveness: a warm and affectionate relationship between children and adults that demonstrates the adults' high regard for the children. Involvement was an active support of children's learning, which encourages exploration and achievement. The third dimension was a positive approach to control, characterised by consistency and explanations, which encourage children to take independent action. Positive control in action works through both responsiveness and involvement.
- Barbara Tizard (1986) highlighted familiarity, responsiveness and attachment. These three themes are the focus of the discussion of the key person approach by Peter Elfer et al. (2003).
- The Scottish *Pre-birth to three* guidance (2010) offers advice about quality in early years practice organised around the four Rs: rights of the child, relationships, responsive care, and respect.

Figure 5.3 Quality in out-of-home care is important for young children

In different ways any serious discussion of attachment considers the ways in which babies and very young children need to become confident that key important relationships will not come and go at random. Different terms are used, which have included that children need to feel kept in mind, or held in mind. This concept most likely originated with W. R. Bion (1962, with thanks to Jane Elfer for this bit of detective work). Bion described how babies become able to summon up the idea of someone who is important, but not physically in front of them. They are then less desperate that that person has gone forever. Bion described how their emotional security depends upon feeling that they are held in mind by an important person in their life, as much as held in body through caring physical contact.

Pause for reflection

Please focus on the concept that young children need to feel that they are kept or held securely in the mind and feelings of the important adults in their life, secure that they have not been forgotten.

Reflect on your own practice:

● In which ways do you behave so as to assure babies and young children that they are 'kept in mind' during the day? What convinces them that it is not a case of 'out of sight, out of mind'?

Then reflect on ways that you let young children know that they are kept in mind by their important adults when those people are not there.

● Think first: what do you say and do that lets young children know that you recall what you did together, or what they told you yesterday or last week?

● In which ways do you help to make close links between children's homes and their time with you? How do you reassure young children that they are kept in mind by their families?

Share your observations and reflections with colleagues.

A personal relationship with child and family

Quality in work with babies and young children can only be delivered through a caring, personal relationship between baby or child and practitioner. Anyone taking responsibility for other people's young children needs to negotiate the careful balance between genuine commitment to individual children and families and the ability to step back: to take a more detached, but not uncaring, view of what is happening. This concept of personal commitment yet with an element of professional detachment is a challenging practical task, and one that team leaders need to understand, in order to support practitioners.

Childminders and nannies face this balancing act within their working life. However, in group settings the personal commitment to children needs to be led through a key person approach to organising time, routines and personal care, records and partnership with individual parents. If you work in England, the requirement of the Early Years Foundation Stage (EYFS) is that all group settings must operate a key person approach. The EYFS birth-to-five guidance has a strong emphasis on the need to establish positive relationships with individual children and their families.

> ### What does it mean?
>
> **Key person approach**: an approach within early years group settings that assigns a named practitioner to develop a close relationship with a young child and his or her parents. (A similar approach works in good-quality residential care for children and adolescents.)

The original impetus for a key person approach in early years provision came from the work of Elinor Goldschmied (Goldschmied and Jackson, 2004) who called attention to the central role of a supportive triangular relationship between the baby or child, the key person and the parent. Goldschmied's practical discussion about the need for warm relationships was taken forward in the work of Peter Elfer and Dorothy Selleck (Elfer, Goldschmied and Selleck, 2003; see also Early Childhood Unit, the *Everyday Stories* resource, full details on page 109). Elfer et al. describe the different nursery patterns that are all called a key person approach. From their observation, quality practice for children needs a version that encompasses a sustained relationship lasting throughout a child's time. Less confident teams or managers are more at ease with a time-limited version, perhaps focused on the settling-in period and on record keeping.

Serious concerns were also raised in some observational studies of English day nurseries during the 1980s. Some of these studies were small scale, and in a review at the time I challenged the sweeping generalisations about day care that were made from some studies (Laishley, 1984). However, there were also reasons to be concerned. Alastair Bain and Lyn Barnett (1986) highlighted the risks to children from what they called 'multiple indiscriminate care', when nursery staff saw no point in making a close relationship with individual children. The concepts described by Bain and Barnett were grounded in psychoanalytic theory and those key ideas have been further developed by Elfer (2006, 2007).

Peter Elfer discusses the feelings and anxieties of practitioners, as well as the emotional needs of young children. He brings to the fore the extent to which early years practitioners (especially those who are still only young adults) may opt for emotional distance from young children, as a way of protecting themselves. It can be hard to deal with normal levels of emotional distress from young children, for instance when they would really rather not be separated from their parent. Julia Manning-Morton (2006) sums up the dilemmas that arise when practitioners are given the impression, or firm directive, that it is not professional to become emotionally involved, even with very young children.

Make the connection with… **Emotional commitment to children**

Babies and toddlers need to develop close and enduring relationships. Uneasy practitioners or managers sometimes say that children must not become 'too attached'. However, this is an adult concept that, in practice, makes no emotional sense for young children. They need to be emotionally and physically close to those familiar adults who are key in their daily life. Some young children spend many hours in out-of-home care.

Adults, practitioners and parents, need to resolve the mixed feelings that undoubtedly exist. Parents who work long hours may well be worried if their young child is clearly fond of her key person. But these understandable feelings need to be discussed between the adults and not 'solved' by disrupting young children's attachments in out-of-home care.

- Reflect on how you are able to make a personal, supportive relationship with young children in your work.

- Explore some of the common 'Ah, but …' concerns about a key person approach. You will find ideas in Peter Elfer et al. (2003) and Lindon (2010a).

- To what extent do these reflect your own concerns, or those of your colleagues?

Attachment and socialisation

Research is undertaken in a time and place, and changes in the social and political atmosphere have affected research into early years provision, especially day care (see page 71). This area of research does not produce identical results each time: methods vary and it is a serious challenge to tease out the cause and effect of early experiences. Making good sense of research data is also complicated by media reporting that demands simplistic messages: that non-family childcare is wholly positive or that working mothers (never fathers) are damaging their children.

Jay Belsky talks of a 'slow steady trickle of disconcerting evidence' (2001, 847) that 20 or more hours of non-family day care, started in the first year of life, increases the risk of insecure attachment between infants and their mother. Some studies, not all, show these children later behaving in more aggressive and less cooperative ways. Early and more extensive day care was associated with less sensitive mothering, as babies moved into being toddlers, and less engagement with their very young children. The expressed concerns, on the basis of research data, are not presented as an absolute cause-and-effect pattern. However, it is not responsible to dismiss the data as inconvenient within a social era in which extensive childcare is viewed as necessary on economic grounds.

I believe there are two broad issues that deserve our attention. Please consider these as 'food for thought' in making sense of the research. I am not saying that research studies prove this explanation: more that it seems very likely from what we know of family life and of child development.

1 *Strong relationships within the family*. Parents – and the primary carer is still often the mother – need to spend enough time with their own young children. The problem of longer hours of day care, especially when started in very early childhood, is that young children may not be given the time really to get to know their parent(s). Just as important, parents may struggle to enjoy short amounts of time with their baby or toddler at the end of an already long and tiring day. Good-practice guidance for early years practitioners stresses the significance of building personal relationships with individual children. The same principle applies to family life. It seems likely that the positive outcomes for young children are ensured by parents who protect time with their baby and young child, despite a busy and/or stressful life.

2 *Guiding children's behaviour*. Babies and toddlers learn how to behave, including pro-social choices, from being affectionately guided by familiar, caring adults. It seems likely that the finding (in some studies) of more aggressive patterns of behaviour in young children who have spent considerable time in day care could be explained by lack of personal guidance. Day care, as such, has not caused the aggressive pattern. The dynamic is more that the day care experience has failed to establish the close relationship between adult and young child that is crucial for early psychological well being. Young children have not been guided away from physically or verbally aggressive ways of dealing with the ordinary social conflicts in daily life. Older children remain stuck at ways of handling disagreements and social skills that are more like those of a two-year-old child.

Take another **perspective**

Think about the two broad issues raised here: strong relationships within the family and guiding children's behaviour.

And for a link back to where the section started … Barbara Tizard (2009) describes how John Bowlby was apparently devastated at four years of age by the loss of his nursemaid/nanny. Bowlby's sense of loss was heightened by a family life (in the first half of the 20th century) where it was normal for him and his siblings to be taken to see their mother for a scheduled hour each late afternoon. As always, young children need to spend enough time with their family.

Relationships between children

The focus in this section has been on affectionate relationships between adults and children. However, babies are essentially social in nature and show interest in other children, as well as adults. Older babies and toddlers seek to make social contact with others of their own age, as well as with older children. An important feature of supportive out-of-home care is that children get to see each other on a regular and predictable basis, so they can discover the shared games and interests that build friendships. This aspect to social development is discussed from page 149.

Figure 5.4 Given the opportunity, children of different ages often play together

The importance of touch

Look back over the key issues raised in this section. You will see that such qualities cannot emerge without a relaxed atmosphere, in which adults touch and cuddle, and children feel able to ask for physical contact by word or gesture. Reviews of good practice with young children, for example Colwyn Trevarthen et al. (2003), describe emotional and other developmental needs that cannot possibly be met without touch.

Research into the workings of young brains has shown that physical contact is part of the whole social and emotional experience for babies and children. A sense of emotional security creates strong connections within children's brains. A positive environment is created chemically in the brain and this balance supports learning and happy exploration. Touch is a powerful non-verbal message, reassuring children that they are liked and welcome. Restrictions on cuddling, for whatever reason, undermine children, creating a sense of emotional insecurity. Young children may redouble their efforts to gain personal attention, and see their peers as direct competitors in this effort.

Make the connection with... **Your practice**

Young children should be confident of your physical comfort in times of distress or uncertainty. But a cuddle, a friendly lap, a hand-hold are all important messages that say, 'I missed you yesterday' (being kept in mind) or 'What a building. Haven't we done well!' Yet misplaced concerns about child protection have created doubts in some early years teams about touch. Do you face such issues in your own mind or in your team?

Young children learn about appropriate touch and boundaries when they experience warm and affectionate touch from familiar adults, and that has to include their key person and familiar practitioners in a nursery setting.

- Children need direct experience of how responsible adults behave and what is affectionate and respectful touch.

- If important adults restrict cuddling, young children can only make sense of this loss by taking it personally. Under-fives and, even more so, under-threes, conclude 'She (or he) doesn't like me' or 'Nobody cares about how I feel' – and the feeling could be 'excited' as well as 'upset'.

- Children who are persistently deprived of affection can be emotionally at risk. The need for affection does not go away, so children are vulnerable to anyone who offers personal attention. They are then doubly at risk because children have not learned how safe adults should behave.

Discuss, with the support of your tutor in a student group, how meeting the emotional needs of young children must be a priority and can be compatible with good practice in safeguarding. You can find more information and ideas in Lindon (2012a).

The need for nurturing

As an educational psychologist working in London during the 1970s, Marjorie Boxall (2002) had many referrals from teachers who struggled with the behaviour of children who were unable to cope with the demands of classroom life. Boxall's observations led her to develop small nurture groups, in which she and her colleagues steadily built up children's social and self-care skills. A revival of interest in the 1990s, along with the same concerns, led to the re-emergence of nurture groups. The high adult–child ratio is more expensive than the usual primary school ratio. Children should be supported for their own sake; it is appropriate to judge any society by how the youngest citizens are nurtured. However, leaving children or adolescents to struggle and fail at school brings a high financial cost at a later stage.

What does it mean?

Nurture: used in this context, the word means taking good care of children, in the fullest sense. The word is sometimes used to contrast with 'nature'; see page 6.

Nurture groups: special groups established in primary schools to support those children whose early experiences have not prepared them to cope with the kind of behaviour required in the group life of a classroom.

In the nurture groups, children aged five, six years and older are enabled to experience learning in ways they have missed in their early years. The objective is to combine a nurturing approach, through adult behaviour, with a supportive daily routine. Children are then enabled to learn skills crucial to group life, such as waiting for a short while, taking turns, making choices and seeing an activity through to completion. The children also need to develop a trust in adults and see them as a useful resource.

Make the connection with... *Good early years practice*

The work with nurture groups highlights the ways in which disruptive early experiences of different kinds mean that young children have not built an understanding of a predictable social world. The children's struggles also highlight what is demanded of children for smooth running in a school classroom environment (see also Lindon, 2012d).

- Find out more about nurture groups from the website of the Nurture Group Network: www.nurturegroups.org/index.php.

- Consider how you, and your colleagues, provide a nurturing environment for young children. What do you offer? Do you recognise the importance of this aspect of your practice?

- What may happen to young children if early years practitioners see nurture as an optional extra, to be fitted in if possible after trudging through pre-planned activities and a sense of pressure to 'get children ready ...' for the next stage?

Emotional literacy

The word 'literacy' has usually been applied to written language. But children also become aware of a pattern of verbal and non-verbal communication about feelings. Within their spoken language, children can be supported to learn an emotional vocabulary: words to express their own feelings, and later to talk about the feelings of other people. Children, and adults, can be more, or less, skilled in this area of learning and children are influenced by adult behaviour and attitudes. Adults, in their turn, have been shaped by their own childhood, their social and cultural background. The concept of emotional literacy and the practical applications are linked with the ideas of emotional intelligence.

Emotional intelligence

Daniel Goleman (1996) developed the idea of emotional intelligence as a balance to excessively intellectual definitions of skills and abilities. He wrote about adult development and focused on five broad strands:

1 Knowing your own emotions: the self-awareness of recognising a feeling as it happens to you, being honest with yourself about how you feel.

2 Managing emotions: handling feelings so that they are appropriate for the situation is an ability that builds upon self-awareness.

3 Motivating yourself: dealing with emotions to be able to concentrate, direct and focus your feelings in a productive way.

4 Recognising emotions in others: the ability to empathise includes being able to notice the social signals and tune into the emotions of other people.

5 Handling relationships: social relationships depend on using empathy to support other people and help to manage the emotional content.

Goleman developed a set of ideas applied to adult behaviour and reactions. Children are in the process of learning these skills, or not, depending on their experiences. To support young children, early years practitioners and parents need to have a clear view of how emotional development unfolds and be willing to reflect on their own emotional intelligence. Awareness of emotions can undoubtedly be used to manipulate and undermine others. Practical applications of concepts of emotional intelligence and emotional literacy are underpinned by pro-social values.

What does it mean?

Emotional intelligence: awareness of your own and others' emotions, the ability to harness feelings to motivate yourself and to develop relationships.

Emotional literacy: ability to express your own feelings and to recognise and understand the emotions of other people.

Empathy: sensitivity to the feelings of other people and ability to tune into their emotions; that is, the sense of 'feeling with' and not pity or 'feeling sorry for …'.

Emotional vocabulary: the words that stand for and can describe the invisible feelings. Young children build this aspect to their spoken language by hearing adults use appropriate words in a meaningful context of real events.

Understanding emotions

Throughout the early years, children are learning about their own and others' feelings. Undoubtedly, adults need to be open-minded in how the ideas of emotional literacy are put into practice and that it does not become culture-specific. Aware adults need to recognise that their own feelings are involved, as well as to hold realistic expectations of children:

- Within their first year, babies show a range of emotions that are only partly provoked by their internal physical needs. Babies cry, but they also express contentment, surprise, uncertainty.
- Toddlers show their emotions through facial expression and their whole body movements. They may be uneasy about strong emotions like anger or fear. They start to show embarrassment or pride in achievements.
- From about the age of two years onwards, young children learn some words to express their feelings. A lot depends on their experience. For example, Judy Dunn (1993) noted that two-year-olds who used an emotional vocabulary had mothers who had commented on emotions when children were younger.
- Children aged three and four years start to understand that other people have feelings as well. Even younger children can show caring behaviour towards peers who look distressed.

Pause for reflection

Supportive and affectionate adults can help young children as they:

- Become clearer about their own feelings

- Are more able to name those feelings and talk about them

- Recognise the source of strong feelings, felt by themselves or others

- Find ways to express feelings in assertive rather than aggressive ways.

How do you use opportunities to help children in these ways? Gather some examples of individual interaction and spontaneous conversations: not planned group or circle times.

Be aware that children with disabilities in the autistic spectrum struggle to understand these subtle clues for emotional communication and many aspects for interaction in play (see Beyer and Gammeltoft, 2000).

Self-regulation and emotions

Children aged two and three years tend to express straightaway whatever emotion they are feeling. If they are happy, it shows in their face and whole body posture. If they are distressed, the tears will flow. Between the ages of four and six years, children show an increasing ability to inhibit temporarily the expression of strong feelings, when they judge it is not the time or place. You may especially notice children holding back their emotions when they are upset. They sense the situation is inappropriate, or they do not want to show someone their distress (the idea of 'being brave'). Young children are able, with help, to develop some level of impulse control. Nancy Eisenberg (1992) proposed that what she calls emotional regulation is the basis for a child's repertoire of social skills. Happy social interaction usually needs children to be willing to hold back sometimes on what they want and find ways to express emotions that do not alienate their friends.

What does it mean?

Impulse control: the ability to hold oneself back on inclinations or expression of feelings.

Emotional regulation: children's ability to direct or redirect feelings.

Pause for reflection

In early years provision, you will observe children who are trying hard not to cry, although they are distressed. Parents have many experiences of getting home with children and facing the flood of distress that the children have managed to control in nursery or, more often, during the school day.

Children are also becoming aware of social and cultural expectations, as communicated through family life. They absorb messages about whether and how to express strong emotions. Cultures around the world vary in social rules about expression of feelings, some being more demonstrative than others.

- What do you observe of young children and how they deal with feelings?
- Does it seem likely that some young children are already aware that some emotions are more acceptable to adults?

Families can have a very individual pattern, whatever the broad cultural context. Robin Skynner and John Cleese (1997) discuss the idea that every family has one particular emotion that is hard to face. For example, the emotion of jealousy may be tough to resolve, so parents, who are probably reworking their own childhood, say 'We have no jealousy in our family.'

Adult emotional literacy

If you look back over the previous section, you will realise that much of what you could observe in young children's emotional behaviour will already have been shaped by messages from familiar adults. In order to support the development of emotional literacy and tune into children, practitioners, like parents, have to become aware of their own emotional reactions.

Young children of three or four years of age start to appreciate that adults have feelings too. Children can be puzzled, partly because the adult world is different from the social world of children, but also because adults themselves are sometimes confused, or less than honest. For instance, an adult who is scared because a child has nearly walked into the road may shout at the child. A young boy or girl hears the anger and cannot read the adult's mind to understand 'I was scared you might hurt yourself.'

Figure 5.5 Feelings can arise in conversation like any other focus of interest

Make the connection with… *How does it feel when?*

Tuning into young children is well-supported when adults can access a parallel experience of their own, whether from their own childhood or a carefully organised exercise experienced as an adult.

Elinor Goldschmied described how she organised two different lunchtime experiences for senior day nursery staff to provoke empathy with children's experience (Goldschmied and Jackson, 2004: 165). Lunch on the first day was relaxed, with appetising food on tables, set attractively, and with plenty of social conversation. On the second lunchtime, the course delegates were told to go into lunch without warning, made to wait for their food, which was good in quality but unappetising in appearance. They had to say 'thank you' on demand and everyone had to wait for the slow eaters before getting their pudding. Do you get the idea? The direct experience was very supportive in enabling these senior staff to reflect on how mealtime was run in their own nursery.

I have heard equally inventive ideas from college tutors and nursery team managers. For example, practitioners who are keen on a conveyer-belt approach to 'creative activities' may be provoked to reflect if they have to endure a session when a fellow adult tells them what to do. Alternatively, how does it feel if people ruffle your hair or adjust your clothing without saying anything? How does it feel if a trainer or tutor has asked everyone to bring a significant item from their childhood and the items are just taken and put to one side?

You need to know the group before you try this kind of reflective exercise. There must always be time for debriefing and discussion, with questions such as 'How did you feel about …?', 'What were you thinking when …?' and 'What does this tell you about how children may feel when …?'.

Emotion coaching

John Gottman undertook longitudinal research in the USA with parents in how they dealt with emotions within family life and relationships with children. He interpreted his findings about the psychological and physical well being of children through making sense of the different parental styles of handling the 'negative' emotions of anger, sadness, envy, and so on.

Gottman and Declaire (1997) distinguished four styles in overall approach, which are equally applicable to any adults who are responsible for children:

1 A *dismissive* approach was taken by some parents. They ignored or trivialised children's negative emotions. Children took the message that their parents did not notice their feelings, or that such feelings were silly and unimportant compared with proper adult concerns.

2 Some parents were actively *disapproving* of children when they showed what were judged to be negative, unacceptable emotions. Parents criticised and punished the children.

3 A *laissez-faire* approach was taken by parents who accepted their children's emotions, but failed to guide their children in the expression of strong feelings and did not set limits to behaviour.

4 A fourth group of parents *accepted* their children's expression of strong or negative feelings and let the children know that their emotions were heard and understood.

Gottman described the fourth option as emotion coaching. He explained that, unlike the *laissez-faire* approach, parents who took an active role with their children's strong emotions also explored what children could do about the situation. Parents acknowledged the emotion, yet guided children towards expression in ways that were less harmful to others.

What does it mean?

Emotion coaching: an approach in which adults actively support children to understand and control their own feelings, and to have empathy with other people.

Pause for reflection

- Gather observations of how you and other people react to children's expression of strong emotions.

- What evidence can you observe of patterns of dismissive, disapproving or *laissez-faire* adults?

- To what extent can you see the emotion coaching approach in practice?

- Use your observations to reflect on your own practice and talk ideas over with a colleague.

Some adults, parents as well as practitioners, resist accepting that young children have strong feelings, especially that they can be very sad or emotionally hurt. It can then feel more appropriate to try to jolly children out of sadness with a suggestion such as 'Let's go and do a picture.' Yet the best approach, and an emotionally literate one, is to say, 'You look sad,' or 'I know you miss Daddy' and offer the child a cuddle or other physical comfort.

Why do you think some adults take the 'jollying' approach?

- Is it easier to believe that young children 'get over' upsets quickly? Is it maybe also that adults struggle with their own distress at seeing an upset child?

- Some practitioners may learn the 'jollying' approach from apparently more experienced colleagues. It just seems to be the right thing to do.

- Some adults are concerned that acknowledging a child's upset will make them more distressed. The opposite is usually the case; acknowledged children tend to become calm. Children get very confused if they are sure they look upset and nobody seems to notice at all.

- Do some practitioners feel that distress in a child is an implicit criticism of their professional skills: they should be able to bring a child round swiftly?

What do you think? And what can be done to support early years practitioners in taking more of an emotion coaching, or emotionally literate, approach?

Also, look back at the research of James and Joyce Robertson (page 74). Why do you think that medical staff preferred to believe that children in hospital were not really upset?

Self-esteem

The term self-esteem has become familiar within supporting children's emotional development. There are several aspects to what is usually meant by the term:

- In the broadest sense, your self-esteem emerges from an overall evaluation of your own self-worth.
- Your level of self-esteem is created by the gap you perceive between what you wish to be and what you believe you are. So a person's self-esteem could be anywhere between very high to extremely low.

However, the judgements are subjective. Individuals vary in the standards they apply and the areas of their life in which they feel achievement really matters. One person may feel that musical talent is very significant, yet their close friend could be desperate to experience success in sports.

Children's potential development of a sense of self-esteem progresses hand in hand with the rest of their development. Their abilities of communication support close relationships and friendships. Thinking and reasoning abilities help them to make sense of what they experience, sometimes reaching very different conclusions from the adults who are involved the same situation.

- By about seven years of age, children's experience builds towards their personal internal judgements that create a sense of self-esteem. They have by then a sense of the gap between 'what I am' and 'what I ought to be'.
- The level of a child's self-esteem and the room for positive or negative shift are affected by the support they experience from family and friends. However, individual children vary in temperament: how harshly they judge themselves and how resilient they are to criticism from others.
- Children have learned to focus on those areas of their life that they believe are important for success, mainly because other people have indicated these areas are to be valued and others to be dismissed.
- Children's level of self-esteem is affected by the extent to which they feel accepted for what they are and treated as people who can continue to learn.
- The level of self-esteem is not fixed from middle childhood. However, children have developed the framework of belief, in which they make sense of experiences. Supportive adults will have to work hard with individual children whose view of themselves is already that they will never be 'quite good enough'.

Pause for reflection

The psychological literature on self-esteem suggests that a healthy level is built through five broad areas:

1 Feelings of competence or lack of ability in learning. Can I do it? What about my mistakes?

2 Confidence in physical skills and abilities.

3 Social acceptance: having friends, people who want to be with me.

4 How I behave. Am I acceptable, what if I do something wrong?

5 Physical appearance. How do I look and is that fine?

Take each of these in turn. Reflect and observe the ways in which you support children in each area, while helping them to have realistic expectations for what they can manage.

It is not helpful for children to be convinced they can do something when that is not the case. Children can have a secure and strong self-esteem and still accept that they do not know something or still need to practise a skill.

Dispositions: where feeling meets thinking

Learning is not all intellectual or rational; feelings are just as much involved. It is important that children develop in confidence that they can learn. Part of healthy personal development for young children, including self-esteem, is a growing sense that they are competent individuals. During middle childhood, once children are within statutory education, it often dawns on them that there is a great deal that they do not know and is yet to come. Children can feel overwhelmed by this prospect, unless they have already developed confidence that they are learners. Children need to feel that tackling new challenges, in school or elsewhere, is not all their responsibility, because adults are supposed to help.

The positive disposition to learn

Lillian Katz developed the concept of dispositions: habits of mind and a pattern of behaviour that are directed towards a broad goal. Her focus reminds practitioners that knowledge and skills are not the only worthwhile goals: that children's overall disposition and related feelings matter just as much. One of Katz's practical examples is poignant, given the misplaced pressure, especially in England, to push young children into formal reading and writing. Lillian Katz made the forceful point in the early 1990s that it cannot be useful for children to learn skills if in the very process of learning them the children's disposition to apply the skills is damaged. The most accessible summaries of Katz's ideas are on the internet, for example **http://www.ericdigests.org/1994/goals.htm**.

Margaret Carr (2001) was part of the team that made positive dispositions a strong theme in *Te Whāriki*, the bicultural early years curriculum for New Zealand. Knowledge, skills and attitudes are seen to combine as dispositions, such as the habit of mind to be curious. Dispositions are encouraged by adults; they cannot be formally taught, and the task of supportive practitioners is to create a learning environment that enables and promotes positive dispositions in children. Young children may be able to kick or catch a ball, but that ability does not mean that they will be disposed to play at ball games. If children have been teased about their lack of skill, they may be disinclined to practise. On the other hand, if the children have been encouraged, they are likely to have a positive disposition to learning, not only for ball games but probably other skills.

What does it mean?

Positive dispositions to learn: an outlook, attitudes and pattern of behaviour that will support children to be, and want to be, learners.

Margaret Carr described five broad domains of learning dispositions:

1 Taking an interest

2 Being involved

3 Persisting with difficulty or uncertainty

4 Communicating with others

5 Taking responsibility.

She then considered each domain in three parts:

1 *Being ready*: that children see themselves as someone who can participate in the learning. This outlook needs to be supported by the second part.

2 *Being willing*: children feel their environment has opportunities and, from their perspective, is safe for learning

3 *Being able*: children have, or are developing, the knowledge and abilities that support their inclination. Feelings of competence can support being ready and willing.

It is useful to link these ideas back to Lillian Katz's crucial point that the methods which practitioners use to promote specific learning for children must protect and encourage the children's disposition to use those skills out of choice.

Pause for reflection

Children's positive disposition to learn includes:

- Curiosity and the wish to find out and explore

- A desire to become competent, to be able to do or say something

- Motivation to keep trying, even if something is difficult or confusing

- A sense of satisfaction for children when they manage a new skill or idea.

This positive outlook can develop over time with adult support. Reflect on your own practice. In which ways are you promoting this positive disposition? What is done to support children, either from adult behaviour, or the way that the learning environment is organised?

Children will always learn something from experiences, which might not always be positive for their well being. If adults highlight mistakes in a critical way, children may learn there in no point in trying.

Be honest; are there aspects of your practice or that of your colleagues that you need to raise diplomatically, to turn back from this situation?

We need to hold developmentally appropriate expectations. You could make short observations to show how curiosity or perseverance could appear with:

- Toddlers, younger than two years old

- A four-year-old child

- A six- or seven-year-old child

- Perhaps also an adult like yourself.

Engagement and involvement

Ferre Laevers was interested in the links between learning and children's sense of well being. He observed that you could conclude that children felt at ease, and therefore were in a positive emotional state for learning when they felt able to act spontaneously in their nursery, expressed their feelings, exuded vitality and looked as though they were enjoying themselves. A sense of well being eased deep involvement in learning, a full engagement, but did not ensure it. Laevers was concerned that the layout of the learning environment was crucial, including use of space and sufficient, but not too many, play resources. He stressed the need for children to be able to make genuine choices and that adult support needed to follow the child.

Figure 5.6 Friends become engaged in sustained pretend play

Laevers made the point that when children are impressed with materials, they are keen to get involved; they do not need to be pushed. He suggested that children's involvement in learning was encouraged by challenges that were neither too easy nor excessively hard. The challenge needed to be at the edge of the children's current competence (see Vygotsky's zone of proximal development on page 174). You can access articles about Ferre Laevers's ideas by searching 'Laevers + engagement' on the internet, but can also read about the concepts in Pascal and Bertram (1997).

Christine Pascal and Tony Bertram developed Ferre Laevers's ideas in their Effective Early Learning (EEL) project. This action research with early years provision has focused on a range of adult behaviours, summed up as engagement. They define this term as a set of personal qualities of adults who are involved in supporting children's learning. The EEL observational research has worked to ground these qualities in what adults actually do and in differences between adults who work with children.

Pascal and Bertram have identified that the key features of more, or less, constructive behaviour with children are:
- *Sensitivity* of the adult to the feelings and emotional well being of children. The term also refers to empathy and genuineness on the part of the adult. Sensitive actions acknowledge children's sense of insecurity and offer encouragement.

- *Stimulation* refers to the way that an adult intervenes in the learning process. Pascal and Bertram have observed how adults introduce or offer an activity. Adults can be more, or less, stimulating in the ways they offer information or join an ongoing activity to promote thinking or communication.
- *Autonomy* describes the degree of freedom given to the child to experiment. Effective adults support children to make judgements, choose activities and express ideas. The dimension of autonomy includes how adults deal with conflicts, rules and other behavioural issues. A positive approach includes the participation of children in rule-making.

Mastery or learned helplessness

Kathy Sylva (1994) reviewed the research into the effect of the well-funded, carefully planned early educational intervention programmes. Long-term tracking of the children has pointed to the great importance of how adults encourage children to view learning. The results are equally relevant whatever your setting or your professional background, because the research did not come out with simple answers that a particular kind of setting or specifically trained adult was inevitably best for children. What mattered most was the impact that different adult styles exert on children's outlook, their dispositions towards learning and themselves as potential learners.

Kathy Sylva draws on the concept of mastery behaviour in children, developed through research about academic motivation by Carol Dweck in the USA (Dweck and Leggett, 1988). Significant differences between individuals were explained by the idea of an orientation of mastery, or learned helplessness. (The concept of learned helplessness has also been developed with application to adults.) Children with a mastery approach saw new learning tasks as a challenge, rather than a threat. Their outlook when faced with a difficult problem, or one at which they initially failed, was to look carefully at their strategy and try another approach. In interviews, children with a mastery orientation showed that they believed effort usually paid off. They did not think that difficulties arose because they were stupid. The children valued persistence, took a problem-solving approach and felt good about themselves and their capacity to learn.

What *does* it mean?

A mastery orientation: a positive outlook that assumes problems can be resolved and that it is worth persevering.

Learned helplessness: when children (or adults) regularly give up swiftly, feeling that they are incompetent and cannot deal with new challenges.

In contrast, children who had learned a sense of personal helplessness were far more likely to view new or difficult tasks as a threat to be avoided. This group did not persevere or try alternative strategies, when the experimental tasks became difficult or children experienced initial failure. They started to chat or engage in other kinds of off-task behaviour. In interviews, these children expressed beliefs that failure showed you were 'no good' at something. They felt negative about themselves and so wanted to get out of the situation. The children had taken on an idea of innate ability: that people are either naturally good at something or useless, and practice will not help.

Make the connection with… *Good early years practice*

Mastery and learned helplessness are not absolutes. Children (and adults) show greater or lesser degrees of their orientation, neither of which are linked with measurable intelligence. A child could be potentially very able, yet feel helpless and hopeless. The outlook may be influenced by temperament, but mainly depends on children's learning experiences. The practical food for thought is that:

- It does not help children if they are made to be unrealistically optimistic about their ability. An honest awareness of current strengths can go hand in hand with a desire to learn more.

- Children seem to be helped to develop a mastery orientation when adults encourage them in the satisfaction of learning a skill, or gaining more knowledge.

- When adults organise children's learning towards specific success on particular tasks, children may learn more to focus on what they can or cannot do currently. With a narrow focus, children have less sense of continuing to learn, which links with the idea of dispositions (page 101).

What can you do in your practice to promote a mastery orientation with children? In what ways do you set a good example, modelling to children how you can react to something new or when something goes wrong? Reflect on what type of adult behaviour could push children towards learned helplessness.

Constructive feedback

The idea of how to give useful, accurate and supportive feedback has been explored largely within organisational psychology and with application to adults in the work setting. Yet much of this area is equally relevant to children, with some minor adjustments of language. Constructive feedback, given to children at the time, was identified as important in the EPPE project and the detailed observation of the most effective centres (Siraj-Blatchford et al., 2002).

Children become disheartened when adults find fault or only notice the mistakes.

Parents or early years practitioners may genuinely believe they are being helpful. Perhaps their own childhood has left them thinking, 'Children have to know what's wrong; how else will they learn?'

How may adults, who struggle to be encouraging, turn their own style around to support young children?

Children can be resentful when adults mainly criticise, but it is not helpful to hear an undiscriminating stream of positives. Some less helpful materials about self-esteem have suggested that adults should drench children in praise for anything and everything they do. Such a pattern of adult behaviour does not help children in the long run and can create older children and adolescents who are intolerant of any feedback, however carefully expressed. Additionally, if adults always say 'That's lovely' or 'wonderful drawing', some children do not feel that the praise can be genuine. There will be many times when children have not grasped an idea, or could manage better with a different technique. Children do not fall apart if their mistakes or misunderstandings are pointed out with warmth and respect. The problem comes when adult intervention is dismissive and fails to be balanced by recognition of what has gone well.

Useful, constructive feedback for children addresses feelings as well as facts:
- Positive feelings can be expressed in words of encouragement to children, along with positive body language and smiles.
- Less positive feelings, if appropriate, should be worded carefully. There may be times to say, 'I'm disappointed by …' but what follows has to be constructive and avoid blunt criticism. Concerns should be expressed factually. Adults should, however, acknowledge and deal sympathetically with children's negative feelings about their abilities.
- Positive factual feedback is useful for children: what has gone well and why or how a child's perseverance has paid off.
- What could be negative factual feedback can be valuable if given in a constructive way – covering what has gone well and what has gone awry – and a genuine help to children to learn from mistakes. The skills of problem solving are often supported when something has gone awry, since there is a real problem to be puzzled over and resolved.

Make the connection with... *Good early years practice*

Watch and listen for examples of constructive feedback: from adults.

Reflect on your practice and how you could catch an opportunity for constructive feedback next time.

Here are some suggestions to consider in your own work. Of course, you need to find a form of words that sits comfortably with your personal style. But make sure, by watching a child's face and listening to any words in reply, that the overall impact is encouraging and not daunting.

- Knowing a child well can help adults to boost children's confidence. Perhaps you can remind a child of how 'You told me you'd never ever be able to do up your buttons. And look at you now. Don't worry, we'll work out this problem with the water and the guttering.'

- Providing that adults help, children can learn from mistakes. You might hear the frustrated comments, or see the struggle and say, 'Are you having trouble with the scissors? Let's see how you're doing it.' Careful observation helps you to pitch the level of your help.

- Invite other children to help by saying, for example, 'I think Chris worked out how to ...' or 'I'm sure Tanya knows a lot about ...'.

Pause for reflection

In a family home or early years provision, where constructive feedback has been established, you will find that children treat each other this way as well. Perhaps one child tells another, 'Well done,' or a genuine 'Thank you for helping me,' or pays the compliment of 'I like your picture.'

Listen for any examples of this kind in your own provision. If you hear none or very few, then reflect on whether children can imitate your model.

Resources

- **Bain, A., Barnett, L.** (1986) *The design of a day care system in a nursery setting for children under five*. London: The Tavistock Institute of Human Relations, Occasional Paper No. 8.
- **Batmanghelidjh, C**. (2006) *Shattered lives: children who live with courage and dignity*. London: Jessica Kingsley.
- **Belsky, J.** (2001) 'Emanuel Miller Lecture – Developmental risks (still) associated with early child care', Journal of Child Psychology and Psychiatry, Vol 42 , no 7, 845-859. **http://cep.lse.ac.uk/seminarpapers/23-02-07-BEL.pdf**
- **Beyer, J., Gammeltoft, L.** (2000) *Autism and play*. London: Jessica Kingsley.
- **Bion, W.R.** (1962) *Learning from experience*. London: Heinemann.

- **Carr, M.** (2001) *Assessment in early childhood settings*. London: Paul Chapman Publishing.
- **Clarke, Ann, Clarke, Alan** (1998) 'Early experience and the life path', The Psychologist, September 1998, pages 433–6. **www.thepsychologist.org.uk/archive** (from this page, go to the correct year and month and download this paper)
- **Dunn, J.** (1993) *Young children's close relationships beyond attachment*. London: Sage.
- **Dweck, C.S., Leggett, E.** (1988) 'A social-cognitive approach to motivation and personality', Psychological Review, 95 (2), 256–73.
- **Early Childhood Unit**, *Everyday Stories* (Descriptive observations from the research undertaken of under-threes in day nurseries during the mid-1990s by Elfer, P. and Selleck, D.). **www.everydaystories.org.uk**.
- **Eisenberg, N.** (1992) *The caring child*. Cambridge M.A: Harvard University Press.
- **Elfer, P., Goldschmied, E., Selleck, D.** (2003) *Key persons in the nursery: building relationships for quality provision*. London: David Fulton.
- **Elfer, P.** (2006) 'Exploring children's expressions of attachment in nursery', European Early Childhood Education Journal, vol 14, no 2, 81–95.
- **Elfer, P.** (2007) 'Babies and young children in nursery: using psychoanalytic ideas to explore tasks and interaction', Children in Society, vol 21, no 2, 111–22.
- **Gerhardt, S.** (2004) Why love matters: how affection shapes a baby's brain. Hove: Routledge.
- **Goldschmied, E., Jackson, S.** (2004) *People under three: young children in day care*. London: Routledge.
- **Goleman, D.** (1996) *Emotional intelligence – why it can matter more than IQ*. London: Bloomsbury.
- **Gottman, J., Declaire, J.** (1997) *The heart of parenting: how to raise an emotionally intelligent child*. London: Bloomsbury.
- **Healy, J.** (2004) *Your child's growing mind: brain development and learning from birth to adolescence*. New York: Broadway Books.
- **Henry, M.** (1996) *Young children, parents and professionals: enhancing the links in early childhood*. London: Routledge.
- **Laishley, J.** (1984) 'Taking responsibility for young children: Who? Where? When' – a consideration of issue, evidence and implications Discussion Paper 1 for the National Nursery Examination Board, London: NNEB.
- **Learning and Teaching Scotland** (2010) *Pre-birth to Three: Positive Outcomes for Scotland's Children and Families*. www.ltscotland.org.uk/earlyyears/
- **Lindon, J.** (2009) *Parents as partners*. London: Practical Pre-School Books.
- **Lindon, J.** (2010a) *The key person approach*. London: Practical Pre-School Books.
- **Lindon, J.** (2011b) *Supporting children's social development*. London: Practical Pre-School Books.
- **Lindon, J.** (2012a) *Safeguarding and child protection 0–8 years* (4th edn). London: Hodder Education.
- **Lindon, J.** (2012d) *Understanding children's behaviour: play, development and learning* (2nd edn). London: Hodder Education.

- **Manning-Morton, J.** (2006) 'The personal is professional: professionalism and the birth to three practitioner', Contemporary issues in early childhood, vol 7, no. 1.
- **Oates, J.** (ed.) (2007) *Attachment Relationships – Quality of Care for Young Children*. London: Bernard Van Leer Foundation. **www.bernardvanleer.org**
- **Pascal, C., Bertram, T.** (eds) (1997) *Effective early learning: case studies in improvement*. London: Hodder and Stoughton.
- **Rutter, M.** (1972) *Maternal Deprivation Re-assessed*. London: Penguin.
- **Rutter, M.** (1999) 'English and Romanian Adoptees Study (ERA)', in Ceci, S., and Williams, W. (eds) The nature-nurture debate. Blackwell: Malden Massachusetts.
- **Siraj-Blatchford, I., Sylva, K., Muttock, S., Gilden, R., Bell, D.** (2002) *Researching Effective Pedagogy in Early Years: Brief No. 356.* **www.education.gov. uk/publications/standard/publicationDetail/Page1/RB356**
- **Skynner, R., Cleese, J.** (1997) *Families and how to survive them*. London: Vermilion.
- **Sylva, K.** (1994) 'The impact of early learning on children's later development', in Ball, C., Start right: the importance of early learning. London: Royal Society of the Arts.
- **Tayler, C.** (2007) 'The brain, development and learning in early childhood', in Centre for Educational Research and Innovation, Understanding the Brain: the Birth of a Learning Science, Part II, 161-183. **www.oecd.org/ dataoecd/39/53/40554190.pdf**
- **Tizard, B.** (1986) *The care of young children: implications of recent research*. London: Thomas Coram Research Unit Occasional Papers, no. 1.
- **Tizard, B.** (2009) 'The making and breaking of attachment theory', The Psychologist, October, vol 22 no. 10. **www.bps.org.uk/thepsychologist**
- **Trevarthen, C., Barr, I., Dunlop, A., Gjersoe, N., Marwick, H., Stephen, C.** (2003) *Meeting the needs of children from birth to three years*. Edinburgh: Scottish Executive. Download the summary on **www.scotland.gov.uk/ Publications/2003/06/17458/22696** or the full report on **www.scotland.gov.uk/ Resource/Doc/933/0007610.pdf**

The importance of physical skills and movement

Chapter **6**

Most theorists and researchers have been more interested in cognitive development or communication than physical development. Developmental psychology has tended to describe physical growth and change in skills and then moved on, without much theoretical speculation about the significance of such changes for children. A greater understanding of brain development, along with the risks of discouraging active play, has now highlighted why we should not take physical development for granted.

The main sections in this chapter are:
- Physical development and children's experience
- Learning through the senses
- The importance of outdoor learning.

Physical development and children's experience

Arnold Gesell and his team documented physical skills, as well as other areas of development, as they established norms for child development (page 15). Gesell (1954) identified an important connection between aspects of young development when he said that a two-year-old 'thinks with his muscles'. Alert observation of young children soon dispels any tendency to undervalue the importance of physical skills and a sense of personal control over their own body. Children's physical development is important for their whole development and well being:

- Children's growing physical competence makes new behaviours possible and some combination skills take time and practice. Young toddlers put in the effort to gain the balance to walk with confidence and be able to carry something at the same time. Young children love playing with a ball. But even six- and seven-year-olds struggle to hit a ball with a bat or racket, especially if the ball reaches them through the air, rather than along the ground.
- Children's physical growth determines their potential experiences within their everyday life. A crawling or walking toddler can take independent action to cross the room to something of interest. Three-year-olds, who are able to manage their clothes in the toilet, gain the satisfaction of greater self-reliance, although they may still welcome help with some aspects of this personal care routine.

- Confident physical skills support cooperative play between children, enabling them to take pleasure in organising themselves, whether it is in respect of their construction projects, gardening enterprises or pretend play sequences.
- Children's growth affects the responses of other people. Children who are smaller or larger than average, compared with their peers, often get treated differently by children and adults.
- A sense of physical competence, or incompetence, can affect a child's sense of self-esteem. All children need to learn the skills of coordination, but some feel 'clumsy', compared with their peers. Some may be living with a disability such as dyspraxia, which will affect their physical skills in daily experiences.
- Children need to be active in childhood, because regular and lively physical activity builds muscle strength, lung capacity and bone density. Basic physical fitness is laid down in childhood and there are limits to how far you can repair serious deficiencies later. Insufficient physical activity, especially accompanied with unhealthy eating habits, increases the health risks associated with obesity.
- Physical confidence, through plenty of practice in large and fine physical movements, is crucial for children in order to manage the bodily control needed later for actual writing and reading. Enjoyable opportunities for mark-making, with a wide range of tools and materials, are vital on the learning journey towards literacy.

Figure 6.1 Toddlers need to work on their balance

Physical growth changes a child's social world

Contrast your mental picture of a newborn baby with a mobile and active seven- or eight-year-old. Human newborn babies are helpless, especially compared with other young mammals, such as lambs who struggle to their feet and follow their mother relatively soon after birth. Human babies have reflex actions at birth, but they are scarcely able to make deliberate physical actions. If all has gone well, a child of seven or eight years old is physically coordinated, able to choose from a wide range of large physical movements and fine skills to achieve different purposes. It is an impressive achievement.

Getting the hands free

Young children's physical development underpins many of the other learning tasks that they face, because the growth of physical skills is not simply more of the same. The development of skills changes the qualities of experience for a young child. Elinor Goldschmied (Goldschmied and Jackson, 2004) developed the Treasure Basket as a resource for babies whose muscle control had developed to the stage where they were able to sit securely. Elinor Goldschmied described this significant shift as being that babies now had 'time on their hands'. Anita Hughes (2006) describes the play opportunities of this resource and you can see it in action in the visual material of Goldschmied (1986) and Siren Films (2006).

Independent mobility

Observation of babies demonstrates their powerful drive for physical control. Before they become able to move themselves from place to place, babies spend much of their waking time working on developing their current physical skills. Babies' ability to control their body moves steadily downwards, with control of their relatively heavy head being the first task. If you watch babies under one year old, it is very noticeable how much effort they put into moving their limbs, getting hold of objects and, by the middle of their baby year, attempting to move by whatever method they can manage. Mobility becomes a key issue for them and for their carers, since an immobile baby is very dependent on what adults or other children bring to them or take them towards.

Young children develop their ability to use, practise and add further physical skills. Yet physical development is not separate from everything else that they are learning. Annette Karmiloff-Smith (1994) shows how careful watching of babies' and toddlers' physical abilities often highlights other, less immediately obvious, aspects to their development. You will see their persistence, creative attempts to solve problems such as, 'How do I get hold of this?' and 'How do I make that work?' and their delight with achievements. The example from my own family diary illustrates how Drew's developing physical skills opened the door for a great deal of learning within other aspects of his development.

- Lance has started a game with Drew, where Lance says 'One, two, three go!' and Drew runs and throws himself into Lance's arms. Drew now makes sounds in the same rhythm when he jumps on his own, or throws himself onto the floor cushions, with a 'Dah, do, da, dah'.

- Drew is safe when allowed to walk into the garden from the back door. He has his little watering can and wants to water the flowers, as well as smell them.

- He wants to use a damp cloth to wipe up his highchair tray, as he sees me do. He likes putting objects into containers, so he is happy sometimes to help in tidying up his toys.

- He can get out the books he wants from his low shelf and has learned to work the pulls in the books with movable parts.

- He is so pleased with himself when he makes something work. He can get all the cones onto his rod and, if one of us engages the mechanism, Drew can press the lever and shoot them into the air. He stamps his feet in appreciation, or applauds himself by holding one hand steady and clapping the other against it.

1 The highlights are all led through physical development, but what other skills are shown in these examples?

2 Make an observation of a toddler of a similar age. What can he or she manage in terms of physical skills? Then consider how these skills open up other areas of development.

Figure 6.2 Plenty of practice builds confidence

The importance of doing it again, and again

The research into brain development in very early childhood has confirmed that babies and toddlers need to be able to move. They need plenty of hands-on learning, and safe feet-on and mouth-on contact to learn through their senses. The enjoyable practice of crawling, grasping and handling objects builds vital neural connections in young brains. Babies and children need to repeat and practise, in order to firm up those connections. The neuroscientists express the idea as 'the cells that fire together wire together'. This need for happy practice is not restricted to physical development, but so much of early learning is led through the drive to move. Continued experience in any area of development firms up neural connections, until they form the complex neural pathways on which babies build more learning. Those connections that are not strengthened by repeated experience are less strong and may fade away.

Pause for reflection

Observe one or more babies over the time that they learn to crawl. (Not all babies crawl; some move by bottom shuffling.) You will see the external version of what is being built in the baby's brain.

- Babies who are ready will have built the muscle strength to be on all fours, but the problem is 'How do you move?' Babies often rock to and fro, looking up perplexed because, despite all the vigorous movement, they have not actually travelled at all.

- Then, quite often babies manage to move but, because the top half of their body is currently stronger, they go backwards. They sit on their bottom, look around expectantly and their face often crumples in disappointment.

- But babies keep trying and are soon rewarded with forward motion, which they practise enthusiastically over the days. You will see the gleam in their eye, as they spot something of interest, move from sitting to crawling, reach their destination, sit back on their bottom and reach out their hands.

- You have observed the development from an immature set of neural connections to a fully functioning neural pathway that is linked also to baby thinking and forward planning.

Sally Goddard Blythe (2004, 2008) has pointed out the dangers of failing to appreciate what babies and toddlers learn through movement and the long-term consequences of undervaluing the importance of physical development. In one sense, Sally Goddard Blythe travelled backwards from her work with older children who had coordination difficulties, or a diagnosis of dyspraxia. She also explored when limited physical experiences seemed to be a factor in dyslexia and Attention Deficit Hyperactivity Disorder.

Goddard Blythe talks about 'the first ABC': attention, balance and coordination are the crucial building blocks for later learning. She stresses that:
- Children need confidence and competence in large movements, as well as fine coordination. So, pushing young children into writing exercises does not help them to learn to write at a younger age. Such pressure creates unsuitable

UNDERSTANDING CHILD DEVELOPMENT 0–8 YEARS

physical habits for handwriting and gives children negative experiences that could well put them off attempting to write when they are finally ready to learn (the link with dispositions, page 102).

- Babies and children should not be rushed through their physical skills. For example, the actions of crawling help babies and toddlers to fine-tune their sense of balance and are often the first experience of synchronising the left and right sides of the body. Incidentally, Goddard Blythe points out that the necessary coordination of moving hands and vision in crawling is undertaken at the same distance that children will use years later in reading and writing.

- Children need plenty of relaxed opportunities to move, in order to understand the messages from their body. This physical feedback about touch, grasp and balance is called proprioception.

- From her research, Sally Goddard Blythe agrees with other observers of early years practice, for example with outdoor play (page 127). Children in the first years of primary school, let alone younger children, cannot be expected to sit for long periods in adult-directed activity without physical breaks.

Pause for reflection

Sally Goddard Blythe observes that the most advanced level of movement is the ability to stay totally still. You may recall that dilemma from learning to ride a two-wheeled bicycle.

- Watch some toddlers who are mastering the skills of walking. Notice that they have to keep moving to maintain balance. You will see that toddlers wobble when they come to a stop and plump down on their bottoms. It is only after plenty of practice that confident walkers are then able to stand still.

- Observe how the most difficult part of learning to ride a two-wheeled bike is the slow-moving part between being still and getting enough speed to hold the momentum.

What does it mean?

Proprioception: the ability to recognise and use the physical sensations from the body that give feedback on balance and the position of our limbs.

Physically active play and learning

There has been increasing concern about the physical well being of children when they are not encouraged to develop physically active habits. A sedentary lifestyle, combined with an unbalanced diet, is a recipe for poor health: physically, emotionally and intellectually.

For as long as practitioners continue to encourage active and playful experiences, or regain this perspective, young children will build their own muscles and robust health through lively play, much of it outdoors. Children do not need structured physical development programmes, unless they have a physical disability or chronic ill health that has created special needs. Also, physical play is not the same experience as PE, as offered in primary schools. The problem with adult-organised physical games is that children often spend too much time standing around, waiting to be directed into action. There is a parallel here with concern about the communication skills of young children (see page 155). They need adults who are genuinely interested to chat, in a personal way, just like children need adults who are good play companions.

Take another **perspective**

- Thoughtful adults have to ask themselves how such a situation can have arisen, when the usual state of babies, toddlers and young children is to be on the move, active and 'into everything'. It takes serious discouragement from key adults and a depressing learning environment to create young 'couch potatoes'.

- One of the key problems, arising from misguided early years and school practice, is the view that valued learning mainly happens indoors and when children are sitting 'nicely' at a table (see page 125).

- An additional problem arises from over-protection: a risk-averse outlook that focuses on the worst that could happen and leads adults to remove opportunities for physical challenge and adventures (Gill, 2007; Lindon, 2011a).

There is a place for what could be called organised encouragement of the adults, when practitioners need support to understand what it is that children gain from physically active play, with generous time for self-chosen activities. The practical ideas of Development Movement Play, promoted by the organisation Jabadao (**www.jabadao.org/dmp_theory.html**), lead through a general focus on the value of free-flow active play and a specific focus on early movements that seem to be especially important.

Theory and practice focused on physical skills highlight the importance of plenty of floor time; babies, toddlers and young children need the easy option to spread out on a comfortable floor. Very young children are not well-served by a rush to get them to sit up to a table, except for mealtimes. Once babies have the muscle control to hold their head and shoulders steady, they need to spend time on their stomachs. Sleeping babies should be placed on their backs (page 75) but wakeful 'tummy time' is ideal for older babies to give them the opportunity to practise lifting their head and upper body off the floor. They are then in the best position to get into the 'all fours position' for crawling. The floor indoors and a safe enough outdoor surface are ideal for rolling and moving from side to side. Beyond babyhood, toddlers and children often like the stretch-and-roll that starts from the lying-down position.

Children need time, space and resources to explore their ability to push, pull and stretch. Babies and toddlers will extend these skills with open-ended play resources, but soon they will use equipment that supports skills of climbing, clambering, hanging and swinging. From larger- to smaller-scale movements, young children will hone their physical control, coordination of movement as well as supporting information from their senses, and sheer pleasure in deliberate activity.

Learning through the senses

Young children learn a very great deal through direct physical contact. They need the reassurance of touch, cuddling and being rocked. Also they learn about the world through their senses. Researchers who are concerned to bring back awareness of the outdoors often highlight the power of learning through the senses and the opportunities of the natural world. The delights of a sensory room, or a sensory corner, have in some cases reached early years settings through an awareness of the special needs of disabled children. However, such resources are truly inclusive.

The importance of hands-on learning

Elinor Goldschmied worked with day nurseries in England and in Italy and was influential in bringing the importance of learning through the senses back to early years practice. By the 1960s and 70s Goldschmied was very concerned about over-reliance in family homes and nurseries on commercially made, plastic toys. (The situation has definitely worsened since that time.) She developed the Treasure Basket to promote relaxed exploratory play that enabled babies to discover for themselves. She stressed the importance of materials that support all of children's five senses: hearing, vision, touch, smell and taste. She also identified a 'sixth sense' in children's sensitivity to their own bodily movement and recognition of what physical skills feel like when they are used. This idea is very similar to that of proprioception (page 117).

Figure 6.3 Sensory experiences remain important throughout childhood

Toddlers often still enjoy playing with the Treasure Basket or with collections of similar types of materials. This activity extended naturally into discovery or Heuristic Play that Elinor Goldschmied developed for day nurseries, with Anita Hughes (2006) and Gwen Macmichael. The term 'heuristic' was taken from the Greek word *eurisko*, meaning 'serves to discover'. A heuristic play session is a special time when mobile toddlers and young children have access to a rich resource of recycled materials, none of which are conventional toys. As with the Treasure Basket, the aim is that toddlers play as they wish and adults watch with interest. Adults help if asked, or offer as appropriate, but do not direct children's play by actions or words. You can watch this kind of exploratory play within a nursery in the visual materials of Goldschmied and Hughes (1992) and at home in Siren Films (2006).

What does it mean?

Treasure Basket: a play resource developed by Elinor Goldschmied for babies who can sit unassisted. The low basket contains a range of safe and interesting objects that are not conventional toys.

Heuristic Play: an exploratory play resource for toddlers and young children, developed by Elinor Goldschmied with Anita Hughes and Gwen Macmichael that uses a wide range of ordinary objects and recycled materials for children to play with as they choose.

Pause for reflection

Gather observations of sitting babies who are able to enjoy the Treasure Basket on different occasions.

- How do individual babies approach the choice in the basket? What do they like and what do they do with items? Do some babies return to the same item over time?

- Two babies can sit with the same basket. Do they have different styles of exploration? Does one baby offer any items to the other?

Gather observations also of a Heuristic Play session.

- What interests individual children? What do they want to explore? Do they watch each other, or hand over items?

- In what ways do children invite your help or interest?

- What have you learned about the skills, interests and preferred ways of exploration of the babies or the toddlers?

Learning through schemas

Chris Athey (1990) developed Piaget's idea of schemas (page 34) as part of a series of early educational intervention projects, based at the Froebel Institute, throughout the 1970s in Roehampton, south London. The objective was to support children from less socially advantaged homes and the project worked in close partnership with parents. The approach through schemas was a successful method for creating common ground between the teachers and parents, who in this project were mainly mothers.

Chris Athey described schemas as 'cognitive constants'. They are often a repeated sequence of similar physical actions that show a combination of young thinking and exploring. Schemas are patterns of behaviour that are linked through a child's current interest and which form the basis of exploration and play for individuals. For example, the play behaviour of one child may be described through a fascination with a schema of 'enveloping'. Perhaps this child explores many different ways of covering herself or objects, or investigates the possibilities through craft activities that include wrapping.

Chris Athey developed the concept of schemas far beyond Piaget's academic interest in children's cognitive development. Use of the schema approach in nurseries has been a positive route to help practitioners and parents to respect toddlers' play explorations, when it might seem like 'just messing about' or not 'proper playing' to adults. For instance, a child who is thoroughly absorbed in his exploration of an 'inside-outside' schema may move objects from place to place and may put items inside others. Unreflective adults may become annoyed that the child wants to put play materials where they do not belong, at least from the adult perspective. A child may be more interested in nesting various containers and items than making the model that a practitioner had planned for today.

What does it mean?

Schemas: patterns of persistent behaviour that are linked through a child-chosen focus of interest and from which a child explores in different situations.

The interest in schemas has continued and the use of this concept as part of partnership is strongly shown in the work of the Pen Green Centre in Corby, England. Cath Arnold (1999, 2003) describes ways of using the concept of schemas through the early development of individual children. For example, Harry is at one point very interested in connection and disconnection. Georgia spent several months exploring a schema of enveloping, which first appeared to arise from her concern that the rabbits would get wet without a protective covering. Sally Featherstone (2008) also offers examples of schemas in action.

Figure 6.4 Observation will reveal a child's persistent play patterns

Carmel Brennan (2004:24) describes examples, in words and photographs, of how young children organise their own play exploration through their current schema. Ali is a girl who likes to envelope: she is busy wrapping up her doll in the visual example, but Ali also likes to wrap presents for her friends and to make her baby dolls cosy. Martin is very absorbed in filling bags and moving materials around his playgroup. Sometimes he plays at being a customer in the shop corner, but his interest in filling and transporting is more extensive than this role play.

Pause for reflection

When my daughter was 18 months old she liked moving bricks and dolls around in her wooden trolley indoors, anything in the small wheelbarrow out of doors and her older brother in his buggy when we went on walks. Tanith had a bag, in which she carried around objects that were important to her. However, she also added items that were important to us, such as her father's watch and the remote control for the television. It was crucial that we did not get irritated with our daughter: she had not taken these objects with the intention of causing trouble and she kept them safe. So, we explained that Daddy's watch should be left where he put it and we asked Tanith to empty her bag, if we could not find something.

One way of making sense of Tanith's behaviour is to say she was exploring a 'transporting' schema. It was not her only way of exploring at 18 months, but it was a strong theme in how she worked with and on her environment in the latter half of her second year.

Think about and observe children you know. Can you see the pattern of a schema in their play? For instance, you could look for:

- Rotation: an interest in things that turn like wheels, objects that roll, or a child's physical exploration of spinning around herself, or waving her limbs in a circular motion.

- Orientation: a fascination with how things seem from another angle, explored by turning objects around or the child twisting or hanging upside down.

- Connection: how things are or could be joined together. A child might explore this in crafts, in stringing together toys or showing connections in a drawing. The opposite schema of separation can lead to havoc when children have the physical skills to disassemble objects that adults would rather they left assembled.

Make notes and compare your observations with a colleague.

Early brain development and learning

Advances in computer imaging have greatly extended understanding of how human brains work and of brain development during early childhood. Reviews like those of Jane Healy (2004) or Collette Tayler (2007) show that many insights give strong support for existing good early years practice that shows awareness of what and how young children learn. Thorough knowledge of child development, linked with the brain research, can make daily interactions with young children more supportive of their learning. However, there is still a great deal we do not know about how the brain works and exactly what happens during early childhood.

Take another **perspective**

Early years practitioners, and parents, need to be wary of commercial interests that have seized the research as a way to sell toys, DVDs and other resources.

You will find many claims for products that will 'boost your child's brain power'. Some materials may be useful, even though the promises are overblown. However, you can support young brain development through using simple play resources, combined with your attention and a warm relationship.

For example, singing and music are beneficial for young children. But an entire industry has grown around the claim that listening to Mozart will boost measures of intelligence. The original research was on college students; the effect was short-lived and the experiment has not been successfully repeated. Look at **www.skepdic.com** for discussion of the 'so-called' Mozart Effect, as well as other claims based very loosely on research.

Prior to advances in neuroscience, research and theory about the process of learning highlighted the importance of time for learning and doing something again and again, to firm up skills. These ideas of a cycle of learning have been around in the literature for practical psychology for many years. (I have been unable to track who originally laid out this cycle, although an internet search will show interested readers that many people have developed the basic ideas.)

There are four general stages in awareness:

1   Unconscious incompetence: you are unaware of an area of knowledge or skill; you do not know that you do not know.

2   Conscious incompetence: you are only too aware that you do not know, cannot understand or manage a skill, but you want or need this ability.

3   Conscious competence: you are able to use knowledge or manage a skill, but you have to attend carefully while you do it.

4   Unconscious competence: you have practised enough that this area seems automatic; ideas are obvious and you do not have to concentrate.

This concept could have been placed in other parts of the book. It has been located here in order to add emphasis to the message that children need to be active. Supportive early years practitioners realise that children's enthusiasm will be to learn what engages them right now and they will be motivated to practise and get better, or understand more thoroughly, when they can share a great deal of the control over 'what we're going to do today'.

Pause for reflection

- Adults already have a great deal of learning experience. You may be aware of stress or discomfort when you need to learn something new. Use the four stages to reflect on a skill that you learned as an adult, such as driving a car.

- Now, look at the process of learning from a child's perspective. Skills that seem easy to you are less than obvious to children; ideas that are crystal clear to you may be a mystery to them.

- Do you allow generous time for children to 'do it again' out of choice? Do they have the enjoyment of realising that a skill, physical or otherwise, is now 'easy peasey'? Do they experience the positive pride of being able now to show another child how to do something?

Physical movement and well being

Practical lessons from an understanding of early brain development have influenced early years and school practice; this is sometimes called the 'brain-based learning approach'. There are some very positive ideas in some materials. However, careful research reviews (Howard-Jones, undated, about 2008; Blakemore and Frith, 2000) raise some serious questions over claims from some of the commercial brain-based learning programmes. Howard-Jones summarises the lack of support for claims about how some activities exert a specific effect on different parts, or sides, of the brain.

Thoughtful practitioners need to take into account that some brain-based claims may be considerably exaggerated, although the broad practice implications can be beneficial. One such impact is an increased awareness of the importance of physical activity to support and promote learning.

- The opportunity to move is linked with mental alertness and emotional well being. Children are disadvantaged by adults whose view of learning is that children do a great deal of 'sitting nicely'.
- Good primary school practice has embraced the idea of 'brain breaks': children need active interludes to aid concentration. However, good early years practice should mean that young children provide their own brain breaks, through ease of movement and free flow between indoors and the outside resources.
- Children cannot learn if they are hungry or dehydrated. They do need sufficient drink and easy access to water. They need a healthy diet, and regular and sufficient rest and proper sleep is essential for young brains to work at their best capacity.

Preferences and styles for learning

The two research reviews of brain development challenge the basis for some approaches to categorising learning styles and individual preferences. The argument is again that there is no clear brain-based evidence for the more specific programmes. The positive impact has been when practitioners, often within the school system, have been provoked to consider their main approach to teaching.

One practical example is an approach to learning that draws on the senses, especially visual, auditory and kinesthetic, known as VAK for short. There is no brain-based evidence to place children in closed categories, or label them. However, the approach can be constructive in helping practitioners to think about their own preferred style, as well as taking children as diverse individuals.

1 Visual: good practice includes the use of images to show and not only tell. For example, early years settings practitioners who use photos and friendly captions to remind children that 'Now we wash our hands' or 'Our books are happy when they are stacked like this.' Cartoons and photographs, some with the additional interest of an invitation to 'lift the flap', help young children to follow a sequence for a routine. Gestures support communication and the visual element works together with the sound of spoken words.

2 Auditory: learning is well supported when practitioners are alert to noise levels, ease of hearing and the rhythm of sounds. Selected use of music can help children, as they move from one part of the day to another routine. You need to choose carefully, since music creates or supports a mood. Avoid fast music that increases in volume if you wish children to relax. Children need to be able to distinguish pieces of music. Their brains are not 'stimulated' by non-stop background sound; children just learn to ignore it. The auditory aspect to learning is triggered when you encourage children to voice their thoughts (see also page 167) or talk through their plans before plunging into action.

3 Kinesthetic: the power of touch is used as a resource for learning when children have access to natural materials, a variety of textures (not all plastic) and comfortable furnishings and dens. They benefit from space and 'permission' to move, rather than being harassed to 'sit still and concentrate'. Gestures also add the communication of movement to meaning from spoken words.

Pause for reflection

Consider the three strands of visual, auditory and kinesthetic.

- In what ways do you use each of these possibilities to support learning?

- On reflection, does your practice tip more in one direction than another?

- Can you identify your own preferred learning style? Do you tend to want to get your hands on something, to have a go? Do you like to see a demonstration and not only listen to an explanation?

The VAK approach does not mean that you overlook the other two senses: smell and taste.

- Think about smells. Pleasant and unpleasant aromas can affect a learning environment.

- Taste is important for everyone, not only babies who put everything into their mouth. Good food (taste and smell) is a powerful support to young children's learning, because they feel that important adults care about them and care for their enjoyment and well being.

Innovative early years practice has emerged from the benefits of making ideas more visible. For example, Nicola Call and Sally Featherstone (2003) describe how to create a visual map with children for a topic that is being introduced by the practitioner. The adult starts with a short explanation of the topic, some key words on paper and maybe a simple picture. But then the children take over with their ideas, fetching items and drawing pictures to illustrate what will be included. String or wool is used to connect together the visual ideas. There is good reason to argue that if you cannot easily engage children in this kind of visual mapping, then the topic you have planned probably does not connect well with their current knowledge and understanding of the world. It is a step too far in terms of their zone of proximal development (page 174).

Claire Warden (2006) describes her ideas of Big Book Planners, in which children make their thinking visible and work alongside adults in forward planning. The approach is to bring ideas and possibilities alive by laying them out in the 2-D Talking and Thinking Floorbook format as well as 3-D when children gather together relevant objects. Both these approaches are a jumping-off point for further talking, thinking and planning as a joint enterprise between children and equally enthusiastic adults.

The importance of outdoor learning

Early years practice in the UK developed in the first half of the 20th century, with a strong emphasis on the value of the outdoor environment. Yet changes in practice during the last quarter of that century worked steadily to undermine outdoor learning. There is good reason for optimism that the importance of the outdoors is being recognised once again. But it remains necessary to recognise the blocks that can still undermine a full view of children's learning.

What does it mean?

Outdoor play: opportunities for children to learn in the outdoors, in a garden or other open-air space.

Physical play: activities and opportunities that especially help children to use, practise and apply the full range of their physical skills.

How did outdoor learning become devalued?

Nursery schools were established in the UK, with a strong emphasis on children being outside and physically active. Pioneers like Margaret McMillan built their early years curriculum upon the value of outdoor experience and play for young children. The first nursery schools were set up largely for children who could be at a social disadvantage. But an equally strong concern was that the traditional primary school model was inappropriate for younger children. The generous nursery garden was never envisaged as a school playground, so it was not an area to be used only for short 'breaktimes'. Margaret McMillan saw no distinction between the bodily development of a child and the growth of their mind, their intellectual capacity.

Make the connection with... *Top-down pressure*

The loss of outdoor learning is symbolic of the whole top-down pressure that unbalanced much of early years practice in the last quarter of the 20th century and continues to need to be challenged.

- Look through this section and find your own connections with the imposition of a school model and pressure to 'get children ready ...' for that next stage.

Respect for the outdoors continued for many years until an alternative model of early learning developed through the last decades of the 20th century. Several strands came together in order to push outdoor play and related physical play to the sidelines for early years settings, back to activities that took place in environments that were more like school breaktime.

- During the 1970s the whole concept of early education as compensatory shifted to a much stronger focus on cognitive development. A wide range of pre-school compensation programmes were launched and tracked for measurable changes in children's development. The more valued learning was now believed to happen indoors, not out in the garden.

- The task of early years provision in the UK came to be defined as preparing children for school, and more specifically not to fail in school. In contrast, many European early years systems see their task as contributing to the raising of the next generation, preparing children for life in society, not exclusively to fit the role of school pupil.

- A top-down school model affected early years teams from the 1970s and 80s and many accepted a working definition of 'learning' and 'concentration' as something that happened when children were sitting still at indoor activities. The outdoors became the place where 'children let off steam'.

- Marjorie Ouvry (2000) adds that early years settings linked with a primary school also risked taking on the view that physical activity was the same as PE, traditionally a low-priority subject in the school curriculum.

- By the late 1980s and 90s, discussion about early learning in different settings had became very focused on intellectual development. Anxieties about children's later achievement in school, and pressures about inspection, made matters worse, especially if early years teams lacked the confidence to promote children's all-round learning and the genuine opportunities to learn outdoors.

Figure 6.5 Anything involving water is usually welcome

Sufficient time to play and learn outdoors

Marjorie Ouvry (2000) describes the need to challenge the circular logic that develops when outdoor learning is dismissed. Adults find excuses for not using outdoor learning: these include the weather, the length of time it takes to set up outdoor equipment or that children get too noisy when outdoors. Any excuse is found to limit time outside, with the consequence that children do not have an enjoyable time, so there is the proof that using the outdoors is a waste of effort. Over-anxiety about safety outside can be another reason for adults to limit time and activities, rather than engage in problem solving with the children. In contrast, good early years (and school) practice takes a robust approach to risk assessment, which usually ends with results that include, 'Yes, so as long as we ...' and not 'We'll have to stop them' (Lindon, 2011a and 2012a).

Over several decades, the image of nursery life became closer to that of a school day and a classroom, with the garden as breaktime. Even the key concept of 'learning through play' (page 228) became much more defined as activities planned by adults for their educational purposes. Free play became too often something that happened as a reward; for example, 'When you've done your work, then you can go and play.' Yet this inappropriate practice can be challenged. Margaret Edgington (2002) and other researchers in this area describe how every aspect of what practitioners hope young children will learn can be experienced outside. Generous time spent outdoors benefits all children, but especially those boys and girls who are keen to move and have a sense of space.

Jane Devereux and Ann Bridges (2004) describe the many ways in which children learned through being directly involved in the development of their nursery garden. In what they call 'The story of the bark chips', Devereux and Bridges recount how an unexpected event was converted by the children into an absorbing and exciting afternoon. Large sacks of bark chips for the nursery garden were left by the delivery firm on the pavement outside the school. The children were keen to tackle this problem and discussed what to do. Teamwork flourished, as boys and girls organised their wheeled trolleys and the transport routes. They moved the entire batch through the school and into the nursery, ready for use in the next stage of garden development.

Vivian Paley (1984) noted the changes when she increased the amount of free and outdoor playtime and spread it over a longer period in the day. The boys, in particular, became more willing to use table-top activities, when they were less constrained by time or personal space. Helen Bilton (2002) recalls her action research study of outdoor time in the early 1990s. She observed the changes in children's behaviour when a 15-minute timetabled outdoor session was changed to free flow between indoors and the garden. The 'mad dash' to the outside stopped, because children who were keen to play in the garden realised there was no time limit. The play outside became less manic and more sustained; children were no longer trying to pack all their favourite activities into a scant quarter of an hour.

Children flourish when they are given experience to connect themselves to the outdoors, nature and the natural world. Champions of the outdoors, like Claire Warden (2005), document the richness of experience in the natural world and address practical problems and reservations. Positive moves to re-establish the potential of outdoor learning are helped by initiatives such as the Forest School movement and outdoor action research, for example the Rising Sun Woodland Project of Sightlines Initiative (2001).

Figure 6.6 Physical skill and strength are often needed in play

Forest schools and dedicated outdoor spaces have developed across the UK. The Greenwich forest school initiative, led by Liz Buck and Lucy Nettleton (2007, also some descriptions in Lindon, 2009), showed that it was possible to get a forest school established across an urban borough. This emphasis on the outdoors is not only an issue for urban children. The Bridgwater Forest School project in Somerset is situated in what looks to a city visitor like a more rural area. But the team working with four-year-olds in the woodland resource realised that some children had scarcely visited the countryside that surrounds their town.

Pause for reflection

Practitioners can best support outdoor learning when they become aware of how the outdoors is experienced by children.

- On your own, or with colleagues, stand close to the edge of a flower bed or other planted area in your garden. Stand still for a short while and take in what you can see and hear.

- So long as you are steady, close your eyes and focus on sound alone.

- Then bend at the knees and go straight down vertically. What can you see now; what is the child's-eye view on this bit of outdoors?

- In which ways do you enable the youngest children, even the babies, to enjoy the outdoors?

Resources

- **Arnold, C.** (1999) *Child development and learning 2–5 years: Georgia's story.* London: Paul Chapman.
- **Arnold, C.** (2003) *Observing Harry: child development and learning 0–5.* Maidenhead: Open University Press.
- **Athey, C.** (1990) *Extending thought in young children: a parent–teacher partnership.* London: Paul Chapman.
- **Blakemore, S., Frith, U.** (2000) *The implications of recent developments in neuroscience for research on teaching and learning.* **www.tlrp.org/pub/acadpub/Blakemore2000.pdf**
- **Blythe, S.** (2004) *The well balanced child: movement and early learning.* Stroud: Hawthorn Press.
- **Blythe, S.** (2008) *What Babies and Children Really Need: how Mothers and Fathers Can Nurture Children's Growth for Health and Well Being.* Stroud: Hawthorn Press.
- **Brennan, C.** (ed.) (2004) *The power of play: a play curriculum in action.* Dublin: IPPA.
- **Buck, L., Nettleton, L.** (2007) *Forest School in Greenwich: Principles into Practice October 2006 – July 2007.* London: Greenwich Council.

- **Call, N., Featherstone, S.** (2003) *The Thinking Child: brain-based learning for the foundation stage.* Stafford: Network Educational Press.
- **Devereux, J., Bridges, A.** (2004) 'Knowledge and understanding of the world developed through a garden project', in Miller, L., and Devereux, J. (eds), *Supporting children's learning in the early years.* London: David Fulton.
- **Edgington, M.** (2002) *The great outdoors: developing children's learning through outdoor provision.* London: Early Education.
- **Featherstone, S.** (ed.) (2008) *Again, Again: Understanding Schemas in Young Children.* London: A&C Black.
- **Gesell, A.** (1954) *The first five years of life.* London: Methuen.
- **Gill, T.** (2007) *No fear: growing up in a risk-averse society.* London: Calouste Gulbenkian. Summary and full book on **www.gulbenkian.org.uk**
- **Goldschmied, E.** (1986) *Infants at Work: Babies of 6–9 Months Exploring Everyday Objects* (DVD). London: National Children's Bureau. **www.ncb.org.uk**
- **Goldschmied, E., Hughes, A.** (1992) *Heuristic Play with Objects: Children of 12–20 Months Exploring Everyday Objects* (DVD). London: National Children's Bureau.
- **Goldschmied, E., Jackson, S.** (2004) *People under three: young children in day care.* London: Routledge.
- **Healy, J.** (2004) *Your child's growing mind: brain development and learning from birth to adolescence.* New York: Broadway Books.
- **Howard-Jones, P.** (undated, *circa* 2008) *Neuroscience and Education: Issues and Opportunities.* London: Teaching and Learning Research Programme. **www.tlrp.org/pub/commentaries.html**
- **Hughes, A.** (2006) *Developing play for the under 3s: the Treasure Basket and Heuristic Play.* London: David Fulton.
- **Karmiloff-Smith, A.** (1994) *Baby it's you: a unique insight into the first three years of the developing baby.* London: Ebury Press.
- **Lindon, J.** (2009) *Parents as partners.* London: Practical Pre-School Books
- **Lindon, J.** (2011a) *Too safe for their own good? Helping children learn about risk and life skills.* London: National Children's Bureau.
- **Lindon, J.** (2012a) *Safeguarding and child protection 0–8 years* (4th edn). London: Hodder Education.
- **Ouvry, M.** (2000) *Exercising muscles and minds: outdoor play and the early years curriculum.* London: National Children's Bureau.
- **Paley, V.** (1984) *Boys and girls: superheroes in the doll corner.* Chicago: University of Chicago Press.
- **Sightlines Initiatives** (2001) *Rising Sun Woodland Pre-School Project.* Newcastle-upon-Tyne: Sightlines Initiative. **www.sightlines-initiative.com/index.php?id=56**
- **Siren Films Ltd** (2006) *Exploratory play* (DVD and booklet). Newcastle-upon-Tyne: Siren Films Ltd. **www.sirenfilms.co.uk**
- **www.skepdic.com** – useful website that challenges some popular areas of research and 'everybody knows'. I found it when researching the 'Mozart Effect'.

- **Tayler, C.** (2007) 'The brain, development and learning in early childhood', in Centre for Educational Research and Innovation, *Understanding the Brain: the Birth of a Learning Science,* Part II, 161–83. **www.oecd.org/dataoecd/39/53/40554190.pdf**
- **Warden, C.** (2005) *The potential of a puddle.* Perthshire: Mindstretchers.
- **Warden, C.** (2006) *Talking and Thinking Floorbooks: using 'Big Book Planners' to consult children.* Perthshire: Mindstretchers.

Chapter 7

Understanding and supporting children's communication

The majority of young children learn to speak and many around the world learn more than one language within early childhood. You can directly observe the development of spoken language and note down the ways in which children's spontaneous communication extends over the months and years. Spoken language is only part of full personal interaction. Children and adults also communicate by the many ways in which words can be said, through variations in tone, volume and different patterns of emphasis. Non-verbal communication coexists with the words, with messages expressed through facial expression, gestures and whole-body movements.

The main sections in this chapter are:
- How do children learn spoken language?
- Early social interaction
- The learning journey towards literacy.

How do children learn spoken language?

There can be no disagreement about the fact that most children manage what, from the outside, looks like a very tough task. The arguments have arisen among psychologists and linguists about how to explain satisfactorily what very young children 'just get on and do'. There have been several main theoretical approaches to the impressive reality of learning to speak. No single theory has been able to explain all aspects of language development.

Learning through imitation and reinforcement

The first attempts to explain children's acquisition of language were through the basic principles of behaviourism. B. F. Skinner proposed that young children learn to speak, because their parents systematically reward correct versions of the language and do not reward mistakes. Young children seem to flourish with positive feedback for their early attempts at language. They also become daunted if parents or practitioners highlight mistakes in an unkind way. However, most adults are considerably more flexible than a reinforcement explanation would predict. Parents and carers respond meaningfully to a wide range of grammatical constructions and pronunciations from toddlers. Correcting all, or most, of children's mistakes seems to inhibit communication rather than encourage it.

The ability to imitate explains partly how babies' sound-making moves towards the language that they hear and children's accents become those of the people they hear around them. Yet simple imitation cannot work as a complete explanation. Toddlers soon produce word combinations that they have not previously heard and some of their endearing phrases are self-created. Young children need to hear spoken language, so imitation is significant; but children are soon very creative in using their experience of what familiar people say.

Make the connection with... Understanding the structure of language

It is important for early years practitioners to have a sound, basic grasp of the structure of spoken language, especially such a rich and complicated language as English.

Young children's logical mistakes in grammar, such as 'I goed', show the results of over-applying a rule system for how to create a past tense. These sensible mistakes are evidence of active thinking, since children are using the standard '-d' ending that works for example in the sentence, 'I walked to the park yesterday.' However, the verb 'to go' is an irregular verb and does not follow the usual pattern: the correct past tense is 'I went'.

Speech and language therapists are alert to those children whose mistakes do not fit the pattern of logical mistakes in cracking the language code.

Pause for reflection

Children reach sensible conclusions from what they have heard. The following examples are from the diary I kept of my own children.

- At 18 months old Drew used the word 'more' for water. This puzzled me, until I heard myself saying, as he waved his empty watering can at me, 'Do you want some more?'

- At 23 months old Tanith used two words 'helpme' and 'helpit', which communicated different messages. 'Helpme' was said with a questioning tone and was an offer to help an adult, whereas 'helpit' was said with a pleading tone and used when she could not manage something. I traced these special words to my own phrases of 'Do you want to help me?', which was often said when we were in the kitchen and 'Do you want some help with it?', used when Tanith looked stuck with dressing or in play.

Listen for examples of sensible mistakes in the words that young, familiar children use.

- Note down what the children say and the context.

- Reflect on the words or phrases. Can you track the source of their logical mistake?

- Discuss your observations with children's parents.

- If appropriate, share that the best adult response is to provide the correct word naturally in your reply to a child. There is no need, and it is not respectful of young children, to insist that they now say the right word. In a friendly atmosphere, you will sometimes find that children choose to repeat the correct word, in a useful echo of what you have just said.

Children who have experienced a severely deprived childhood, with very limited human contact or care, do not learn to speak in isolation. It is a skill that needs appropriate experience, although babies and young children are very flexible about the topics of conversation. Children who hear plenty of language seem to develop their vocabulary slightly faster than those whose experience of language is limited. Babies and toddlers who have experience of infant-directed speech (page 146) also seem to develop some facets of their language slightly faster. Young children are helped by friendly extension of their short phrases, or slightly recasting what they say. For instance, the child says, 'Moggle village, little houses, little mans, little boats'. Her parent expands and gently corrects by saying, 'Yes, we went to the model village, didn't we? And everything was so little. There were little people and even the little boats. And the little train, do you remember the little train?'

Figure 7.1 Children need to be confident you will listen to them

Biological programming

Language development is not fully explained through the details of individual children's experience. So, some theorists proposed that an innate biological system must be involved: a process within the brain that is present when a baby is born. On this argument, language emerges as part of the process of maturation: the unfolding of characteristics programmed by a genetic code. This theoretical approach argues that children need to hear language spoken to trigger the system. Such an innate readiness has to be for language in general, not a specific language, and human infants need to be poised to listen to sounds and rhythm, to the beginnings and ends of sound sequences and to how sounds are stressed. This kind of explanation started with the work of Noam Chomsky in the 1960s and Steven Pinker (1994) has continued the emphasis on an inborn linguistic structure that functions to guide children's language learning.

Babies are born potentially able to produce all possible sounds and sound combinations. But by about one year, they have lost the ability to discriminate and make sounds that are not in the language(s) spoken around them. Their tuneful babbling has taken on the sound patterns of the language(s) that they hear. The concept of an innate predisposition to spoken language overcomes the difficulties of explaining how the majority of infants 'home in' on language so successfully. Toddlers appear not to receive enough feedback on their early attempts to support a learning theory explanation. A theory or innate predisposition would predict that the pattern of learning language would be very similar from one language to another. When this approach was first proposed, it looked as if children learning different world languages did follow very similar patterns. But more recent and detailed research has also found many differences.

Research findings from neuroscience support aspects of a brain-based innate theory. Part of this explanation for language development is that human infants are born predisposed to tune into spoken language. The part of the brain attuned to hearing, and vision, can be observed to work before birth. Brain activity gives off small electrical discharges, which can be tracked by computer imaging. Their pre-birth listening enables babies to show recognition of their mother's voice and, in some cases, familiarity with music or songs that they will have heard from the womb. However, there is no basis for enthusiastic commercial claims that parents can boost their unborn baby's brain power by playing specific CDs or DVDs.

Human infants appear to be designed to be social and to pay attention to the human voice. Lynne Murray and Liz Andrews (2000) describe how even very young babies are already alert, imitating and using all their senses in interaction with their social world. Visual material, for example from The Children's Project *The Social Baby* (2004) or Siren Films with *The Wonder Year* (2008), enables practitioners, or parents, to observe the clear evidence that babies are very responsive, and so the quality of adult communication really matters. Involved parents notice when infants are unresponsive and their concerns are often the first sign that some kind of disability is affecting infant social skills. For instance, blind babies may respond only to the sound of a parent's voice and deaf babies wait for the familiar face before a smile spreads over their face.

Figure 7.2 Very young children communicate clearly without words

Language linked with thinking

Innate models of language development allowed for the abilities of children and not just the input of speaking adults. Theorists, whose interest started from cognitive development, focus more on how language is a vehicle for expressing thoughts.

Lev Vygotsky (1962, 1978) proposed that young children's use of speech started as a means to guide themselves, as the words accompanied their actions. Then language began to precede the actions, with a function of planning what the child could or would do. The idea is that language frees children's thinking process from their immediate experience; it enables a mental step back for reflection, memory and making connections. Vygotsky pointed out how children and adults might use the same words, but that did not mean that children fully understood the concept represented by that word. Concepts are not given to children ready made with the words; development in thinking also has to take place.

The social constructivist tradition (page 49) stresses that children learn words primarily because they connect with what the young child is already thinking. Words do not introduce new meanings, but give expression to thoughts that the young child has developed pre-linguistically. One source of support for this theoretical stance is the extent to which children initiate exchanges, so long as they are confident of the interest of their parent, or other key adults. Subtle experimental research (Gopnik et al., 2001 and Gopnik, 2009) has shown that babies and very young toddlers show evidence of causal thinking, months before they are able to put their knowledge of their world into actual words. (See the discussion on page 164.) Another support comes from the observation that the emergence of pretend play, a significant form of symbolism, coexists with early spoken language.

Pause for reflection

Observation of babies and toddlers has highlighted links between how they play and their early language. The pattern is as follows:

When children's play is:	They will probably:	At about this age:
Exploring objects and people close at hand	Communicate with gestures and sounds	0–10 months
Relating one object with another in play	Produce many patterns of sounds	9–15 months
Simple pretend actions applied only to them	Utter their first words	11–18 months
Simple pretend actions that involve other people or toys	Make two-word combinations, short phrases	12–30 months
Sequences of pretend play and other play involving other people and play materials	Make three-, four-, and five-word sentences	19–36 months

Make some observations that could link the play of babies and toddlers with their developing communication.

- What patterns do you observe as you watch and listen to a baby or a toddler? Note the wide variation in the ages given above.

- Do you see children whose language is a little later than average following the same route?

Young children, learning a wide range of world languages, tend to start slowly, adding one word at a time, specifically linked with familiar objects and people. Then, somewhere between the ages of 16 and 24 months, toddlers launch themselves into what has been called 'the naming explosion', when they add new words at a rapid pace. It certainly looks as if they have understood that people and objects have names that can be said out loud. Their pointing, questioning tone of voice and, soon, a question word like 'Wassat?' show that toddlers want some answers.

Young children's spontaneous vocabulary develops alongside their intellectual grasp of categories. They need to learn that there are many examples of familiar objects. However, they are also about to learn that their familiar world is grouped into types of objects, or people, and some words apply to whole categories.

- Before the naming explosion, toddlers tend to show under-extension of their current vocabulary. They act as if the word 'cup' only applies to their familiar cup or beaker, almost as if it is a personal name for that item.
- After the naming explosion, very young children switch to over-extension: they often use one word to apply to similar objects or creatures. Children's mistakes are logical; for example, 'cat' is applied to any creature that is furry and has a long tail. Foxes are clearly cats by this reasoning, as may be animals like meerkats that children see in a television nature programme, or in a zoo.
- Other examples could be that any round fruit is an 'apple' (the most familiar fruit to this child, for example) or any adult male is a 'daddy', for children whose father is part of their family life. Very young children have grasped the idea of categories, but they do not yet know where to stop. Their knowledge and understanding of their familiar world will soon encompass the concept of categories and the subtle learning that all horses are animals, but not all animals are horses.

What does it mean?

The naming explosion: the phase of language development, often in the second year of life, when very young children add new words to their spoken vocabulary at a fast pace.

Under-extension (of known vocabulary): the phase when very young children act as if a known word applies only to the specific, familiar person or object.

Over-extension: the phase when young children tend to apply a familiar word across too broad a category.

Pause for reflection

- Identify some young children who are in the phase of language development before the naming explosion. Note their words and how they use them. Gather examples of under-extension.

- Keep observing the same children at regular intervals and note when the naming explosion starts. Watch out now for over-extension in their use of words.

- Reflect on what you find and what it tells you about this very young child's learning journey. Share your observations with parents.

UNDERSTANDING CHILD DEVELOPMENT 0–8 YEARS

Figure 7.3 New experiences introduce new words to young children

So how do they do it?

Academic books and papers about language acquisition are tough to read: full of complex sentences and often new words created for the purpose of a particular theory or specific piece of research. I find it amusing that toddlers, who would understand none of these weighty concepts, just get on with the job of acquiring language. All of the competing theories have some merit. But no single theory offers a full explanation of how young children make the impressive leap between what they hear and the sophisticated language they eventually produce.

It seems that human children make the powerful leap into spoken language because their brains are programmed ready for human communication. However, children's learning is then shaped by their experience of language, especially the communication behaviour of the key adults in their environment. But it is equally important what children do with this experience; they are active linguists, just as they are active thinkers.

Make the connection with... **Your communication skills**

The practical implications of research point to simple actions from adults to support communication, not to complex techniques. Babies and young children respond well to friendly, personal attention and communication linked with those children's current interests.

Work your way through this chapter, and then weave in Chapter 8 to read about thinking. Draw out the practical applications for 'What do I do?' Compare your ideas with colleagues and fellow students.

Early social interaction

A major part of how you help full communication and language development is to notice and value the early social interaction that builds the foundations. Sally Ward (2004) developed her 'Baby Talk' programme from her work as a speech and language therapist, seeing not only children with language difficulties, but also children whose early experiences did not support the development of communication.

Babies and very young children with few words need to use non-verbal forms to convey meaning. But fluent speakers, both older children and adults, still continue to communicate non-verbally, sometimes giving a different contradictory message from the verbal language. For instance, the spoken words may say 'I believe you' but the body language shows doubt.

Meaningful gestures

Gestures are an important aspect of early communication and form part of babies' body language, sending messages long before recognisable words can be heard. The ability to gesture is linked with babies' increased physical control. But gestures are also a clear sign that babies want to gain and direct the attention of others. They use gesture to communicate a range of messages, for example:

- Requests: from the age of about five months, babies use hand gestures to indicate wants. A hand stretch and a look communicate 'I want that and I can't get it.' An open and close of the hand can say 'Put it in my hand.'
- Refusals: babies and toddlers use a variety of limb and full-body gestures to indicate reluctance, or full refusal to cooperate. Then they add a firm head shake for 'No'.
- Social contact: gestures and sounds are used to attract and hold the attention of adults and other children. Pointing, which starts from about the age of eight months, is a direct way of requesting adults to fetch something for a baby who is not yet mobile. Soon, babies use pointing to direct attention to something interesting, to ensure an adult gazes in the same direction.
- Babies and toddlers often repeat patterns of gestures and sounds, like blowing raspberries, if this behaviour has provoked a laugh.

Take another **perspective**

I call young children 'language detectives'. For example, when they understand only a few words, toddlers use the clues from familiar context. You may say, 'Please put your tissue in the bin.' They recognise 'tissue', 'bin' and your gesture towards the corner of the room. They know that tissues go in the bin (not on the floor), are pleased to follow your request and be thanked by words and smile.

Children who are perplexed by adult questions use all the clues of your eye movements and gestures to fill the gap. In normal life, you need to be generous with those clues. If you want to check exactly what a child understands from the words alone, you need to remove the clues.

Figure 7.4 Babies use gestures to communicate a range of messages

Signs as symbolic gestures

Linda Acredolo and Susan Goodwyn (2000) studied the way that toddlers who have no words, or just a small number, use specific signs to communicate an association that they cannot say in words. The signs are a reflection of the child's personal experience, so very young children do not necessarily make the same signs as each other. Linda Acredolo's interest in signs was stimulated by realising that her young daughter made a blowing motion when she saw a fish and rubbed her hands when she saw a spider. Both these signs were the result of the toddler's alert observation: her mother used to blow on the fish mobile over Kate's cot to make it revolve, and the rubbing motion was from the hand movements in 'Incey Wincey Spider'.

Acredolo and Goodwyn found many such personal signs in the toddlers they studied. If parents took the signs seriously as communication, this approach encouraged the development of spoken language. The key was that parents responded to their toddlers' signs, and took the trouble to understand the meaning of those signs. Parents also then talked with their toddlers about what had interested them.

Take another **perspective**

Attention to infant sign language can support adult interaction with babies and young children. Meaningful signs or gestures should always be used alongside simple spoken communication. Linda Acredolo and Susan Goodwyn take a naturalistic approach, encouraging parents, or early years practitioners, to use the baby's symbolic gestures as the starting point.

'Baby signing' training programmes are now a franchise in the UK. The idea came from the US research of Joseph Garcia into the development of hearing babies of deaf parents. Children seemed to benefit from the signing they learned, in order to communicate with their parents.

Many speech and language therapists are wary (and I share their concerns) that a commercial programme can imply parents are unable to use symbolic gesturing unless they are trained. Sign systems work well to support children with learning or communication disabilities. But there is no consistent research that suggests young children need this organised approach to promote language development, in general. There is also some concern that unreflective adults, either practitioners or parents, may focus on signing to the detriment of spoken language.

Strong views are expressed on both sides of this debate. Take a look at the website given below, which is part of the National Literacy Trust, to support your own thinking and discussion with colleagues, or fellow students:

(**www.literacytrust.org.uk/talktoyourbaby/signing.html#view**)

What does it mean?

Infant signing: the pattern of symbolic gestures that babies develop to aid their message; this is a natural pattern of non-verbal communication.

Early social communication

Detailed observational research has shown just how much babies are primed to interact with adult carers from the earliest weeks and months. During the 1970s, video technology created the possibility of analysing communication exchanges in very fine detail. In observing a baby or young toddler hand an object to his mother, researchers were able to get beyond 'Child stretches out hand' and 'Mother takes the object.' Later, watched frame by frame, this kind of exchange is shown to be a whole series of subtle moves by baby and mother. In this interaction, and similar ones, the moves of both baby and adult are responsive to changes in signals coming from the other. Such sensitivity is an important part of how babies make, and sustain, contact with caring adults, and how those adults develop a communicative and affectionate relationship with the baby.

Figure 7.5 Communication and affection are essential ingredients in an effective relationship between adults and children

Lynne Murray and Colwyn Trevarthen (1985) looked at the reactions of babies aged six to twelve weeks under different conditions; when mothers gave their babies full attention; when the mothers gazed without reacting; and if they turned away.

- When babies had the full attention of their mothers, the infants reacted with smiles, coos and away-from-their-body gestures.
- When mothers gazed but did not react, the babies made similar efforts of communication. Then they became tenser, until they looked away from their mothers.
- If mothers turned away, for instance to talk with the researcher (a planned interruption in the experiment), babies looked less at their mothers, gazed at the researcher and made vocalisations and gestures that seemed to be an attempt to regain their mother's attention.

These very young babies were active in relating to their mothers and their behaviour changed in response to varied conditions. Colwyn Trevarthen has developed the concept of musicality to describe the partnership of these very early social exchanges. But the concept also refers to the alertness of babies to tuneful communication, the rhythmic flow of conversation from an adult who looks and sounds interested.

The precise and sensitive interaction was further highlighted when Murray and Trevarthen played back to the babies the video sequence of their attentive and smiling mother. This experience led to distress in the babies. Although their mother was gazing and smiling, what she did was not responsive to the babies' behaviour at the time the video was running. Babies were aware of this mismatch and their upset reaction shows how attuned they are to seeking a genuine exchange with important carers.

Pause for reflection

Spend some time watching the communication efforts of babies aged six months and younger. You may find opportunities in your place of work, but there can also be chances to watch in daily life: babies with their parents on the bus, in the supermarket or in the park.

Watch out especially and make some notes (discreetly) on:

- Those early 'conversational' exchanges when baby and adult take turns.

- How the baby reacts if the adult turns away, or does not respond.

- How babies use sounds and actions to get, and hold, others' attention. For instance: squeals, yells, blowing raspberries or vigorous hand gestures.

- Listen and watch the adults, or older children, in the exchange. Can you observe the qualities of infant-directed speech?

Infant-directed speech

Research has established that babies respond enthusiastically to a modified version of talk that is:

- Higher pitched and said with more expressiveness than normal adult conversation
- At a slower pace, with more pauses, when the adult looks expectant
- Full of simple repetitions and a circling quality to the phrases ('Hello ... have you woken up then? ... Have you just woken up? ... Come on then, let's have a cuddle ... a nice warm cuddle ...').

Babies have been found to prefer listening to this kind of adjusted talk, even when the language spoken is not their family language. A modified form of language is also used with toddlers, but often with far more links into what the adult and toddler can both see. For instance, an exchange can circle with 'Where's Asha's foot? .... Where's your foot then? ... Has it gone? Has it gone forever? ... No, I can see it. I've got it now ... I've got Asha's little foot ...'.

The 1970s research into early communication patterns studied mothers and their babies and, consequently, called this modified speech 'motherese'. But it is more accurately called infant-directed speech, because this form of communication is not restricted to mothers, or even to women. Men, as fathers or carers, modify their speech in the same way and so can some children, for instance with younger siblings. Infant-directed speech seems to exert a broad effect, because adults who adjust their speech patterns for babies and toddlers are also paying attention and are physically close. Infant-directed speech has been found in a considerable number of cultures, but is not universal.

What does it mean?

Infant directed speech: the modified version of spoken language, with lively tone and facial expression that are suited to adult communication with babies.

Musicality: the sensitivity of babies to tone and rhythmic flow in communication.

Pause for reflection

Children as young as two years old can adjust their language, depending on the listener. You will observe that young children talk in a different way among themselves, in contrast to their words and intonation used with an adult.

By the age of four years, children usually discriminate between different forms of speech. For instance, they will simplify their language when talking to a much younger child. Five-year-olds usually explain in more detail to an unfamiliar adult than to a friend; they have grasped that adults do not necessarily know everything that they do.

- I have observed children as young as three and four years of age engage babies through infant-directed speech. The children imitate an adult model and the pleased reaction of the baby is encouragement to continue.

- Watch and listen for examples from your own work with children

- If you struggle to gather any observations, then reflect on the extent to which children are able to interact with babies, especially if you work in a group setting where the ages are kept separate. This is lost opportunity for both children and babies.

Make the connection with... Family support

Observation of very depressed mothers has shown that they are considerably less likely to use infant-directed speech. Their children still learn to speak, but the language is often not as rich or conversational. There is basis for concern because young children need the social context and experience of predictability in an important relationship. Family support services, appropriately, aim to get supportive, non-judgemental help to families where the main carer is depressed.

The intense, uninterrupted exchanges filmed in a special observation suite are not typical of all interaction between adults and young babies. In family life and out-of-home care, communication with babies is sometimes interrupted. Parents and practitioners have to share out their time and attention. However, the results from very detailed observation are a crucial reminder, for anyone involved with babies, of just how much is possible and the need to make the most of the many opportunities that will arise within a normal day.

There are important practical messages for everyone caring for babies and young children, whether in the childminding situation or in group provision.

- Communicative exchanges need to be sustained and not rushed. There should be a relaxed pattern of give and take, providing time for babies to respond.

- Exchanges with babies should not be interrupted regularly, as if they do not matter.

- The routines of physical care provide rich opportunities for close and sensitive communication between adult and baby. Good practice in group settings is that the key person is responsible for the personal care of the individual baby or toddler.

The importance of nurture and respect for personal care routines must never be under-estimated within a holistic approach to best practice. A clear focus on care and caring should apply across early childhood.

Communication between very young children

The difficulty for babies and toddlers is that their physical moves to contact another child of the same age are inevitably less subtle than those of older children. Touches may be more of a poke than a pat and adults become concerned about possible hurt from toddlers' whole-body clasps and semi-wrestling. However, any assumptions that toddlers are uninterested in relationships do not survive observation of the under-twos.

Elinor Goldschmied gathered observational material in England and Italy. Her films of babies and toddlers exploring materials in her Treasure Basket (Goldschmied, 1986) and with Heuristic Play (Goldschmied and Hughes, 1992) show that gazing, touching and offering play materials are regular exchanges between very young children. Toddlers and young children develop relationships with their peers that show friendly behaviour, a wish to be together and mutual enjoyment in shared activities, however simple.

Pause for reflection

Mobile toddlers show preferences, which may persist for months, in their choice of play companion in out-of-home care: with a childminder or in a day nursery. Make your own observations over several weeks, following the preferences of a few children.

- When the young children arrive in the morning, which other children do they regularly approach?

- Given the choice, do children sit beside one, or more, individual children?

- Do they take play resources, or particular books, to show specific children?

Figure 7.6 Even very young children communicate with each other

A persistent myth about very young children is that they cannot play with other children and that they exclusively play alongside them: parallel play. This belief is largely a misunderstanding of research that showed how older children spent relatively more time in cooperative play and less in parallel, or solitary, play than the younger ones. Research into the social and communicative abilities of very young children corrects this misunderstanding.

Carol Eckerman (1993) observed very young children in contact with each other and noticed deliberate patterns of social play, for example:

- Mobile babies establish a joint focus of interest, by making physical contact with an object that another young child (or adult) is manipulating. The baby then imitates the 'play partner'. This copying action seems to signal a message of 'I like this,' or 'Let's do it together.'
- In toddler interaction, imitative acts seem to open an exchange, because they often happen swiftly after the first contact. The other toddler is encouraged to imitate in return and a social connection is established.
- Reciprocal imitative games are common between toddlers; for instance, taking turns to do the same action, such as jumping off the sofa. Adults may say furniture is not play equipment, but that does not discount toddlers' actions as real play.

- From the age of two to three years, young children begin to integrate words into their play. Children begin to be able to coordinate their actions towards new play sequences, in addition to familiar rituals. Verbal and non-verbal language is used to guide the interaction.

Pause for reflection

Look out for examples of play between toddlers in your own setting, or from opportunities that arise in everyday life.

Some years ago, my wait in our local health clinic was greatly enlivened by watching two young children in a double buggy. One child looked about two years old and the younger was about 18 months. They amused themselves for at least ten minutes. The older one usually started a game. But the younger one restarted a sequence, once he had played it a few times. The two of them played 'I touch your knee and then you touch mine', 'We stare into each other's faces' and 'We shake our heads hard, so our hair swings about'. Pauses were filled with loud chortling. Then one child, not always the same one, started a new game, or a repeat of a previous turn-taking game.

Play communication between the different ages

Much of the play research has been undertaken by observing same-age groups of toddlers. Sometimes researchers also seem to take an inappropriately strict line over what can be defined as 'play' and what is not. Carol Eckerman's observational research challenged claims that very young children do not really play together. But another perspective is to observe mobile babies and toddlers in interaction with older children. Judy Dunn's research in families (1984, 1986, 1993) produced examples of two-year-olds who were drawn into pretend play sequences with an older sibling. When children of different ages play together, the younger ones are often assigned a part, and increasingly understand how to take a pretend role in long sequences that they would be unlikely to manage with their peers.

Mainly friendly relations with older siblings also give the younger ones a chance, sometimes, to exercise some direction over the play, perhaps by clowning around and making the older ones laugh. Some years ago I watched an 18-month-old hold the attention of three older children (ranging in age from three to seven years) by running along a hallway and then sliding along on her bottom, cushioned by her nappy. The older children fell about laughing and Anna repeated her run and slide six times, delighted with the full attention of the older ones. I watched this event in my personal life, on holiday with another family. However, such events are not unusual in out-of-home care, when children have the opportunities to mix with more than a narrow age span.

Make the connection with... **Play across the ages**

These excerpts are from my family diary. They show how an older sibling can lead a younger one and create games that the younger would not develop alone, or with peers. Tanith was born four days before Drew's second birthday. We involved him safely in her care and Drew gave Tanith toys from the time when she was able to grasp. He liked to show her how to work resources, such as their bath toys.

Once Tanith was a confident walker, their play became a more active interaction and she was drawn into games that were possible from a three-year-old's knowledge and understanding of the world.

- Tanith, 13 months, Drew, three and one month: D. has started a chasing game with her. Mainly he gets her to chase him along the hall by calling her name. Also, D. builds brick towers, says, 'What about this, Tanith?' and then she knocks them down. They both laugh loudly. Sometimes T. brings him the brick box as a way to ask Drew to start the game.

- Tanith, 14 months, Drew, three and two months: They still play the chasing game but sometimes T. starts it now by hovering until D. sees her. They spend time together in the playhouse we made out of a huge cardboard box, playing peep-boo through the windows. They wrestle together.

- Tanith, 15 months, Drew, three and three months: T. sits beside D. and hands him Lego for his models. They still play the chasing games and growl at each other as monsters. D. has created a rescue game. He lies down and calls out 'Tanith! Help, help!' T. comes up, gives her hand and they walk off.

- Tanith, 18 months, Drew, three and a half: D. has invented more games for him and T. Most revolve around chase and rescue: sharks, traps and something to do with heat. They both chant, 'Hot, hot' and drag the pink bath towel around. (I was puzzled by this game at the time. Tanith explained years later: it was about escaping from volcanoes.) T. copies D. a great deal in her play: how he handles the play dough, pretending to eat and drink with the tea set, counting like him and trying to jump as he does.

- Tanith is two, Drew is four: T. is as likely now to start their games together as D. As well as jumping about together, they spend a lot of time in the playhouse and they jointly run a pretend cafe from behind the sofa.

Pause for reflection

You could observe play between the ages if you work in an early years setting that enables easy contact between younger and older children. Or you could talk with parents who have two or more young children.

- What do the children do together? Who leads and who follows?

- In what way is the play environment different for the second child, or third child, than for the firstborn?

- What strategies do the parents take to deal with squabbles?

The learning journey towards literacy

During childhood, girls and boys have another substantial task to manage: understanding the written system of language. Whatever language(s) children are learning, early childhood is the best time for them to build knowledge and understanding that will support the skills that are viewed as 'proper' reading and writing. It will be a tough task for children eventually to learn to decipher the written word in reading, to form correct handwriting and spelling and to put their thoughts on to paper. A crucial task for adults is to provide experiences throughout early childhood that build the related skills and offer a learning journey free of harassment. Young girls and boys also need to have developed personal reasons for them to be enthusiastic about learning to read and write, when they are developmentally ready.

English is a very complex language

In order to read and write, children have to learn how the system of sounds in the words of their familiar spoken language is written down in terms of symbols: letters or other forms of writing. However, this task is especially tough for English, a language with historical roots in many other languages, with the result that it is a highly non-regular language. Some reading and linguistic specialists describe English as the most inconsistent world language in terms of the rules for how spoken sounds from different words are transcribed by written letters from the alphabet. Some cross-national studies report data that children in the UK learn to read and write later than some of their European peers. Informed writers such as Usha Goswami (2003) or Carol Togerson et al. (2006) point out that there is nothing the matter with children in the UK; they face a much harder task than children learning the more regular languages across Europe.

A problematic situation arose in England, when the Foundation Stage, for three- to five-year-olds, was launched in 2000. Developmentally unrealistic early learning goals for reading, writing and handwriting (Lindon, 2007) were pushed into an early years framework. Early years and reading specialists challenged these goals at the time and have continued to argue that such specific expectations of 'most' five-year-olds are more realistic when applied to seven-year-olds. These goals crossed into the 0–5 Early Years Foundation Stage (again for England) without any relevant changes. A 2009 review for the previous Labour government, led by Jim Rose, refused to concede that there was a problem. The disputed goals have passed, with few changes into the revised EYFS to be implemented in 2012.

Building skills for literacy

Young children are helped by practitioners, and parents, who understand the skills that need time within early childhood and who do not try to fast-track young girls or boys into structured, formal literacy lessons. The main building blocks for later literacy include:

- Children's confidence in their spoken language and a large vocabulary, built through personal exchanges and spontaneous, not organised, conversation.

- Enthusiasm for books, both fiction and information books.
- Storytelling and story making, also the narratives that children weave when they have plenty of time for pretend play.
- Alertness to sound and sound-making, rhythm and rhyme and the steady beat of music making and singing.
- Confidence and enthusiasm for meaningful mark-making, using tools and, in time, making the deliberate marks that begin to look like writing in the child's spoken language(s).

Some of these issues are discussed in this section, especially good early years practice during oral communication. Readers can also extend their understanding from written materials such as Robin Campbell's (1999) detailed account of how his granddaughter, Alice, steadily learned the skills to support literacy. Visual materials such as Siren Films (2009) show the firm foundations of early literacy.

Take another **perspective**

The most useful way to look ahead for actual literacy during early childhood is to think about what needs to happen before there will be any point in teaching children how to read and write.

- What do young children need to be able to do?
- What do they need to understand?
- What do they need to be enthused about?

Reflect on these key questions as you read this section.

Rich oral communication

Children need to hear, experience and use language from an early age. They will be seriously disadvantaged in trying to crack the written code, if they have a limited confidence and vocabulary in their spoken language. A considerable number of children across the UK learn more than one language during early childhood. They will become successfully bilingual, but their task is to build a generous vocabulary in their two, or more, languages. Charmian Kenner (2000, 2004) describes the ways in which children learn to distinguish the key features of the written form of their familiar languages, including the fact that they may be written in a very different script.

Spontaneous and enjoyable conversations with young children support their learning of words and boost their motivation to be understood, with ever more complex ideas. Children benefit from the enjoyable experience of playing with the sounds of their own language(s). Barbara Tizard and Martin Hughes (2002) describe 'games for fun', as children extend their own language skills by playing with words in joking interaction with their mothers. Relaxed, young children often lark about with their vocabulary: putting words together in a way that sounds funny to them, or saying something that they know is wrong and laughing. I call this 'nonsense talk' and it is often between children, but may be shared with adults who show a capacity to have fun.

Cathy Nutbrown et al. (2005) explain the importance of oral language as a crucial building block to literacy. Sharing nursery rhymes and chants is an effective way of alerting children to slight differences in sound patterns and encourages them to play with language. Books are important, but so is a more general enthusiasm for creating stories, with adults who start a story, perhaps with a puppet as well as generous time for children's own pretend play narratives. These kinds of experiences, which enable children to understand the basic structure of stories, are very helpful since children in primary school are often motivated to try to write a story. Children also benefit from the enjoyable conversation that Cathy Nutbrown called literacy talk: expressing opinions about books and stories and having the words to talk about what happens, how a story makes the reader feel and the effectiveness of the characters.

Take another **perspective**

Children need confidence in spoken language for thinking out loud and developing ideas for what, and how, they will write. Writing is partly the technical skill of handwriting, which is itself a combination of physical skills and cracking the code of letters and how they link to sounds. But writing is also about the writer creating content, otherwise the child is simply using a technical skill to copy.

Without the base of rich oral communication, children may learn to write words. But they are ill-equipped to reflect on what they want to write and to plan the details, whether it is a fictional story, an account of a real event, a letter, or set of written instructions. On the other hand, authentic experiences of play and everyday life, during early childhood, give children many good reasons to want to write.

Do children lack communication skills?

In the first edition of this book, I noted that local speech and language teams and national organisations like I CAN (**www.ican.org.uk**) had expressed concern about the rising numbers of young children who seem unable to express themselves clearly or understand simple requests. The delayed or restricted language development cannot always be explained by disability; limited early language experience seems to be the main factor for much of the increase. In the intervening five years since I first wrote this section, there has been increasing concern and the launch of national programmes, such as Every Child a Talker.

Lack of simple conversation?

Rather like working out what has gone awry with the diet of some children, there seem to be several strands to unpacking the problems. Reviews like those of Liz Attenborough and Rachel Fahey (2005) point to a range of possible explanations. Some families are very pressed for time, but some parents are also unaware of the huge importance of simple, personal interaction during early childhood. Some limited communication with babies and very young children seems to arise from the belief that there is no point in talking with children until they can talk back; this is a desperate misunderstanding that derails early development.

Apparently small changes may sometimes open the door to more conversation. Suzanne Zeedyk (2008) looked at the communication between parents and their under-twos, when the children were in buggies that faced the adult pusher, or faced towards the pavement ahead. Parents using the toward-facing buggies were more likely to be engaged with their baby or toddler.

Pause for reflection

Read the report by Suzanne Zeedyk about type of buggy and communication on

www.literacytrust.org.uk/resources/practical_ resources_info/1555_whats_life_in_a_baby_ buggy_like

- What practical issues can you apply to your own practice?

- Bear in mind that the children in these two studies were all under two years of age. Slightly older children may well want to see what is coming up on a local trip out and not what is disappearing into the distance. How should conversational adults behave when out and about with over-twos in a buggy? (The aim is also that over-twos will sometimes be walking.)

- Buggy design is not, of course, an answer in itself to limited communication. Wheeled equipment can only offer opportunities; it is not more, or less, emotionally healthy or able to promote communication. The power lies with the people who push the buggy with legs, a voice and ears. (However, there is nothing positive for children when they are sitting in the lower section of the two-layer buggies.)

- I have seen adults pushing a towards-facing buggy with a toddler who is clearly awake. But the adults talk animatedly on a mobile phone. What message does this give to very young children?

Trying to explain exactly how young children learn spoken language is difficult. However, what helps them to learn most is very straightforward: it is neither complicated techniques nor a special language programme, unless this child's language development is complicated by a disability. What works for young children is generous time and interest from familiar adults, who are focused on what has engaged this baby or child today. Communication is between real people who know each other.

Bilingual children need to hear language from adults that is pitched appropriately for their vocabulary, but which also acknowledges their likely knowledge and interests, given their age. Four-year-olds for whom English is currently their least fluent language will be thinking very differently from two-year-olds who have the same number of words in their first and only language.

Delegating communication to technology

Some children watch a considerable amount of television, or are sat in front of DVDs, marketed with inflated 'educational' claims, right down to the baby year.

Robin Close (2004) reviewed research on the effects of television and concluded that children who were heavy viewers of television were more likely to have delayed language development. As you might guess, it is difficult to prove exactly what is happening in this relationship between television and children's development. But part of the explanation seems to lie in all the activities that children give up, if they sit in front of a screen for hours every day. Rich language development needs social interaction, and television is one-way. Even good-quality programmes for young children are unlikely to exert the possible benefits, unless a familiar adult watches with the child and can make connections, either at the time of watching the programme, or later.

Dimitri Christakis et al. (2009) have shown that, with every extra hour that the television was left on in family homes fewer words in total were spoken to under-twos by their parents. The screen time was actually reducing personal conversation and the crucial need for babies and very young children to hear meaningful spoken language in context. There has been challenge and counter-challenge about the growing list of DVDs that purport to support early language development. Given what is understood about the interpersonal nature of how babies and toddlers make sense of the spoken word, it seems very unlikely that use of such products will actively support the spoken vocabulary of very young children.

Misguided early years practice?

However, concerns about the limited communication skills of a proportion of young children cannot be focused exclusively on family life. Some researchers have raised the problems arising from over-structured, adult-dominated experiences in some early years provision. I am optimistic that many practitioners and teams are now turning away from micro-managing children's play and conversations. The practical lessons of the EPPE research about sustained shared thinking (see page 171) and the strong focus on self-chosen experiences in the Early Years Foundation Stage have been a positive boost for English practitioners (Lindon, 2010b). However, the possibility for continued improvement has to rest on understanding what goes so wrong, when early years practitioners lose sight of their role as proper conversational and play partners.

Jacqui Cousins (2003) drew on years of research, and experience as an Ofsted inspector, to express deep concern by the late 1990s that some practitioners were dismissive of children's spontaneous language as a vital tool for their thinking. Adults had lost their way as good role models and saw worthwhile conversations as exchanges in which they asked the questions and children produced the answers. She gathered many examples of four-year-olds' ability to ask searching questions and showed how sustained conversation was a window on to young children's passion to extend their knowledge of the world. Some of these conversations happened between children, without the need for direct adult involvement, except to listen and learn. Yet in some settings the children themselves had accepted the adult view that 'just chattering' was worthless; you had to get on with your work.

A lesson plan view of early education has also misdirected some practitioners into attempting to pre-package children's learning, rather than trusting a well-resourced learning environment. The adult energy needs to go into watching what children do and listening to what they say. Thoughtful practitioners have caught themselves in their back-to-front unwise practice. Joy Roberts (2000) recounts the lesson she learned by looking closely at her practice as a reception teacher. She had persuaded children to colour in a drawing of a road with cars in a line, and then asked questions about the relative position of the cars. Then, later the same day, she observed the same children playing with vehicles and spontaneously using positional language, number, talking about speed and describing characteristics such as colour, size and shape. The adult-led worksheet activity was redundant, and a waste of precious playing time.

The pressure to get children reading and writing, especially in England, has been a specific source of disruption to spontaneous conversation; this is a tragic own goal since oral communication is the crucial building block to understanding written communication. Ann Locke and Jane Ginsborg (2003) assessed the introduction of 'Teaching Talking', a spoken language programme, in two nursery classes in a socio-economically deprived neighbourhood. The language skills of the three- and four-year-olds did not improve as predicted, in comparison with the two control nurseries. Locke and Ginsborg tracked what had happened and discovered that, although committed in theory, one nursery team had only partly implemented the programmes and the second nursery had barely used it. These practitioners were unwilling to engage in conversation with the children. They felt strong pressure to ensure children would meet targets, especially related to literacy. Many staff felt they could not waste precious time on 'just talking', when they had so many activities to be completed with children in the day.

Firm foundations for reading and writing

Children need plenty of enjoyable conversation and other uses of spoken language. They also need adults to use developmentally appropriate methods to demystify the whole reading and writing business.

Jessie Reid (1983) interviewed children who were having difficulty in learning to read or write. She discovered that most of the children were unaware of writing as a system. Children had not realised that the marks in books represented different letters, or that there was a separate letter and number system. Their attention had not been drawn to the writing all around them, on buses, shops or street signs. So the children remained puzzled about the point of reading or writing, except that teachers seemed to want them to do it.

The children interviewed by Jessie Reid will now be well into their adult life, yet the points she made are as relevant as ever. Many young children in the early 21st century are surrounded from babyhood by disconnected letters, as part of plastic toys, on quilts, friezes or bricks. The misleading message is that such resources will help young children with literacy. In contrast, Cathy Nutbrown (2005) has promoted the concept of alerting young children to environmental print: the idea that writing is all around and young children learn to recognise writing-type shapes and logos. They also need to grasp the context, that writing does a job.

What does it mean?

Environmental print: meaningful writing and logos that are present within the family home, other settings and in the neighbourhood; this is writing that is there for a purpose of communication.

Meaningful mark-making: the range of marks that even very young children choose to make for their own purposes with any tools available.

Emergent writing: the deliberate mark-making by children that moves towards the shape and flow of the writing that they observe. Children may say now that they are writing.

Figure 7.7 Children will make marks with many different resources

Children need plenty of practice in meaningful mark-making and then their marks move towards emergent writing. Robin Campbell (1999) describes how Alice moved on from drawing to creating deliberate shapes that look more like writing. Children imitate how an adult writer looks, as well as the flow of mark-making on the page or whiteboard. Anne Hughes and Sue Ellis (1998) suggest that the major difference in literacy support between early years settings and primary school is the balance between:

- Responding to young children when they choose to do meaningful mark-making, and
- Recruiting children into writing, following a shared agenda in the group.

They describe that primary school teachers do more recruiting because of the different staff–child ratio and demands of the curriculum. But more direction is feasible, because the children are older, and if they have had suitable early years experiences. The balance for early years practitioners should be much more on responding to exploration chosen by three- and four-year-olds and the way they want to apply their skills. Young potential writers can be undermined when early years practitioners believe the aim is to recruit this age group into worksheet copying and tracing of letters.

Anne Hughes and Sue Ellis (1998) describe the process for children of becoming a writer. They highlight the need to establish positive attitudes towards writing, just as much as encouraging the technical skills. Consider these questions with colleagues, or fellow students.

- Do you provide experiences that enable children to realise that writing is used for a whole range of purposes in real life?

- Do children see you writing for a purpose? Do you obviously look back at what you noted earlier, showing how the written word keeps ideas for you and helps memory?

(**www.ltscotland.org.uk/earlyyears/Images/writingitright_tcm4-124463.pdf**)

Supportive adults watch and listen in order to grasp the perspective of young children, who may still be puzzling out what exactly this skill of reading is. Penny Munn (1997a) interviewed four-year-olds about their understanding of reading several times during their final year before going to primary school. They were asked the following questions: 'Can you read?', 'Who do you know who can read?', 'When will you be able to read?' and 'What will you have to do to be able to read?' Almost all the children were very familiar with a story read to them and their behaviour towards books did not change much at all. However, over the year their beliefs altered about the process of reading.

Before they entered primary school, most of these young children had made a significant shift. As young four-year-olds, many had believed that you read by turning the pages and telling a story. As a nearly or young five-year-old, many children now understood that reading meant decoding print in a specific way. Over the year many of the children had realised that they could not yet read; it was a skill they needed to learn. When children were familiar with books, from home and not only nursery, they were less daunted by this task. Children with a family background that was low in literacy appeared less confident and more likely to find ways to avoid the risk of 'failure'.

Take another **perspective**

Parents may be anxious about evidence of 'proper' reading and writing, even with three-year-olds. Partnership with parents means acknowledging the concern, but not agreeing to impose activities that are developmentally inappropriate in early childhood.

It is crucial that early years practitioners understand how to build firm foundations for a confident literacy. Then it is possible to share evidence of all the skills, understanding and a positive disposition that will enable children to tackle the challenging task of written English.

Consider how you show and share appropriate early literacy through partnership with parents. You will find some useful ideas in the work of Anne Hughes and Sue Ellis (1998) but also in some of the leaflets in the Learning Together Series from Early Education, such as *Making their mark* and *The road to reading* (**www.early-education.org.uk**).

- **Acredolo, L., Goodwyn, S.** (2000) *Baby signs: how to talk with your baby before your baby can talk.* London: Vermilion.
- **Attenborough, L., Fahey, R.** (2005) *Why do many young children lack basic language skills?* **www.talktoyourbaby.org.uk**
- **Campbell, R.** (1999) *Literacy from home to school: reading with Alice.* Stoke-on-Trent: Trentham Books.
- **Christakis, D.** (and a team of seven colleagues) (2009) 'Audible television and decreased adult words, infant vocalisations and conversational turns', *Archives of Pediatrics and Adolescent Medicine,* vol 163, no 6. Summary on **http://archpedi. ama-assn.org/cgi/content/abstract/163/6/554**
- **Close, R.** (2004) *Television and language development in the early years: a review of the literature.* **www.literacytrust.org.uk/Research/TV.html**
- **Cousins, J.** (2003) *Listening to four year olds: how they can help us plan their education and care.* London: National Children's Bureau.
- **Dunn, J.** (1984) *Sisters and brothers.* London: Fontana.
- **Dunn, J.** (1986) 'Children in a family world' in Richards, M., and Light, P., *Children of social worlds: development in a social context.* Cambridge: Polity Press.
- **Dunn, J.** (1993) *Young children's close relationships beyond attachment.* London: Sage.
- **Eckerman, C.** (1993) 'Imitation and toddlers' achievement of co-ordinated actions with others', in Nadel, J., and Camaioni, L. (eds), *New perspectives in early communicative development.* London: Routledge.
- **Goldschmied, E.** (1986) *Infants at Work: Babies of 6–9 Months Exploring Everyday Objects* (DVD). London: National Children's Bureau. **www.ncb.org.uk**
- **Goldschmied, E., Hughes, A.** (1992) *Heuristic Play with Objects: Children of 12–20 Months Exploring Everyday Objects* (DVD). London: National Children's Bureau.
- **Gopnik, A.** (2009) *The philosophical baby: what children's minds tell us about truth, love and the meaning of life.* London: Bodley Head. Also a conversational feature on **www.edge.org/3rd_culture/gopnik09/gopnik09_index.html**
- **Gopnik, A., Meltzoff, A., Kuhl, P.** (2001) *How babies think: the science of childhood.* London: Phoenix.
- **Goswami, U.** (2003) 'How to beat dyslexia', *The Psychologist,* volume 16, no. 9. **www.thepsychologist.org.uk/archive/archive_home.cfm?volumeID=16&editionID=9 8&ArticleID=598** (This is a useful general article about the task of reading.)
- **Hughes, A., Ellis, S.** (1998) *Writing it right? Children writing 3–8,* Learning and Teaching Scotland: Dundee.
- **Kenner, C.** (2000) *Home pages: literacy links for bilingual children.* Stoke-on-Trent: Trentham Books.
- **Lindon, J.** (2007) *Understanding children and young people: development from 5–18 years.* London: Hodder Arnold.
- **Lindon, J.** (2010a) *The key person approach.* London: Practical Pre-School Books.
- **Lindon, J.** (2010b) *Child-initiated learning.* London: Practical Pre-School Books.

- **Locke, A., Ginsborg, J.** (2003) 'Spoken language in the early years: the cognitive and linguistic development of three- to five-year-old children from socio-economically deprived backgrounds', *Educational and Child Psychology,* 20 (4), 68–79.
- **Munn, P.** (1997a) 'What do children know about reading before they go to school?', in Owen, P., and Pumfrey, P. (eds), *Emergent and developing reading: messages for teachers.* London: Falmer Press.
- **Murray, L., Andrews, L.** (2000) *The social baby.* Richmond: The Children's Project.
- **Murray, L., Trevarthen, C.** (1985) 'Emotional regulation of interactions between two-month-olds and their mothers', in Field, T.M., and Fox, N.A. (eds), *Social perception in infants.* Norwood NJ: Ablex.
- **Nutbrown, C., Hannon, P., Morgan, A.** (2005) *Early literacy work with families: policy, practice and research.* London: Sage
- **Pinker, S.** (1994) *The language instinct: how the mind creates language.* New York: Morrow.
- **Reid, J.** (1983) 'Into print: reading and language growth', in Donaldson, M., Grieve, R. and Pratt, C. (eds), *Early childhood development and education: readings in psychology.* Oxford: Blackwell.
- **Siren Films Ltd** (2008) *The Wonder Year* (DVD and booklet). Newcastle-upon-Tyne: Siren Films Ltd. **www.sirenfilms.co.uk**
- **Siren Films Ltd** (2009) *Firm foundations for early literacy from 0 to 5 years* (DVD and booklet*).* Newcastle-upon-Tyne: Siren Films Ltd. **www.sirenfilms.co.uk**
- **Tizard, B., Hughes, M.** (2002) *Young children learning: talking and thinking at home and at school.* Oxford: Blackwell.
- **Togerson, C., Brooks, G., Hall, J.** (2006) *A systematic review of the research literature on the use of phonics in the teaching of reading and spelling.* **www.education.gov.uk/publications/RSG/Developingreadingwritingand numericalskills/Page1/RR711**
- **The Children's Project** (2004) *The social baby* (DVD). Richmond: The Children's Project/NSPCC. **www.childrensproject.co.uk/**
- **Vygotsky, L.** (1962) *Thought and language.* Cambridge MA: MIT Press.
- **Vygotsky, L.** (1978) *Mind in society: the development of higher psychological processes.* Cambridge MA: Harvard University Press.
- **Ward, S.** (2004) *Baby talk.* London: Arrow.
- **Zeedyk, S.** (2008) *Do Baby Buggies Affect Development?* **www.literacytrust.org.uk/ talk_to_your_baby/news/1553_do_baby_buggies_affect_development**

Thinking and learning

You will have noticed that much of the discussion in Chapter 7 about communication also shed light on children's thoughts. But are very young children thinking before they can express ideas in spoken words, and how do you know? Researchers have shown increasing interest in the cognitive abilities of young children, rather than assuming that their thinking must be an inferior version of what their older selves will manage. Careful study has supported reflective early years practice in terms of how adults can best help young thinking and learning.

The main sections of this chapter are:
- Very young thinkers
- The sounds of the children thinking
- Working within the zone of proximal development.

Very young thinkers

Young children use their spoken language to think out loud. You will hear two-year-olds guide themselves in an activity, with expressions such as 'No, not dat' or 'Put in there'. Slightly older children talk themselves through a task, as well as using their language in pretend play. It is crucial that adults view this 'talking out loud' in a positive way, and certainly do not tell children to 'be quiet'. This type of self-directing speech becomes quieter, as it develops into a low mutter that older children (and some adults too), use when they are tackling a difficult task. Otherwise this type of self-directing language remains silent as internal speech.

Thinking shown through actions

The behaviour of very young children shows evidence of thinking, planning and use of memory. Their spoken language may be a work in progress, but their actions 'talk' to any alert adult.
- Crawling babies and toddlers remember where their toys are kept. They can be persistent in searching out objects they are not supposed to have, which is a source of frustration to parents at home.
- Under-twos recall and show you that personal objects belong to a particular person. Very young children demonstrate this understanding by taking a bracelet to their mother, or pointing to a bag and saying, 'Nana'.
- Very young children show recognition of people and places. Older babies may kick their legs in glee, as they recognise the last part of the walk that enables them to reach the park, or their grandparents' home.

Figure 8.1 Hands-on experiences support children's thinking

Alison Gopnik and her colleagues (2001) show that it is possible to design simple experiments that explore how very young children are busy thinking. One of my favourites is an experiment in which toddlers were shown two bowls, one with cheese crackers and the other with florets of raw broccoli. Given a choice, every toddler ate the crackers, rejecting the broccoli. Then the researcher tasted food and indicated, by a delighted face and saying 'yum', that she liked one choice but with a disgusted face and saying 'yuk', that she disliked the other. Then she put the bowls back near the toddler, held out her hand and said, 'Could you give me some?' The 14-month-olds gave her their own preference, a cracker, whatever she had indicated. But toddlers who were 18 months old gave the researcher broccoli, when that had been her preference. Think about the results of this experiment: such young children deduced an adult's choice from their own observation, and gave her raw broccoli, although their personal experience did not support her choice.

Researchers are people too and Alison Gopnik (2001, 2009) shares a personal event. She had returned home from an extremely hard day at the university to find she had failed to defrost any dinner. It was the last straw; she sat on the sofa and burst into tears. Her son, who was not yet two years old, fetched a box of plasters and proceeded to put them on her at random. Her toddler did not know what was wrong, but it clearly needed a lot of patching up, and his strategy worked because his mother stopped crying. Such examples are utterly endearing, but they are also a window on to very young thinking power.

Even babies seem to have a very basic idea of number, long before they can count (or make any sense of the written numbers that are on so many plastic toys). Annette Karmiloff-Smith (1994) describes a family example from the *Baby it's you* project. The parent of five-month-old Sarah had noticed that this young baby seemed to have a sense of how many toys should reappear in a hiding game. Her parent dropped one of the toys by mistake and only two reappeared on Sarah's highchair. This young baby looked surprised.

Alison Gopnik (2009) reports an experiment that showed how nine-month-olds have a grasp of number and relative amount. They were shown a transparent box with red and white ping-pong balls. Sometimes the box had mainly red balls and only a few white ones, sometimes the reverse. Next the researcher covered the sides of the box and then took five ping-pong balls out of the box in succession: either four red and one white, or four white with one red. Every possible variation, using the full box and the selected balls, was run. There was no doubt that these older babies looked longer at the researcher when she had pulled mostly white ping-pong balls out of a box filled mainly with red balls, or mainly red balls out of a box mainly filled with white balls. The babies were able to process the visual information and notice unlikely probabilities.

Pause for reflection

Toddlers use rich non-verbal communication to say what they cannot yet express in words. At the age of 16 months, my daughter used to fetch her outdoor shoes and wave them at me when she wanted to go out for a walk. If I was slow to react, Tanith would then get my shoes and push them at me, until I cooperated.

- What does this example tell you about toddler communication, memory and thinking?

- Gather some examples of meaningful gestures and actions from under-twos.

- Discuss them with your colleagues and share with children's parents to support the view 'She's thinking already.'

Make the connection with... Knowledge and understanding of the world

Children learn not only their own personal name and those of other family members, but also the cultural tradition of family names.

At two years, two months, our son Drew had grasped that Mama was also called Jennie and Daddy was also known as Lance. He was prepared to believe that Lance had another name, Lindon, and that he, Drew, also was called Lindon. But he laughed uproariously and gave a disbelieving, 'No!' when told that Mama and baby Tanith were also Lindons. He seemed to accept there could be two people with the same name in the house, but it was clearly a joke to suggest there could possibly be four. He reacted in the same way when told that he had once been a baby, like Tanith.

- Watch out for examples of the children in your care, as they build a picture of themselves in relation to others.

- Do you find that children's current knowledge leads them to conclude you are making a joke, when what you say makes no sense to them?

What happens outside the laboratory?

Alison Gopnik and Annette Karmiloff-Smith are happy to combine evidence from experiments with observations in family homes. However, experimental research and the underlying theory have sometimes led to firm statements about children's lack of ability that do not survive observation in naturalistic settings. From the 1980s, Judy Dunn and her team chose to watch and listen to children in their own home. Dunn challenged the reliability of conclusions about early thinking, when so much information was lost for experimental control. Judy Dunn was also convinced that it was impossible to make sense of children's cognitive development, while it was treated as separate from their key relationships.

Judy Dunn (1984) showed the subtleties of children's social and play behaviour with siblings in the family. Very young children are drawn into pretend play, a form of activity that is often claimed to be beyond the understanding of this age group. She quotes the example of two-year-old Rose, who entered into the pretend play of her sister Nell, who was four years old, by insisting that she (Rose) was one of Nell's imaginary friends. Rose had shown a complex level of thinking, although it would appear partly with the motivation of teasing Nell. One can imagine the kind of argument that probably followed this sequence.

Make the connection with... **Very young children and play**

Judy Dunn's observations of shared play sequences illustrate that very young children must be thinking, remembering and planning. Look back also at the description of Carol Eckerman's research on page 149.

Reflect on your own practice, especially with very young children.

- Are you expecting children's play to be longer, more complex, or without minor squabbles? 'Real play' does sometimes end in tears.

- When you look through the eyes of a toddler, you may be able to redirect play in a friendly way, without stopping an entire game.

- A positive and friendly adult approach to setting boundaries can coexist with appreciation of the playful nature of some of children's actions.

The sounds of the children thinking

The heading of this section is taken from the words of Vivian Gussin Paley, who wrote up a series of reflective accounts of her experience as a kindergarten teacher of three- and four-year-olds in the USA. Paley explains the significant turning point in her practice, when she realised she was unhelpfully wedded to her adult plans and questions. Once she focused on the children and their absorbing interests, she realised that what she had viewed as distractions in group time were actually 'the sounds of the children thinking' (Paley, 1988: 7).

Learning through social conversation

Vivian Gussin Paley is honest that she had envisaged circle time as an event planned and led by her as the teacher. She listened to her tape recordings and realised that children were highly motivated to discuss issues that arose in their play. The most impassioned discussions, and arguments, arose from the children's pretend play. Following her recognition of what really enthused children, Paley started to record other parts of the nursery day, and so built up her observational material on children's thinking and learning. Her reflective observations continue (2004) to highlight what it is that children lose when early years practitioners try to control the input and outcomes of conversation and play. One significant application is for practitioners to be wary about how group time is planned and run. Young children learn most usefully from interactive, personal conversation. There is a limit to what they can manage and enjoy within sit-down, group time, let alone large groups in which they have to put up a hand and wait for ages for an opportunity to speak.

Make the connection with... *Good early years practice*

Reflect on your own practice and what it is that will genuinely support young learning. Do you even 'have to get' young children into a group?

- Reflect on the words of Vivian Gussin Paley: 'It did not occur to me that the distractions might be the sounds of the children thinking.' Are you tempted verbally to pull children back on to what seems like the 'right' track for their attention, or use of communication?

- Young children have a short time span between thinking of something that is very interesting and needing to say it out loud. They cannot wait for long.

- In fact, children who regularly 'interrupt' group times may well be the only ones who are really listening to you. Yet unreflective practitioners can label the children as disruptive or rude.

The intellectual search

In the early 1980s Barbara Tizard and Martin Hughes (2002) undertook a small-scale research project that had some large-scale repercussions. They observed the conversations of 30 girls who were four years old in a half-day nursery class with their teachers and also at home with their mothers. The researchers made the observation that the girls usually had longer, more complex, conversations at home than in their nursery. They also observed that the girls' nursery teachers tended to underestimate these children's language competence and how they handled many abstract ideas.

Tizard and Hughes acknowledged that the adult–child ratio was different between home and nursery, although in fairness they pointed out that mothers were trying to do many tasks, in addition to talking with their daughters. The major point made for early years practice was that the nursery staff's view of their role was limiting the potential for conversations. The practitioners were focused on the questions they wanted to ask, and they frequently used talking time to serve an adult educational agenda.

In the mid-1970s and early 80s good early years practice in the UK had been influenced by the ideas of Joan Tough, an educational psychologist who promoted a dialogue led by adult questioning techniques. Tough (1976) built on Marion Blank's concept of cognitive demands and led a practical research project, involving many nursery classes and schools. Barbara Tizard and Martin Hughes challenged the 'everybody knows' platform that directive adult behaviour was best for children's learning, as well as the assumption that nursery must be a richer learning environment than a family home.

Make the connection with… **Willingness to reflect**

Barbara Tizard and Martin Hughes posed a legitimate challenge, but their research provoked a defensive reaction, at the time, from some early years professionals and writers. However, good practice cannot be led by the words 'because we say so …' or the belief that outsiders cannot grasp the intuitive knowledge possessed by insiders. The ideas raised by this research are equally relevant now.

Wise practitioners (and trainers or writers) take account of different kinds of evidence to guide them. There were some very positive ideas in Joan Tough's project. I still value what I learned about the different uses of language for children and adults. But the first edition of Tizard and Hughes's book in 1984 (a later edition is referred to below; see Tizard and Hughes, 2002) was a crucial 'take a moment' turning point, and not just for me. I have spoken with early years practitioners, whose careers also encompass that era, who describe how children's reactions made them rethink their language behaviour.

One experienced nursery head, who was involved in the project led by Joan Tough, told me of her own turning point. One day a four-year-old boy had agreed that she could sit down beside him, yet said firmly, 'But you are not to ask me any questions,' which was emphasised with body posture and finger waving.

Barbara Tizard and Martin Hughes developed the concept of 'a passage of intellectual search' to describe some of the conversations that they had recorded. They define this kind of pattern as 'a conversation, in which the child is actively seeking new information or explanations, or puzzling over something she does not understand, or trying to make sense of an apparent anomaly in her limited knowledge of the world' (2002: 91).

What does it mean?

Passage of intellectual search: a sustained conversation, led by the children's own questions, in which they work to make sense of an event or idea.

The typical pattern of these episodes is a sequence of questions put by the child to the adult. Children consider the adult answer and relate it to their current knowledge. The fit, or lack of fit, then often leads to further questions. Careful observation of children's intellectual search led Tizard and Hughes to the useful distinction that young thinking develops along two equally important tracks:

- Children need to learn details and they are hungry for information. Children whose enquiries meet with a positive adult response go on to ask other questions when they are ready.
- But four-year-olds are also working hard on a framework to enable them to make sense of the information. Their questions sometimes show an awareness that something does not fit, a sense of 'But that can't be right because …'.

Pause for reflection

Barbara Tizard and Martin Hughes (2002) give several examples of conversations between daughters and their mothers, in which the young children are trying to make sense of something that puzzles them. Look at any of these examples:

- Penny and how Father Christmas knows what you want, and whether he gives birthday presents too (2002: 91).
- Rosy trying to unravel the mystery of money, why and how the window cleaner gets paid (2002: 95).
- Beth and the mysteries of sloping roofs (2002: 99).

See if you can identify what the child currently understands and what is puzzling her. How is she trying to make sense of the situation? And how her mother does, or could, help.

The examples also show that, even if you know children well, it can still be difficult to work out what they do not understand. See also the conversation on page 177 about working within the zone of proximal development.

Collect your own examples of conversations that children themselves are using to drive a passage of intellectual search. Listen to four- and five-year-olds.

Do you struggle to collect examples or, indeed, searching questions from children in your care?

- Then you need to reflect (with colleagues, if you work alongside fellow practitioners) about opportunities for genuine conversations in your early years provision.

- There is also the possibility that children in your setting have yet to develop the confidence and vocabulary to support what would usually be within the intellectual grasp of four-year-olds and some threes. What are you doing to help them?

The intellectual search is often not restricted to a single conversation. Children who are confident of adult attention return to the same subject days, or even weeks, later. Early years practitioners who are serious about supporting young learning will follow children's lead. You let them determine the precise direction of adult-initiated topics and develop their own projects.

- I was able to track how my son Drew explored many issues around his knowledge and understanding of the world over the year in which he was a four-year-old child. Some of his questions addressed issues of family relationships, the natural environment, death and why unhappy things happened in the world. With his permission I documented his intellectual searches in *What does it mean to be four?* (Lindon, 2008: 44).

- In cooperation with children's parents, you could track the absorbing interests of some individual three- or four-year-olds over a period of months.

In a relaxed and warm emotional environment, at home just as much as in nursery, children lead their own intellectual search. Jacqui Cousins (2003) continued this line of research with Martin Hughes and other colleagues. She heard many perceptive questions posed by four-year-olds about issues that intrigued them at that moment. Children's searching questions showed how much they wanted to make sense of new experiences, which they realise are currently outside their knowledge. Among many fascinating questions quoted by Jacqui Cousins were those in which four-year-olds asked directly what she was doing, in her capacity as one of the mysterious 'Ofsted ladies' and what she would do with her written notes as a researcher.

Pause for reflection

Reflect on your use of questions with children, either as you think about your individual practice, or in team discussions. Do you consider sometimes 'Is this a genuine question that I am asking?' You can check by asking yourself:

- Do I really want to know the answer from the child(ren)?

- Do I already know the answer?

- Does the child have the answer and I do not?

My thanks go to Saplings Nursery in South London for these points. Their development team first started my thinking around 'questions about questions'.

It is well worth considering 'Do I ask a lot of questions?' Or 'Do I ask a lot of testing questions, to which I know the answer, but I want to know whether the children can give the correct reply?' Practitioners are often encouraged to focus on open-ended questions and avoid closed questions to which there can be only a one-word answer. But there is definitely a place for this kind of question, when the child has the answer, and you do not.

You need to reflect on children's replies to your questions:

- Do children give me 'odd' answers? 'Wrong' answers?
- What can I learn from their replies?
- Do the children seem confused but keen to cooperate?
- Do they go silent, change the subject, or 'wander off'?

Maybe children want to cooperate, but they are confused about what you are asking. Perhaps you and the children are not actually talking about the same thing (page 185). Perhaps your question does not connect closely enough, or at all, with their current understanding. You are out of the zone of proximal development (page 174).

Jacqui Cousins (2003) also suggests valuable open-ended questions from adults: 'What made you ask that question?', sometimes, 'Do you mean …?' and when appropriate, 'I wonder what you were thinking then'.

Sustained shared thinking

The Effective Provision of Pre-School Education (EPPE) research project identified that effective early years settings had practitioners who used their attention and communication skills to promote what the team called 'sustained shared thinking' with young children. This concept has much in common with the passage of intellectual search (page 167), not least that helpful adults need to listen and be careful about overuse of questions. Iram Siraj-Blatchford et al. (2002) observed in more detail 12 settings identified in the main EPPE study, as especially effective in supporting young children to learn. In their report they give transcripts of conversations, which also highlight that helpful practitioners make moment-by-moment, small decisions about whether to comment, or to listen and look without adding words. Today's attentive listening by an adult may connect with tomorrow's provision of appropriate resources, or next week's adult-initiated experience.

Figure 8.2 Sometimes you just watch

Opportunities for sustained shared thinking were unlikely to happen unless children were able to interact on a one-to-one basis with an adult, or with a few of their peers in a very small group. Such a process was simply not possible in adult-led, larger group time. The team linked this observation with the importance of a learning environment that enables a great deal of child-initiated and self-chosen activities, rather than a balance towards adult-led activities. The Early Years Foundation Stage (for England) included the EPPE focus on a balance in favour of 'child-initiated' experiences. This positive focus, nevertheless, highlighted that some practitioners, bogged down by an adult-dominated view of 'planning', were perplexed about what 'child-initiated' meant (Lindon, 2010b).

The EPPE concept of 'sustained shared thinking' is promoted by adults who join child-initiated play and conversation, but do not seize control. Genuine conversations – and those that truly support young learning – are based on close connections between what a child is doing or saying and the adult contribution. When children are excited about finding a spider, wise practitioners do not hijack the moment and insist on talking about 'How many legs does a spider have?' It is a different matter, if children voice or show an interest in spiders' legs. You listen and add your part in a conversation that may be about spiders' homes, whether spiders can fly, have babies and why they make webs, whatever interests the children today.

Sustained shared thinking, by words and actions, also happens through carefully considered adult-initiated, and maybe adult-led, experiences. In the early years, these activities should still share a great deal of control with the children. So today's child-initiated experience may be a self-chosen development from something that was started and led by an adult last week, and vice versa. Visual material from Marion Dowling (2005, 2008) shows aspects of sustained shared thinking in action.

What does it mean?

Sustained shared thinking: communicative interaction between adults and individual children that supports them to explore, understand and extend their knowledge about experiences and ideas.

Child-initiated experiences: events and activities that are freely chosen by children from their learning environment, directly requested of adults, or explorations started from a child's remark, shared family experience, and so on.

Adult-initiated experiences: events and activities that are started by adults, possibly, but not always, planned in advance, and may be led or guided, if children need tips on technique.

Pause for reflection

Look at examples of sustained shared thinking given in the research of Iram Siraj-Blatchford et al. (2002). For instance:

- The lively exchange between two four-year-olds about how God made us, blood and bones (2002: 45). Note in that sequence that the teacher sat and mainly listened as the conversation flowed to and fro. But she brought in relevant resources later in the week.

- Joining in pretend play about being a dog (2002: 44).

- Participating in children's imaginative use of playdough (2002: 47).

(**www.education.gov.uk/publications/standard/publicationDetail/Page1/RR356**)

In any of these examples what can you learn about:

- What each child probably understands so far? What is confusing to any of the children at the moment?

- The current interests of any of the children?

- How the different practitioners come alongside the children? Can you identify any of the supportive approaches discussed in this chapter?

- What could have happened if the practitioner in any of the examples took over the conversation, or asked lots of testing questions?

Experiences worth talking and thinking about

Children are not provoked to think if their experiences are pre-packaged. The approach of Diane Rich et al. (2005, 2008) evolved from deep concern that too many early years and school practitioners had moved away from engaging, first-hand experiences for children. Anxiety about paper evidence and a misguided belief that adults could determine what children would learn today had led to nonsensical situations, such as topics about fruit during which no real fruit was ever available.

Alison Gopnik (2009) describes how young children become able to manage counterfactual thinking: the ability to reflect on what might have been and not only to recall what actually did happen. Some of this 'What if …? or 'Supposing that…' thinking is explored through spoken language. However, children's counterfactual thinking flourishes in 'young scientist' mode, when they can get their hands on a generous resource of open-ended materials. It is then possible to try building the cardboard box spaceship differently from the method that led it all to collapse. When children enjoy familiar, local outings, it is feasible to explore directly what happens if you turn right at the library and not left; and consider looking for the correct route to re-find the garden with the amazing sunflowers.

The more directive techniques, such as questioning, are so tempting, because adults feel they are making a more active contribution to children's learning. Yet overuse of questions by adults, especially testing questions to which they already know the answer, is more likely to block genuine conversation and positive learning. It is often more effective to comment on what a child is doing, putting into words the interesting event that is unfolding in front of you both. Adults as equal play partners need to feel comfortable to talk out loud about what they are doing. Children close by are busy listening and looking, even when they appear absorbed in their own play.

Children feel encouraged, and valued, when familiar adults simply stay close and look genuinely interested in what has caught the attention of an individual child or a small group. Alert observation, often an informal 'keeping your eyes and ears open', is the way to get close to understanding what it is that young children currently understand. Their thinking and knowledge become visible to adults through what children do. You will see children's assumptions in action when they work on their chosen constructions, or persevere in using a magnifying glass. You will see the buzz of new learning when they paint glue on their fingers and patiently watch it dry.

Make the connection with... **Holistic development**

The EPPE research confirmed that the best outcomes for children emerged in those settings in which early years practitioners behaved as if cognitive and social development were equally important. Staff gave time and attention to personal interaction and emotional support.

- Look at the example of Rosie and Ben's pretend play in *What does it mean to be three?* (Lindon, 2008: 60). What is happening between two friends when they are absorbed in play and supportive adults are close by and attentive?

- Consider a sustained play sequence, involving two or more children, that unfolds in your provision. On reflection, what do you think they were learning and from which broad areas of development?

Working within the zone of proximal development

Lev Vygotsky (1962, 1978) was especially interested in how adults could best help children to learn. He saw the adult task as a far more active role than Jean Piaget proposed, not least because Vygotsky viewed intelligence partly as the ability to benefit from instruction. Like Piaget, Vygotsky saw play activity as a crucial means for young children to learn, but he saw adults as important resources who would guide children and share ideas and strategies.

Moving on from current understanding

Vygotsky's description of the zone of proximal development (ZPD) guides an active role for adults to intervene wisely in children's learning. Children's ZPD is the area of possibilities that lies between what they can manage on their own – their level of actual development – and what they could achieve or understand with some appropriate help – their level of potential development.

Vygotsky believed that the focused help could come from either an alert adult or from another child whose understanding, or skills, were slightly more mature. The size of the zone is not fixed; some children may have a larger ZPD than their peers. Assistance enables children to go slightly beyond their current competence; it is a supported stretch, not an almighty shove. The help builds on the child's existing ability, understanding or skill, rather than trying to introduce completely new ideas or ways of behaving. This pattern of support is sometimes called the Vygotskian Tutorial and is well illustrated by learning stories from Carmel Brennan (2004). Jacqui Cousins (2003) offers examples of situations when children are active in helping each other.

Pause for reflection

Use Figure 8.3, the diagram of the zone of proximal development, to reflect on individual boys or girls whom you know well.

- What can this child do or understand with full confidence?

- What is she keen to manage but is currently uncertain or puzzled about?

- How could you help him, without taking over, or pushing a step too far?

Lev Vygotsky described that children can help each other as well.

- Look out for examples of situations where one child helps another in play, in such a way that the younger or less sure children extend their learning.

- How could you plan the learning environment, or the routines, so that opportunities are created for children to help each other in this way?

What does it mean?

The zone of proximal development (ZPD): the area of potential learning for an individual child at a given time.

The Vygotskian Tutorial: the helping approach offered by an adult to a child; it is support that is sensitive to that child's current zone of proximal development.

I like to represent the ZPD as shown in Figure 8.3. However, a college tutor I met also had the creative idea that the zone could be represented as a set of three concentric circles. The collected papers from Lev Vygotsky (1962, 1978) do not provide the zone in diagrammatic form. So use the visual image that works best for you.

All the child's current skills, abilities and understanding

We have to start here with the children, for any flexible, adult-initiated activity or joining in their spontaneous play.

Anything we do has to make a firm connection for babies, toddlers and young children with what they can manage now.

The child's level of actual development (now, without any help)

The zone of proximal development, in which help can be given now

All your words, actions, suggestions are a gentle extension of what the child has already grasped, not a great leap forward.

If a child cannot manage something or looks puzzled, then helpful adults go back to a simpler version.

The child's level of potential development (now, with help)

What is yet to come: the future in this child's development

We do not start here with a learning goal that we want young children to achieve.

What is obvious to us as adults may yet be far from obvious to the children.

If our learning intentions are way off children's current levels, then we are wasting our time and that of the children, and we may well distress them.

Figure 8.3 Working within the zone of proximal development

When my son was five years old, his close friend moved house and we were invited to tea at Piya's new home. I drove most of the way and then parked to check my *London A–Z*. Drew and I had a conversation that went like this:

Drew: How do you know where Piya lives?

Jennie: His mum gave me their new address. I know it's round here somewhere. I'm just not sure of the last bit.

D: So how can we find it if you don't know?

J: I've got the map. I'm going to find it on the *A–Z*.

D: (looking at the map) But how can you find it on there?

J: It's OK. I know the name of the road.

D: But there are no houses or anything on it [the map]. How can you find Piya's house on that?

J: Ah, right. The map doesn't show houses and things. But it shows me the roads. Look. We're here now and Piya's road is there. The map tells me we have to turn right, go straight on a bit and then turn left.

D: But what about his house?

J: That'll be all right because I know the number. We get onto Piya's road and then we look out for number 14. The houses will have numbers on the door.

Drew and I talked some more and I understood more about what he needed to know from me, as well as the extent of what he knew already. Thinking afterwards, I realised that Drew had experience of two-dimensional plans that related to three-dimensional settings. For instance, he was able to follow exploded diagrams to make small Lego models. But those instructions had drawings that looked like the Lego pieces in front of him. He had a roadway for his cars, but that had the outline of buildings on it. The *A–Z* was a 2-D representation, with even more detail removed. This example highlights, for one aspect of learning, the current understanding of an individual boy.

- Look and listen for similar examples in your work with children.

Figure 8.4 Children will sometimes provoke each other's thinking

Teaching children road safety is a practical illustration that adults need to become aware of what children currently understand: work within the zone of proximal development. Research projects have highlighted that a long-standing approach of teaching a set of rules, or safety code, fails to transfer into safe behaviour by children, unless there is plenty of actual kerbside practice. Also, young children think from specific examples and then generalise to other similar situations (inductive reasoning). Yet, for many years, road safety training worked mainly in the opposite direction, by stressing general principles and expecting children to apply these rules to specific road-crossing situations (deductive reasoning). The problem can be seen as lack of a shared reference point, of 'Are we talking about the same thing?' (see page 185).

Right into middle childhood, children struggle to apply a rule such as 'Find a safe place to cross,' because they do not share adult knowledge of what would be safe or dangerous. Thomson et al. (1996) found that children often thought that the best place to cross was the shortest distance between two points. Children also reason that they if cannot see any cars, then it is safe to cross. They do not allow for their own relative invisibility and so they emerge from between parked vehicles, sometimes with fatal consequences. Children also have difficulty in judging the combined effect of the speed of a vehicle and its distance away from the crossing point. A series of studies identified that children needed to practise at the kerbside, with adults safely beside them, in order for 'safe thinking' to make sense in terms of choices in behaviour. Actual practice could be supported by working with children on appropriate computer simulation, but time spent at the computer screen on its own does not equip children with the skills to cross the road safely.

Disembedded thinking

A crucial part of working with children's ZPD is for adults to be well-grounded in their level of actual, current development. Margaret Donaldson (1978) developed the key concept that children are increasingly required to manage disembedded thinking. By this term she meant the type of thinking used when children have to handle ideas without concrete reference points. The primary school curriculum requires this kind of abstraction. Children aged six or seven years are increasingly able to manage without a hands-on context, provided that they have a sound understanding of the concepts involved. However, good primary school practice seeks to make close connections for children, frequently through relevant first-hand experiences (Rich et al., 2005, 2008). Growing research has also looked at the need for active experiences to support thinking skills during middle childhood and adolescence (see Lindon, 2007).

Young children are not like their older selves in middle childhood; they need to make very clear connections to the knowledge and ideas that they understand so far. This kind of embedded thinking is usually helped when they can be active with relevant resources and explore within a meaningful context. Margaret Donaldson and her team showed how young children could grasp quite abstract ideas, provided they could relate them to a conceptual framework that made sense (see also page 69 and 70). Alison Gopnik (2009) describes how young children ask for and offer causal explanations about a wide range of ordinary events. Under-fives are very capable of causal reasoning about an event such as 'How did Teddy's arm fall off?' Alert early years practitioners will know that young children can be passionate about the logic of sequences in imaginative play. It may be a pretend bus, but there are definitely rules about how bus drivers are supposed to behave.

Young children may be busy thinking, but they can only work from their current understanding. Margaret Donaldson usefully distinguished children's two main tasks, which still reflect Piaget's broad framework.

- Children absorb a great deal of information to build their knowledge; and it is a positive sign when they are hungry for facts and experiences.
- But at the same time, children are working on a conceptual framework to make sense of new experiences or ideas. Sometimes their spontaneous comments or questions tell you that children have identified a problem with their current theory.

Pause for reflection

Margaret Donaldson (1978:53) quotes a recorded exchange between a five-year-old girl and a researcher. The conversation happened shortly after the death of Donald Campbell, while he attempted to break the world water speed record. A few months before, a researcher, Robin Campbell, had visited the school. The child asked, 'Is that Mr Campbell, who came here, dead?' (with dramatic emphasis). The researcher replied in a surprised tone, 'No, I'm quite sure he isn't dead.' The child replied, 'Well, there must be two Mr Campbells then, because Mr Campbell's dead under the water.'

- Reflect on that short exchange; what does it tell you about the reasoning powers and likely current knowledge of that five-year-old?

- What can the example also tell you about the importance of conversation and children's confidence to ask their own questions, sure that a familiar adult will listen?

What does it mean?

Disembedded thinking: the process of thought when it is necessary to deal with concepts in the abstract, without an immediate reference point in direct familiar experience.

Both Alison Gopnik and Margaret Donaldson point out that Jean Piaget (page 35) sometimes asked under-fives causal questions, such as 'Why do clouds move?', an enquiry that entered uncharted territory for their general knowledge. It is unrealistic to expect anyone to manage causal thinking on a topic about which they know very little. Then, as now, young children understood the conventions of a question and tried their best to provide an answer, often logical given their limited knowledge.

The less a situation makes sense to children through links with their existing experience, the more they are dependent on making some sense through what they guess the adults want them to say. Martin Hughes and Robert Grieve (1983) explored what happened when children were asked meaningless questions by adults, such as 'Is red heavier than yellow?' Further exploration is reported by Amanda Waterman et al. (2001). Studies consistently find that young children work hard to cooperate and give answers that make as much sense as possible out of a nonsensical situation. Some children argued that red was heavier because it was darker, or they explained their answer by reference to specific red and yellow objects close to them. Children created a context to create sense, when the only existing sense was that, when adults ask children questions, they expect an answer, and a working assumption that adults, especially unfamiliar ones, are probably not teasing.

Ways of helping

The basic ideas for supportive adult behaviour are straightforward. Rather like explaining how very young children manage to learn to talk (see page 134), it becomes complicated to explain every detail of the 'how' and 'why' of good early years practice. Yet what works is actually very simple, looked at action by action. Glenda MacNaughton and Gillian Williams sum up the situation neatly with 'While teaching is a complex, highly interactive process, much of the teaching process involves the continuous use of very simple and subtle verbal interactions that may only last moments' (2004: 2). These interactions build into a sustained dialogue and children can return to an interest. Each adult contribution is enough to help, but not so much as to take over from a child.

The supportive technique of scaffolding

Jerome Bruner (1990) studied children's thinking and learning through the way in which they process information. His approach is to look equally at two aspects:

1 How children's experience affects their cognitive development, from external events to internal thinking.

2 How children's ability to think can then shape their experience, inside to outside.

Bruner pointed out that children can enjoy solving problems but that they are not necessarily very skilled or motivated at problem finding. And, of course, in order to identify a problem that needs solving, you also need some grasp of the gap between what you currently know and do not know, what you can and cannot do. This kind of identification and guidance is the crucial role of adults who can challenge children without daunting them. Jerome Bruner developed the concept of scaffolding to explain a positive way for adults to intervene in children's learning (see page 40).

Pause for reflection

Jerome Bruner's idea of scaffolding has been described as not so much directing children, but more a case of leading by following. You have to observe an individual child, before you can judge how best to help.

- Choose one or two children and focus on something they are currently keen to learn. It may be a physical skill such as learning to button up their coat, or the answer to an intellectual search about 'How do rainbows get made?'

- Watch individual children carefully to understand how far their learning has progressed. What kind of help may be most useful now: suggestions by words, showing how by demonstration, encouraging a child to talk thoughts out loud, wondering 'how we might find out about …'?

- Or could it be helpful to offer an experience to help children make more sense of what puzzles them? Perhaps several children are perplexed about how a travel agency works. The best first step would be to organise a visit to a travel agency. Children may then have a clearer idea and want to set up their own pretend agency, which in turn may raise new questions.

- Reflect on what you have done and how your contribution seems to have helped children to extend their learning. But always ask yourself as well, 'What have I learned from this experience?'

The apprenticeship model

Margaret Donaldson (1992) stressed how children want and need sometimes to learn directly from adults. She describes their enthusiasm for the role of novice, which can enable them, with suitable challenges, to experience personal satisfaction and that sense of achievement from 'now I can ...'. Donaldson emphasises that a genuinely child-centred learning environment does not leave children to struggle when direct adult suggestion could help. Her view was that learning should be a shared enterprise, to which adults bring their own contribution, offered with respect. This approach has much in common with the ideas of sustained shared thinking and provides food for thought about the role of helpful early years practitioners.

Figure 8.5 Children do not only learn from play; they benefit from real-life experiences

Barbara Rogoff (1990) developed her ideas of an apprenticeship model of learning through research that highlighted a contrast in cultural traditions. She observed children and their families in the USA and in Guatemala. She noted that the children from Guatemala were expected to learn domestic skills, alongside their parents and other family members, and soon had responsibility for tasks such as care of the animals. In contrast, the children in the families living in the USA were far less likely to be learning in this way. Adults tended to instruct them but did not expect children to take the same kind or level of domestic responsibility.

Rogoff developed the concept of learning as guided participation: the 'apprentice' child learns through appropriate conversation, organisation of the environment and actions and directly from an adult or other child. Barbara Rogoff also emphasised the concept of a community of learners, in which children learn the sociocultural meaning of items and actions. She stressed the idea of co-construction of knowledge that children and adults form meaning together, so adults need to become aware of the child's understanding and share control much more than is usual in an instruction model, led by adult greater knowledge.

Make the connection with... **Your own practice**

You may well be working within an apprenticeship approach, without using that term.

- Reflect on how you encourage children to come alongside as you undertake daily tasks. Domestic routines can be a rich source of learning for children in early years group provision, as much as in your home, as a childminder, or children's own family home.

- Can you also see the links with the technique of scaffolding and the zone of proximal development? An active role for the adult has to rest on the child's current skill or understanding, whether it is an idea or a physical skill.

Early mathematical experiences

Children can manage much better when they are able to embed a potentially confusing abstract idea in a familiar context, either by direct, hands-on exploration, or a visual image summoned up through words. Children's grasp of early mathematical ideas is a good example of how adults need to understand how this area of knowledge is most effectively supported.

Understanding number

Martin Hughes (1983, 1986) demonstrated the impressive thinking power of four-year-olds, as well as the point at which they no longer understood the concept of number as applied by the adult in this exchange.

In one study, Martin Hughes showed that well over half of a group of three- and four-year-olds could manage hypothetical ('what if ...') counting, provided that the imaginary situation, described in words, made sense within children's own experience. So this age group could often give the correct answer to a question such as, 'If there were two girls in a shop and another one went in, how many girls would be in the shop now?' It seemed that young children could transform the words into a familiar visual image in their imagination. They could often produce the correct answer, although they had nothing tangible in front of them to count. However, the same age of children struggled when invited to say 'how many is one and two more', without a further reference point, which could be 'two elephants and one more'. These young children seemed to take the view that, without 'two more something', it was only possible to guess at random.

Money is a complicated idea for young children, but Judy Miller (1996) showed how two-, three- and four-year-olds were enabled to make sense of purchasing decisions about play equipment for their nursery. The children had the same number of discs as the pounds limit in the budget. The familiar adult supported the children as they considered options from the catalogue and counted out the number of discs needed to pay. But soon the children were working with the idea of 'how much', and 'not enough' money. The children were also part of the trip to go and buy the equipment, so they experienced a real-life context of purchase.

Make the connection with… **Tuning into children**

The ideas explored in this section link with other ideas summed up by the whole idea of tuning into children: an approach that needs to be applied as much to emotional fine-tuning as intellectual.

I will add my idea of the 'cognitive wobble', drawing a parallel between intellectual and physical development. When young children are in the process of learning physical skills such as balancing or climbing, you can easily identify the gap between learning the skills and being fully confident. You see the wobble.

Adults have to use more than their eyes to recognise the cognitive wobble. You have to allow that what is obvious to you as an adult, in terms of knowledge or concepts, is far from obvious to a child. You need to backtrack to where children are no longer wobbling, where they are cognitively stable and then move on slowly from this point.

The what and why of counting

Penny Munn (1997b) talked with individual children during their last year in nursery and their first term of primary school. On each of four visits, she asked the children the same basic questions including 'Can you count?' and 'Why do you count?' She found that children generally learned to recite a number sequence before they are able to count a given number of objects, or to select a limited number in answer to the question 'Can you give me three bricks?'

Children aged four years tended to believe that counting was the same as saying the number words, rather like they believed that reading was the same as retelling the story (Munn, 1997a, see page 160). Many of the younger children were perplexed by the question, 'Why do you count?' It was rare for young children to understand the adult purpose of counting until they were old enough to be in primary school. Then the children increasingly gave an answer to, 'Why do you count?' that focused on 'to know how many'.

Penny Munn drew useful conclusions from her research. Early years practitioners should:

- Take children's counting seriously and not dismiss it as rote, perhaps because children use their abilities in what looks like a limited context.
- Avoid assuming that your adult purposes are clear to children, because that is not necessarily the case. You often help children by speaking your processing thoughts out loud ('I wonder how many we will need …?').

- Encourage children through daily routines to experience counting as a useful, practical skill. Give children a reason to check on 'how many' or 'are they the same?'.

Figure 8.6 Practical experiences often give children a reason to estimate and measure

Penny Munn also stresses that practitioners need to take time to understand young children's beliefs about counting before they plan activities designed to help learning about number. Penny Munn and her colleagues in Strathclyde have explored the idea of shared and non-shared reference, in terms of the role of adults in lessons about maths in the early years or primary school. Catherine Ridler (2002) considered examples from her research of when the teacher and children shared the same reference point, because the resources plus the teacher's words made sense. She also observed what happens when a teacher fails to consider 'Are we talking about the same thing?' There is no point in continuing with the lesson plan if you have lost the children, and 'odd' answers, from the adult perspective, are usually a sign that, as far as the children are concerned, the adult is now talking nonsense.

Similar messages emerge from an action research project led by Susan Morton (2002), in which a nursery team was supported to notice how much mathematical exploration was happening within children's self-chosen play and spontaneous conversations. Alert observation then supported practitioners to build on those experiences and to judge in what way adult-planned activities were genuinely needed. Liz Marsden and Jenny Woodbridge (2005) show how an adult-initiated exploration around mathematical understanding was most effective because the children not only shared control in how games were developed, but also their reflections on learning were highly valued by their teacher.

Dorothy Caddell's practical suggestions (1998b) are firmly based in the research about early mathematical understanding (1998a). Her approach will enable children aged three to five years to stockpile many answers to the important question of 'What can numbers do for me?' (During early childhood, young boys and girls need also to have gained personal answers for 'What can reading or writing do for me?') Dorothy Caddell describes what makes sense to young children and will engage them. For instance, numbers give information (prices) but they also help us to make decisions (which bus to catch). She also focuses on how young children need to see adults using numbers for a real purpose. Just as with literacy (Hughes and Ellis, 1998, see page 160), young children need to see the point of early mathematical skills.

Pause for reflection

Over a few weeks, gather examples of how children in your provision use early mathematical skills such as counting, estimating, or measuring as part of their self-chosen play. Look also for ways in which they are using mathematical skills for a practical reason, when they help with regular routines such as tidying up, or laying the table for a meal.

Reflect on your practice:

- Stop and think about planning an adult-initiated activity around number, or another mathematical concept.

- Are you sure that children are not exploring these ideas within their spontaneous play?

- Will your planned activity really work within the children's zone of proximal development?

Link these ideas also with Cathy Nutbrown's concept of environmental print (page 158). In what ways can young children experience environmental number? Look out for written numbers in their learning environment, including the local neighbourhood, that exist for a reason.

Consider also the different ways that young children can make meaningful marks to represent amount. Look at using tallies of lines to show scores when throwing balls into a large container, or the symbolism of drawing a ball each time a throw is successful.

When adults do not understand

A great deal of research on children's thinking has explored those situations when children do not understand what the adult is saying, or trying to show. The practical issues raised in this section put the spotlight on adults' potential failure to understand children's perspective.

Elizabeth Robinson and Peter Robinson (1983) focused on what usually happens when adults are puzzled, when children have not got their message across to the more mature partner in the exchange. When adults did not understand what children meant, the most frequent response from the adult was to ask for a repetition with 'Pardon?' The next most common reaction was to ask questions to encourage more information, such as 'What?' and 'Who?' questions. Some adults guessed what the child meant, repeated and expanded the child's message, or simply ignored it.

In this intriguing research, the least frequently used response was for adults to tell children directly, with a sentence such as 'I don't understand what you mean.' Several experiments within this study showed that young children did not realise adults had failed to understand, unless those adults said so directly. This research made me think about interactions led by adults. Cooperative young children often repeat themselves or answer adult questions. But a strategy of simple honesty from adults is more likely to promote understanding. Adults can also directly model the difference in words between:

- 'I didn't hear you,' or an honest 'Sorry, I wasn't listening,' which leads to 'please say that again,' and
- The different message of 'I don't understand, can you say it a different way?' or 'Please show me.'

These distinct strategies can be helpful to children to highlight the difference between not having heard, and having heard every word and yet the meaning is still not clear.

Make the connection with... Being a positive role model

- Reflect on your own practice, keeping alert to how you handle times when you do not understand what a child says.

- Try letting children know that you are confused about what they are telling you. Use any questions carefully in this context.

Considerate early years, and school, practitioners do not regularly assume that confused boys or girls have not been listening. (Be gracious if they admit that is the case.) I have listened to some very annoyed older children and adolescents who do not appreciate being given the same, incomprehensible explanation, only louder.

Resources

- **Brennan, C.** (ed.) (2004) *The power of play: a play curriculum in action.* Dublin: IPPA.
- **Bruner, J.** (1990) *Acts of meaning.* Cambridge MA: Harvard University Press.
- **Caddell, D.** (1998a) *Numeracy in the early years: what the research tells us.* Dundee: Learning and Teaching Scotland.
- **Caddell, D.** (1998b) *Numeracy counts.* Dundee: Learning and Teaching Scotland.
- **Cousins, J.** (2003) *Listening to four year olds: how they can help us plan their education and care.* London: National Children's Bureau.
- **Donaldson, M.** (1978) *Children's minds.* London: Fontana.
- **Donaldson, M.** (1992) *Human minds: an exploration.* London: Penguin.

- **Dowling, M.** (2005) *Supporting young children's sustained shared thinking: an exploration.* DVD and booklets. London: Early Education. **www.early-education.org.uk**
- **Dowling, M.** (2008) *Exploring young children's thinking through their self-chosen activities.* DVD and booklets London: Early Education. **www.early-education.org.uk**
- **Dunn, J.** (1984) *Sisters and brothers.* London: Fontana.
- **EPPE**: *Effective Provision of Pre-School Education Project.* **http://eppe.ioe.ac.uk/** The project is following the children through primary and into secondary school and you can access research papers on this site.
- **Gopnik, A.** (2009) *The philosophical baby: what children's minds tell us about truth, love and the meaning of life.* London: Bodley Head. Also a conversational feature on **www.edge.org/3rd_culture/gopnik09/gopnik09_index.html**
- **Gopnik, A., Meltzoff, A., Kuhl, P.** (2001) *How babies think: the science of childhood.* London: Phoenix.
- **Hughes, M.** (1983) 'What is difficult about learning arithmetic?', in Donaldson, M., Grieve, R., Pratt, C. (eds) *Early childhood development and education: readings in psychology.* Oxford: Blackwell.
- **Hughes, M.** (1986) *Children and number.* Oxford: Blackwell.
- **Hughes, A., Ellis, S.** (1998) *Writing it right? Children writing 3–8.* Learning and Teaching Scotland: Dundee.
- **Karmiloff-Smith, A.** (1994) *Baby it's you: a unique insight into the first three years of the developing baby.* London: Ebury Press.
- **Lindon, J.** (2007) *Understanding children and young people: development from 5–18 years.* London: Hodder Arnold.
- **Lindon, J.** (2010a) *The key person approach.* London: Practical Pre-School Books.
- **Lindon, J.** (2010b) *Child-initiated learning.* London: Practical Pre-School Books.
- **Lindon, J.** (2012e) *What does it mean to be one? A practical guide to child development in the Early Years Foundation Stage.* A set of four books, for each year of early childhood, so also *What does it mean to be two? (three?, four?).* London: Practical Pre-School Books.
- **MacNaughton, G., Williams, G.** (2004) *Teaching young children: choices in theory and practice.* Maidenhead: Open University Press.
- **Marsden, L., Woodbridge, J.** (2005) *Looking closely at learning and teaching… a journey of development.* Outlane: Early Excellence. **www.earlyexcellence.com**
- **Miller, J.** (1996) *Never too young: how young children can take responsibility and make decisions.* London: Save the Children.
- **Morton, S.** (2002) *Promoting number and mathematical development in nursery through staff development.* www.pre-online.co.uk/feature_pdfs/spotlight88.pdf
- **Munn, P.** (1997a) 'What do children know about reading before they go to school?', in Owen, P., Pumfrey, P. (eds), *Emergent and developing reading: messages for teachers.* London: Falmer Press.
- **Munn, P.** (1997b) 'Children's beliefs about counting', in Thompson, I. (ed.) *Teaching and learning early number.* Buckingham: Open University Press.
- **Paley, V.** (1988) *Bad guys don't have birthdays: fantasy play at four.* Chicago: University of Chicago Press.

UNDERSTANDING CHILD DEVELOPMENT 0–8 YEARS

- **Paley, V.** (2004) *A child's work: the importance of fantasy play.* Chicago and London: Chicago University Press.
- **Rich, D., Casanova, D., Dixon, A., Drummond, M., Durrant, A., Myer, C.** (2005) *First hand experiences: what matters to children.* Clopton: Rich Learning Opportunities.
- **Rich, D., Drummond, M., Myer, C.** (2008) *Learning: what matters to children.* Clopton: Rich Learning Opportunities.
- **Ridler, C.** (2002) 'Teachers, children and number understanding', Conference paper, British Psychological Society Psychology of Education Conference, University College, Worcester.
- **Robinson, E., Robinson, P.** (1983) 'Ways of reacting to communication failure in relation to the development of the child's understanding about verbal communication', in Donaldson, M., Grieve, R., and Pratt, C. (eds), *Early childhood development and education: readings in psychology.* Oxford: Basil Blackwell.
- **Rogoff, B.** (1990) *Apprenticeship in thinking: cognitive development in social context.* Oxford: Oxford University Press.
- **Siraj-Blatchford, I., Sylva, K., Muttock, S., Gilden, R., Bell, D.** (2002) *Researching Effective Pedagogy in Early Years: Brief No. 356.* www.education.gov.uk/publications/standard/publicationDetail/Page1/RR356
- **Thomson, J., Tolmie, A., Foot, H., McLaren, B.** (1996) *Child development and the aims of road safety education.* London: HMSO.
- **Tizard, B., Hughes, M.** (2002) *Young children learning: talking and thinking at home and at school.* Oxford: Blackwell.
- **Tough, J.** (1976) *Listening to children talking.* London: Ward Lock.
- **Vygotsky, L.** (1962) *Thought and language.* Cambridge MA: MIT Press.
- **Vygotsky, L.** (1978) *Mind in society: the development of higher psychological processes.* Cambridge MA: Harvard University Press.
- **Waterman, A., Blades, M., Spencer, C.** (2001) 'Is a jumper angrier than a tree?', *The Psychologist,* vol 14, no. 9. www.bps.org.uk/publications/thepsychologist/search-the-psychologist-online.cfm

Children's behaviour: adults' reactions

This chapter focuses on children's behaviour, but you can only make sense of what children do within the broader context of their development. So, you will find discussion of how children think, as well as what they do. This area of development is also one that throws into sharp relief the impact of children's experience, a large component of which is how adults behave.

The main sections of this chapter are:
- Individual differences and experience
- The journey towards pro-social behaviour
- Social behaviour and play.

Individual differences and experience

Alert observation, within a family or early years provision, shows that individual children do not behave in the same way when faced with what look, to an outsider, like similar events. If you watch the same children some years later, you will almost certainly notice that the child who looked confident and was central in the play is still very much a social leader. The child who stood on the sidelines or who clung to an adult may not cling so much, but probably still seeks more reassurance, especially in a new or anxiety-provoking situation.

Individual differences

The available research does not suggest that children are fixed from birth; there is plenty of scope for the impact of experience. But there is good reason to say that babies have an inborn inclination towards one kind of temperament, shown through a behavioural style. The word temperament is used to mean inborn tendencies for children's reactions and behaviours that probably build the basis for a more enduring adult personality. The two concepts are both attempts to explain continuities in how the same child, or adult, tends to deal with their experiences.

What does it mean?

Temperament: inborn tendencies that shape how a baby and young child react to daily experiences.

Personality: usually the term used to describe continuities in how adults react to experiences.

Behavioural style: the individual pattern of behaviour that a child shows from a very young age, reflecting inborn temperament.

Stella Chess and Alexander Thomas (1996) followed children who were part of a longitudinal study that began in the 1950s. They were interested in temperament as a counterpoint to the theoretical stance that individual differences could be explained solely by experience. From their clinical practice, as well as research, they took the view that environment (nurture) did not explain everything. They considered that young babies tended to fit into three broad temperamental types:

1 *Easy babies:* who reacted in a playful way, moved into regular care patterns and adapted readily to new circumstances.

2 *Difficult babies:* whose biological needs did not slip into a regular pattern, behaved in an irritable way and often responded intensely and negatively to an unfamiliar situation.

3 *Slow-to-warm-up babies:* who tended to be lower on activity level and responded in a mild way. These babies tended to withdraw from unfamiliar situations, but not in the intense way of the 'difficult' babies. These babies were able to adapt, but needed more time than the 'easy' babies.

Pause for reflection

- Look at the three broad categories described by Stella Chess and Alexander Thomas. How could caring adults, either parents or early years practitioners, be affected when they face these inclinations in young babies?

- In what ways could there be an interaction between parental expectations and the baby's inclination? See also the idea of match and mismatch on page 193.

- Draw on your own experience and talk, if possible, with a health visitor, or other professional who offers home visiting to families. They could discuss general themes about support for parents and more, or less, 'difficult' babies, without breaking confidentiality about individual families.

Other research teams have been interested to explore inborn individual temperament. The researchers do not all propose the same types, nor use the same terms; and the useful research does not place children in rigid categories. However, there are shared themes about individuality, which can be summed up by the following dimensions of broad temperament:

- *Activity level*: some children are physically mobile and react in a vigorous way to the possibilities in their environment. Some are considerably less active and may prefer sedentary play activities. Some may react passively, waiting for experiences to come to them.
- *Sociability*: individual differences between children in how they relate to people and to new experiences or objects. Some children are keen to make contact or explore, some are less enthusiastic or outgoing in a social way.
- *Wariness*: a tendency to react with fear or to withdraw from new experiences and people. Children who tend to show such anxiety are often called 'shy', but the wariness is not only about people.
- *Negative emotions:* children differ in their tendency to react to experiences with anger and irritability. All children feel annoyed at some point, but some children are easily provoked by minor frustrations.
- *Effort and persistence:* children vary in how well they are able to focus on what they are doing and to persist, despite distractions. Attention control is partly developmental but some older children struggle to concentrate.

Figure 9.1 Some children will appear more adventurous

Make the connection with... **Balance between nature and nurture**

Individual differences in temperament need to be seen as tendencies; they are not proposed as a fixed characteristic that is unresponsive to experiences. Temperament operates as a built-in bias: possibilities may be strengthened or weakened through what happens to children.

Sociocultural context determines whether children's temperament is experienced as difficult by themselves, or by the key adults in their lives. Adults may judge some temperamental inclinations as appropriate, or inappropriate, given this child's sex. Think of some possibilities here.

Interaction between temperament and experience

Longitudinal research about temperament has established that children rated by adults as having a 'difficult temperament' (getting upset very easily, finding it hard to settle, and so on) are far more likely to show what adults judge to be behaviour problems. But it is not the case that a 'difficult' temperament inevitably leads to later problems.

For example, newborn babies who cried a lot more than average do not necessarily grow into irritable, easily upset toddlers. Babies with mothers who were rated as highly responsive were crying less by the age of five to six months. But babies whose mothers were observed as less sensitive to their babies crying were still doing a great deal of crying at the half-year point. In a similar way, crying babies were more likely to develop into defiant toddlers when their mother had reacted in an angry way to the early crying. Mothers were more able to be responsive to their crying babies if they had the support of family and friends.

Take another **perspective**

Consider the idea of match or mismatch. Some adults, both parents and practitioners, can feel a wide gap between their own inclinations and the way that a child reacts.

An outgoing adult may be baffled by a reticent toddler, who seems to approach new situations as a worry and not as exciting possibilities. On the other hand, a cautious adult may be unnerved by a vigorous young child with an enthusiastic 'leap-then-look' approach.

- Can you think of examples of match and mismatch between familiar children and your own preferences?

- What can happen to a child if their important adults insist on a very different outlook on life?

- Reflect on your own provision. How do you reduce distractions for children who find it hard to concentrate? Are wary children labelled as 'shy'?

Learning from experience

Throughout childhood, boys and girls experience the reaction of familiar adults to behaviour that those grown-ups regard with approval, disapproval or indifference. Children also experience the degree of consistency or inconsistency from the same, familiar adult and between known adults who are part of their daily life. Constructive support for parents or practitioners focuses on helping them to be aware of options and strategies, as well as a willingness to notice what actually happens as a result of adult intervention, and not only what the grown-ups believe or want to have happened. See a detailed discussion of all these issues in Lindon (2009a.)

Remember partial reinforcement

When adults are inconsistent, they can unintentionally reward the exact behaviour they are trying to discourage. For example, a young child may wake at night and cry to be taken into the parents' bed. On the first few occasions, the parents stand firm and settle the child or take her back to her own bed. Then exhaustion or exasperation takes over and, on the third or fourth crying bout, the child is taken into the parents' bed.

Inadvertently, the parents have shown the child that persistence pays off; the child has experienced partial reinforcement (see page 29). Crying does not get you taken into bed straightaway or even every time, but the success rate is good enough. Helpful programmes for parents whose children wake at night advise putting a child back into their own bed again and again, reassuring them and going into the child's room only briefly. Supportive advice must also acknowledge that it is tough for exhausted parents to be consistent.

Learning from negative reinforcement

Negative reinforcement is an unpleasant event, the cessation of which acts to increase a particular behaviour. It is a useful concept to grasp, because adults can behave, unintentionally, in a way that provides negative reinforcement to children.

Imagine a harassed early years practitioner who tries to get some children to tidy up before lunch. She tells them to put the blocks away and then she tells them again but more firmly. She calls them 'inconsiderate' and says they will not get any 'helpful' stickers this week. She threatens that they will not be able to have the blocks out this afternoon … then she runs out of energy to continue, and lunch is ready. The children have not tidied up; they need to eat lunch and the practitioner tidies up the blocks herself. What has happened here and what are the alternative options?

- From the children's perspective their behaviour of not tidying up has been negatively reinforced. They have learned that if they ignore the practitioner, they can avoid tidying up, which seems to be a boring chore to them. They may also know from experience that the practitioner will forget about her threat of 'no blocks this afternoon'.
- The practitioner is puzzled: she has told the children many times and also believes (or has been advised) that it should work to threaten the absence of stickers. In fact, she has been using the ineffective 'hot-air' strategy, where

children learn that if you ignore this adult's nagging, she gives up in the end. Also the children may well feel that they can live without a sticker today.

- If the practitioner asks for help, wise advice will include gaining awareness of the situation from the perspective of the children. They need a friendly time warning and positive incentives (not stickers) to be involved in tidying up time.

Figure 9.2 In a friendly atmosphere, young children like to help

This example highlights how the concept of negative reinforcement is sometimes confused with punishment by some childcare writers. The mistake is to apply the term to the practitioner's nagging behaviour, rather than to the significance from the children's perspective of when that nagging stops.

Being cautious about rewards

Early years practitioners may be aware of the risks of using sweets or money as a reward. However, some teams have found that their use of symbolic rewards, such as stickers or certificates, appears to have reduced, rather than increased, a wanted pattern of behaviour in a group of children. When children are given stickers for specific tasks, they do not necessarily increase this behaviour, when given a free choice. The claim is sometimes then that 'reward does not work' or that 'it does not have a long-term effect'.

Social learning theory explains that the use of tangible rewards has shaped children's perspective on this particular activity. Instead of developing a sense of internal satisfaction, for example 'I lay the table because it's interesting and I enjoy helping', children now think of the task as something they do for the reward:

'I only do this if I want a sticker today.' Some children experience a sense of pressure that operates as a disincentive, for instance that they are only liked and valued if they earn enough stickers.

Using encouragement instead

Rudolf Dreikurs (Dreikurs and Soltz, 1995) developed the ideas of Alfred Adler around using encouragement rather than rewards or spoken praise.

Here are the main differences:

- Conventional praise focuses on the end result, whereas encouragement is freely given for perseverance and improvement, especially given what is a big effort for this individual child.
- Praise or rewards stress a fixed quality about a child, but encouragement focuses on what a child has done. Can you experience the difference between 'Well done for waiting your turn', rather than 'Good boy' and between 'Thank you for helping' instead of 'You're such a helpful girl'?
- Encouragement focuses on feelings: of the adults when they express appreciation for help and of the children by acknowledging their pleasure in a job well done or finished, despite the difficulties.
- Encouragement taps into children's feelings of satisfaction and their strengths. Patterns of praise and reward can be unforgiving of mistakes, or times when children do not feel like being 'patient' or 'helpful'.

Using consequences rather than punishment

Punishment is the addition of something negative to the situation, or the removal of something positive. Some adults are confident, even enthusiastic, about the likely success of punishment to change behaviour. However, punishment by words, removal of privileges or harsh actions can just as successfully make children secretive. Children learn not to let the adults see them doing what is forbidden. The learning dilemma for young children is also that conventional punishment does not direct them towards alternative behaviour; it only communicates 'don't' and 'stop it'.

Rudolf Dreikurs and Vicki Soltz explain the value of using the consequences of children's behaviour. Behaviour that you want to stop or redirect can be guided by ensuring that children experience the consequences of their actions.

- Natural consequences follow as part of the child's behaviour. For instance, a child who insists on tearing the pages of her favourite book may be sad that it cannot be mended so that it is as good as new. Of course, responsible adults do not allow children to experience the dangerous consequences of an action.
- Logical consequences are adult-determined but need to make sense, given what the child has done. Children who throw sand at others can be given a firm but friendly warning but, if they continue, they will be moved away from the sand area.
- However, neither child should lose their chance to join the afternoon walk in the park. Neither book tearing nor sand throwing has any relevance to the ability to walk safely with an adult and enjoy the local neighbourhood. Loss of the walk would operate as an artificial consequence, as a punishment; and children would most likely regard the adult imposition as very unfair.

> ## What does it mean?
>
> **Natural consequences**: results that inevitably follow from a course of action.
>
> **Logical consequences**: adult-determined and pre-warned consequences that make sense, given a child's persistent pattern of behaviour.

The journey towards pro-social behaviour

Prevailing values in UK guidance for the early years lean strongly towards pro-social behaviour. This positive focus sometimes struggles with developmentally realistic expectations for young children and a thorough grasp of the learning journey towards consideration for others. Problems have also arisen within a national atmosphere where a punitive approach towards even mild antisocial behaviour has become more common (Lindon, 2007, 2012d).

What example is set by adults?

The behaviourist approach was developed by Albert Bandura (1986) into a more sophisticated theory of social learning. Bandura emphasised the importance of imitation and adult role models in how children learn to behave. However, his theory also acknowledges that children use their skills of observation and thinking. Bandura found that, when adults' behaviour did not fit their words, then children were most likely to copy what the adults did. So, research does not support optimism about adult approaches of 'Do what I say, not what I do!' Children think about what they are told and do not simply accept a behaviour rule, especially if the adult's behaviour is inconsistent.

Figure 9.3 Your presence will sometimes ease turn taking

Research across cultures has shown how adults behave in ways that shape children's behaviour to fit the values and priorities of that society. Adults are often not alert to the differences, since the pattern of behaviour within their own group is viewed as 'normal'. For instance, Janet Maybin and Martin Woodhead (2003) describe the contrast between an Inuit community in northern Canada and a group of American children in south Baltimore.

- The Inuit parents modelled their preferred behaviour pattern of being nurturing, protective and even-tempered, a concept summed up by their word '*naklik*'. Parents did their best to avoid scolding children or showing anger. They reinterpreted unacceptable actions, for instance, treating an expression of annoyance from a child as if it were amusing. They also commented with disapproval on '*un-naklik*' behaviour from other people.
- In contrast, the Baltimore parents (not assumed to be typical of all parents in the USA) guided their children to stand up for themselves through verbal and physical aggression. Mothers provoked their daughters by teasing and pretend fighting. Adults recounted how they had handled an incident with aggression, or imagined how they would retaliate. However, if the girls directed anger at their mother, they were reprimanded and labelled as spoiled.

The Inuit children were being guided towards a pattern of pro-social behaviour. On the other hand, the Baltimore children were being guided towards a more aggressive pattern. Cultures and subcultures vary in their beliefs of which behaviour patterns are judged to be right and proper.

Potential development of pro-social behaviour

Children's ideas of right and wrong and their understanding of what is expected of them are a blend of several different aspects to development, which are set out below.

1 *Social relationships.* Babies are born morally neutral but inherently social. A growing sense of morality is partly a social development. Rights, wrongs and expectations make sense to children because ideas are grounded in relationships with other people. With positive early experiences, young children are motivated to please their carers and get along with other children.

2 *Moral behaviour.* Young children do not understand adult moral judgements of 'messy' or 'destructive', but they notice adult disapproval. Adults can over-focus on ideas such as 'It's nice to share.' Young children start with actions; an abstract concept like 'sharing' only makes sense from 'What does sharing look like?', along with 'Do they help me to take turns?'.

3 *Moral reasoning and judgement.* So moral development for children is first about behaviour; ideas are harder to grasp and come later in a child's development. Understanding 'why' and making the 'right' decision are related to children's growing ability to think and reason. They begin to follow a pattern of what is expected: of rules about acceptable and unacceptable behaviour. Older children increasingly understand the reasons and values behind moral judgements, and they make judgements in their turn. You will find a detailed discussion of this area of development in Lindon (2012d).

Children apply their growing powers of thinking and reasoning to try to understand ideas of 'right' and 'wrong' and 'why'. The same child who is getting to grips with the meaning of number, or that some squiggles are 'writing', is also trying to make sense of social situations and the behaviour of others.

- Children aged three and four years have the thinking skills to build a working theory about moral standards. They tend to focus on what happened, rather than allowing for intentions. The actual consequences of an act are seen as the same as intentions. Also, behaviour is judged by the seriousness of the consequences: a major mess means a 'naughtier' act.

- But informal observation of children and adults will show you that adults often get more cross about bigger messes. Parents and practitioners who are under pressure do not always pause to explore children's intentions before criticising the consequences.

- So the conclusions of young children may arise at least as much from their observation of how adults behave, as from immature thinking processes.

Practical researchers including Nancy Eisenberg (1992), Judy Dunn (1986, 1993) and Ronald Slaby and his team (1995) highlight whether children's early experience supports them to be able and willing to:

- Become aware of the feelings of other children or adults: the outlook of empathy.
- Behave with a selfless concern for the well being of others: the pattern of altruism

The combination of empathy and altruism is called pro-social behaviour. The key features are that children show intentional, voluntary behaviour that is intended to benefit someone else. It is not inevitable that children learn empathy, or that they choose sometimes to act with altruism. Those skills and choices arise from experience. The events of their early years can just as easily teach children that life is competitive and 'he who shoves gets'.

What does it mean?

Empathy: the ability and willingness to tune into the feelings of others, either children or adults.

Altruism: acting with a selfless concern for the well being of others.

Pro-social behaviour: that children show intentional, voluntary behaviour, which is intended to benefit someone else.

Judy Dunn and her team showed how actions, including those which are allowed and not allowed, are learned within a context that is given sense by the emotional link that is integral to family relationships. Children as young as 18 to 24 months of age had a good grasp of the family ground rules, to the extent that they could talk about them with parents or siblings and deliberately break rules as a source of joking.

Emotionally secure toddlers are able from about 18 months old to notice the distress of others. They know how to get an adult's attention and point out that another child is crying or hurt. Toddlers also sometimes take the initiative to help. Young children may offer another distressed child their own comfort object, which is an act of great generosity in itself. But soon, young children who know each other well (in the same family or early years setting) offer the other child's favourite blanket or teddy. Young children may also pat the hand of a sad-looking adult. By the age of three years, children may imitate and suggest you have a 'nice cup of tea'.

Make the connection with... **Adult choices in behaviour**

Early years settings, like family homes, are undoubtedly happier places for everyone if children behave in a pro-social way, so how can you help?

- Create an affectionate and warm environment. Young children who feel they have to compete with peers for the attention and affection of adults have little emotional energy left to give to each other.

- Be clear about your rules for considerate or helpful behaviour. Be ready to give children simple explanations about why 'we ask, we don't just grab'. Also model using the words that can be used to ask.

- Just telling a child, 'You mustn't hit people' is less effective than alerting him to the consequences; for example, 'When you bit Sam, you really hurt him and made him cry.'

- Create opportunities for even very young children to do something helpful and acknowledge what they have done. Appreciate considerate behaviour with words and not stickers or other rewards.

- The most important step for adults is to behave in a manner that reflects what you would like children to do: model thoughtful and generous behaviour.

In summary, aim for: 'tell–show–do'. It is the combination that works.

Figure 9.4 Children relish taking responsibility in their own world

Support for social skills

Ronald Slaby and his team (1995) looked at applications of the research on pro-social behaviour. Their concern also arose from a goal of redirecting children away from aggressive patterns. The team redefined the area as an adult task to coach children in specific social skills.

- The project worked to identify the kinds of behaviour that children needed to learn if they were to develop an assertive way of dealing with conflict rather than turn to aggressive methods.
- Slaby et al. focused on adult behaviour and how practitioners could shift from dependence on telling and directing behaviours ('You must share') or regularly stepping in on behalf of children ('Let him have a go').
- Attention was paid to how settings operated on a daily basis and the unspoken messages from layout and organisation. Was it relatively easy or hard for a child to take the pro-social option?
- Strategies were also developed for adults to model the pro-social options and find ways for adults to coach children in how to handle situations for themselves.

This reflective approach encourages practitioners to consider the real meaning of moral rules like 'sharing'. What do adults mean in terms of recognisable behaviour and what do children think is expected of them? For example, this research team recognised that 'nice sharing' should not have to mean that children simply feel obliged to hand over an important play item. Practitioners could model suggestions such as 'You can have it when I've finished' or 'I'll swap you the car for your truck,' just as much as how to ask courteously, rather than seize what you want.

Make the connection with... *Getting time on your side*

Vivian Gussin Paley comments about making the time to be kind and the sense of pressure felt by practitioners in US kindergartens. She describes a conference at which practitioners talked about 'the gradual lessening of "ordinary niceness" in the classroom' (2004: 53).

A kindergarten teacher had explained how she and the special education teacher had reintroduced long play periods. The change was led by the needs of children who could not possibly go from one task to another, as was expected of their peers. It dawned on the two practitioners that all the children needed the ordinary, therapeutic support of uninterrupted play. They then observed that these young children were generally 'nicer' to each other.

These adults had not talked more about kind behaviour, nor tried to 'manage' the children's behaviour. In contrast, they had taken up the adult responsibility to manage time with children's best interests at heart.

- Does this dilemma sound familiar?

- What happens when early years practitioners feel they have to harass young children to complete a list of adult-determined tasks?

Social behaviour and play

A considerable proportion of adult concerns about children's behaviour arise within the context of play. Useful approaches have encouraged practitioners to observe what is really happening and to adjust any adult intervention with a full understanding of the flow of play.

Play as part of childhood

Ethology is the study of animal behaviour, but with specific attention to patterns that are shared across different species. Human ethology brings in the study of human behaviour as part of the animal kingdom. Ethologists such as Nicholas Blurton Jones (1967) became interested in the play patterns of children, both for the common ground with other young mammals, and also for continuities across cultures. Children are considerably more complex than 'kittens who can talk'. However, it is worth recalling the proposal that young mammals seem to be biologically predisposed towards play (see page 18). It is a simple explanation of why children persevere with their play, sometimes creatively circumventing adult rules, anxieties and prohibitions. Adult concerns about behaviour within play, or choices about play themes, are met sometimes with a heartfelt cry from children of 'we're just playing' or 'but it's only pretend'.

Take another **perspective**

The biological parallel is reflected in a common phrase used in playwork that:

Play enables children to learn what cannot be directly taught by adults.

This insightful comment is worth reading more than once and reflecting on the implications.

Supportive adults engage with the perspective of children themselves. Adults' behaviour can have a disruptive effect on play when they insist on viewing the activity exclusively from the grown-up standpoint. Disruption can follow when practitioners effectively highjack play, in order to 'deliver' their set of learning outcomes, which is a problem within some early years practice. But it is equally disruptive when children's play choices are restricted by unreflective practitioners who insist that particular play is, for example, too noisy, too rough, too active, or too risky.

Play as a therapeutic process

Alert adult observers of play cannot miss the fact that emotions matter within play. Even very young children express strong feelings about play and by middle childhood, if not younger, children will deliberately explore emotions within their pretend play, with directions to each other, such as 'Pretend that you're really surprised to see me.' One strand of adult interest in play has been to interpret children's behaviour as observed within the context of play, or a play situation devised by the adults.

Anna Freud and Melanie Klein (part of the psychoanalytic tradition, see page 23) believed that the themes and symbols of children's play, especially imaginary play, were a window into the unconscious life of children, including the emotional conflicts underpinning the development of personal identity. Klein and Freud disagreed, however, on the details of theory and therapeutic technique. The pattern for psychodynamic play therapy is that the therapist interprets the true meaning of a child's play, in accordance with Freudian concepts of psychosexual identity and conflict. The role of the psychodynamic play therapist is to identify those meanings and share them with children, or to affirm such meanings, when they are voiced by the child.

Not everyone agreed with this approach, even in the early period of its development. Susan Isaacs, for example, left the mainstream psychoanalytic tradition because she came to believe that children's play had a broader developmental function than reflecting emotional turmoil. Her stance was supported by the very detailed observations she made of children's play, including the years during the 1920s spent running the Malting House School (Drummond, 2000 and Graham, 2009). Susan Isaacs was very clear that her staff should not try to act as analysts for the children. She continued to believe that symbolic and fantasy play could be a release for children's feelings and that children work through deep emotional problems within their play.

Reservations continued about the risks of over-interpreting children's play. Less directive forms of play therapy were developed, which also did not depend on psychoanalytical explanations. Elizabeth Newsom (1992) challenged the rather neat case studies and certainties of interpretation by some therapists. Elizabeth Newsom and her team developed an approach in which children create a 'world' of their own choosing from a sand tray and a wide range of figures, vehicles, buildings and other items. Children are asked gentle, open-ended questions about their completed world.

What does it mean?

Play therapy: an approach to supporting children and helping them with concerns or problems through the medium of their play.

Psychodynamic play therapy: using children's play to resolve conflicts that are believed to arise in childhood and to share that interpretation with the child.

Play, learning and the adult role

An essential feature of play designed and organised by children themselves is that it is often unpredictable; uncertainty is an integral part of many different types of play. Children develop their own rules for some games and sustained pretend play themes often have some predictable characters and scenes. However, these certainties are discussed and, if necessary, renegotiated by the children themselves. The uncertainty of play, left in the control of the children, creates a high level of unease when practitioners are concerned about judgements that will be made about them: that the children have to have 'done something' or 'made progress' in their development.

Over the 1990s, the rhetoric around learning through play, applied a great deal to early years practice, became shaped to ensure that there would be 'play with a purpose', usually very close to what the adults valued as a legitimate purpose. The temptation was then high for early years practitioners to intervene in children's play, to organise resources and direct choices to ensure that children were learning something each day that adults judged as worthwhile. A legitimate question became, 'Whose play is it, anyway?' and 'What makes play genuinely "play-full"?'

There is good reason for optimism about a return to more child-friendly, as well as developmentally sensible, early years practice. A renewed commitment to outdoor learning (page 127) and a greater focus on child-initiated play experiences (page 172) mean that children's understandable frustrations or escape strategies are far less likely to be labelled as 'behaviour problems'.

Adults involved with children across the age range, and not only in early years, need to find a middle course between two extremes: such a low level of involvement that children do not benefit from adults' presence or such a high level of directive involvement that adult actions operate as interference. All practitioners need to consider how they step into the following roles:

- Being a playful companion in play: adults are not simply big children, although children often appreciate a child-like quality in an adult play partner. They want you to look as if you are pleased to be with them, to run around, to help them with a simple board game and hold their tower while they secure the base. Playful companions are co-players who show enthusiasm and are able to add an idea without taking over an enterprise.
- An admiring and interested adult: part of the adult role in play, as in other parts of children's life, is to respond to the calls of 'Look, look'. They want you to watch and be impressed by a bold jump or a tricky manoeuvre on their bike, just as much as to be excited by their large chalk drawing. Jacqui Cousins (2003) reported how four-year-olds wanted to show her the special parts of their nursery or playgroup. I have experienced the same pull on my hand, when I have visited settings, to come and see the snails, to watch this nifty somersault or speedy-run and to crawl into 'our scary jungle'.
- Acting as a facilitator: this role focuses on the adult ability to ease play, to give an appropriate nudge, without taking over the direction of the play or making the children passive recipients of adult ideas and instructions. An adult role as facilitator, or enabler, recognises that children's playful activities happen within a learning environment that is shaped to an extent by the adults. However, children can, and should, have considerable input into the details of their spaces for play. They should certainly have an impact on decisions about possible changes to those spaces.

- Offering a model and sharing play skills: adults can offer a lead in play that still leaves children with choices about how and what to follow. When children lack experience with some play materials, then adults can model ways that these can be used. Useful adult play companions ensure that they know the rules for active games such as 'What's the time, Mr Wolf?' You are a pleasant 'opponent' in games of skill, which means discreetly losing at least sometimes when you play cards or dominoes with under-eights.
- Being the grown-up: the crucial point about having a useful adult play companion is that they can act the grown-up when necessary. Children look towards adults to take a fair and impartial role in their play. You need to be an effective diplomat who can show the skills of problem solving. You are also the safety officer, when necessary and without overreacting.

Play behaviour that concerns adults

The last point above – being the grown-up in play – can require some serious thinking, in order to reach and maintain the right balance. The following broad issues need to be addressed for good early years practice, and are equally important issues for practitioners in school and playwork settings.

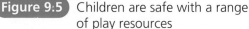 **Figure 9.5** Children are safe with a range of play resources

Risk and play

A sensible adult response to an accident, or series of related incidents, is to have a thorough discussion with everyone involved. Perhaps some changes are needed, or a revisiting of ground rules. However, there are serious disadvantages when adults respond with an absolute ban on play that children regard as enjoyable and legitimate. New 'behaviour problems' are created when children contravene what in their opinion is a stupid rule and adults respond by expending energy to stop and reprimand them.

UNDERSTANDING CHILD DEVELOPMENT 0–8 YEARS

Tim Gill (2007) offers the useful concept of risk aversion: the hopeless task of trying to stop any kind of perceived risk. In play, as in any enterprise shared between adults and children or adolescents, risk management and assessment have to be more constructive.

Children cannot learn to anticipate and consider ordinary risks unless they have been enabled to experience different situations and activities with supportive adults nearby. Children need to encounter manageable risk in play, but they also need to learn practical life skills and how to be safe enough in physical games and adventurous activity (Lindon, 2011a.)

Bans are usually introduced for activities that children like, for example, jumping from the step or balancing on the edge of the flower beds, but which the adults regard as having no intrinsic educational value. Problems that arise during activities that the adults regard as worthwhile are far more likely to be addressed through the behaviour of the individual child. In some school playgrounds, one mistimed kick may get football banned for a long time. But, if children use books to hit one another over the head, there will never be a wholesale removal of books. The children will be reminded firmly that 'Our books are for looking at and reading. We don't use books to hit people.' These contrasting reactions are disrespectful to children and they feel aggrieved about the adult choice. Practitioners have also lost a valuable opportunity to take a problem-solving approach with them.

The basic steps in effective problem solving are to:

- Enable a full discussion about the nature of the problem. Listen to the children: their perspectives and priorities are important too. Be honest when it is you as an adult who feels this is a problem (the children may not think so) and be ready to listen when children tell you, to your surprise perhaps, that there is a problem they want to resolve.
- Generate a range of possible solutions to the problem, rather than jumping at the first proposal. Children often have good ideas and one suggestion may piggyback onto another.
- Decide on the best solution out of those discussed. Talk through how this solution will work. Both children and adults have to be committed; it will not work if adults impose the solution.
- Put the proposed solution into action for long enough to see how it works. Give it time and remind the children, if necessary, of what was agreed.
- Monitor and evaluate the situation and discuss again as necessary. Be pleased with the children; alert them to the fact that 'You had great ideas' or 'We've solved it, haven't we?'

Practitioners, and whole staff teams, need to get into the habit of considering 'can-do possibilities', rather than making swift 'can't-do judgements'. For example:

- 'Why do we say the children can't climb the tree? It is really tempting with the low branches, so how do we ensure it's safe?'

- 'Why do we say to them don't run in the ... Have we noticed whether they actually crash into each other?'

- 'How can we involve and reassure parents about ... and how many parents are actually worried about ...?'

- In your setting, what tends to be the focus of 'We can't let them do that'? What is the impact on children's behaviour of 'don't' prohibitions?

- How could you change your behaviour, welcome some of this play and still be a responsible adult?

- Sensible risk assessment within a play environment (rather than a factory) will most usually reach 'Yes, providing that we ...' and not 'No, you have to stop that'.

What does it mean?

Risk aversion: an unrealistic approach of trying to remove all possible perceived risk, however unlikely.

Risk assessment: a balanced approach to considering genuine hazards, the level of risk they pose and reaching an informed decision about action.

Weapons play

Over the 1970s it became accepted practice in early years provision that imaginative games involving war and pretend weapons were 'aggressive behaviour'. The games were usually stopped on the grounds that children would otherwise develop more generalised violent behaviour. However, the ban steadily extended in many nurseries, and the school playground, to a wide range of good-versus-evil pretend play, including superheroes and play enactments of favourite characters from animated or acted television programmes.

By the late 1990s it had occurred to a number of thoughtful practitioners that years of zero tolerance had achieved little, except to teach children (many of them boys) to be secretive and creative with the truth when confronted with the forbidden pretend weapons (Holland, 2003; Paley, 1984; Rich, 2003). Penny Holland noted how the superheroes looked crestfallen at the regular adult disapproval and turned to alternative behaviours that genuinely disrupted the setting. From my own consultancy experience, I realised how children from military families, and their practitioners, faced the dilemma that guns were the tools of trade for some parents.

Many teams have quietly lifted the ban and found that there is no increase in injuries or mayhem. Key points are:

- Clear acceptance from adults that the play is pretend: the leap of imagination when children create fantasy play.
- Practitioners address, as necessary, that real weapons are dangerous; this is a fact that some older children know because of their neighbourhood.
- Adults who behave as equal play companions are able to contribute generous resources and ideas: a holster for the gun, a base for the superheroes, some play figures and a new twist in a narrative.
- Practitioners address issues of behaviour within the play narrative itself. For example, a child who looks uncertain about the vigorous nature of this 'battle' or the need for ground rules such as, 'not directly in people's faces'.

Some teams rethought their approach to avoid imposing a problem perspective on physically active boys. However, girls are often keen to join this play once they observe that 'superhero-saves-the-world' and 'goodies-versus-baddies' no longer brings adult disapproval. Steve Mynard (2008) provides an engaging account of lively play that evolved from asking boys in his reception class what they would like to do. The choice of knights and castles, with jousting using foam pipes, was a winner for the girls as well as the boys.

Figure 9.6 Children should not be discouraged from participating in superhero play

The Department for Children, Schools and Families (DCSF) published guidance in 2007 specifically aimed at addressing the problems that can arise when lively children, especially the boys, are required to be unrealistically quiet and to stop any games that the adults, often female, deem to be aggressive. The ideas, which were applied within the framework of the English Early Years Foundation Stage, are equally relevant across other countries in the UK.

Rough play?

The issues of 'behaviour problem or just playing?' also arise with play-fighting. A working definition of 'rough play' has sometimes been so elastic that it includes any kind of mutually agreed bumping into each other, play-wrestling and rolling on top of each other in a cosy corner. Anxiety about play-fighting connects with high levels of concern about the risk of accidents in play and also crosses over with pretend play involving superheroes and fantasy weaponry.

> ### What does it mean?
>
> **Play-fighting**: physical games between children, usually boys, including wrestling and close body contact; also called 'rough-and-tumble play'.

However, observational studies of games in the context of the school playground have challenged the accepted wisdom that play-fighting is always aggressive, leads to more serious troubles and therefore should always be stopped. Children and young adolescents definitely want effective adult support when physical contact is not a game and they are being harassed. However, they resent being reprimanded and sanctioned for play behaviour that is regarded by everyone directly involved as 'just a game'.

Nicholas Blurton Jones (1967) became interested in the play behaviour of young children, in particular the rough-and-tumble play that they share with other young mammals. He described 'play-face': a laughing expression, wide enough that children often showed their teeth. He observed that children, who used their play-face, usually stayed together after encounters that he categorised as rough-and-tumble play. This kind of play may include close physical interaction with pulling, pushing and grasping and could be called fighting by watching adults. Children sometimes ran and chased each other in games involving several individuals. They sometimes hit each other with an object or an open hand. This kind of behaviour looked playful, was a voluntary activity and children's physical actions were intended neither to hurt nor to intimidate.

Play researchers like Mechthild Schafer and Peter Smith (1996), David Brown (1994) and Michael Boulton (1994) studied these social clues about rough-and-tumble play by showing children and adults filmed exchanges. Primary school-age children explained how observers should use changing gestures and expressions to identify the point at which a play-fight turned into a bullying incident. The social clues of play-fighting are subtle and it is likely that not all children are able to read them. Dabie Nabuzoka and Peter Smith (1999) studied nine- to eleven-year-olds and found that children with learning disabilities relied on a narrower set of criteria. They were less accurate than their non-disabled peers in distinguishing serious altercations from play-fights, but appeared to be working with a similar set of clues.

A consistent message from this research into play at breaktime in the primary school age is that children and adults broadly agree on how to tell the difference between play-fighting and real fights. The difference is usually that the adults believe a higher proportion of playground fights are real, or generally become aggressive, and so judge that they need to intervene more often than children think is necessary. The breaktime research looks at boys and girls in middle childhood, so it is appropriate to take care in generalising the findings to younger children. However, the messages about possible adult overreaction and the need to listen to children's informed judgements are equally relevant to younger children.

Pause for reflection

The breaktime play researchers view play-fighting as potentially positive, not something that should immediately be stopped by adults. They stress that play-fighting is one way that relationships are formed and friendships gel, especially with boys. It is an enjoyable activity and, in the main, low risk. Early years practitioners need to take note of the research, while fairly making appropriate adjustments for younger children.

It seems likely that play-face is one of the clues that children use to judge whether this current lively activity is a game or not, is pretend or real.

- Watch out for play-face as you observe play in your setting.

- Look for opportunities to explore with children how they tell when something is 'just a game' and when the activity does not feel like play any more.

Undoubtedly, some kinds of play behaviour should catch the attention of responsible adults, because the pattern is significantly out of the ordinary for this age group. Some behaviours may raise the possibility of abusive experiences for this child. Even the most experienced child protection specialists have to be grounded in a sound knowledge of child development and an understanding of patterns of play. You have to balance what you observe against what you know to be ordinary, or out-of-the-ordinary, behaviour for this age, or this individual boy or girl. The same balance applies when you hear concerns expressed by somebody else about the behaviour of a child. Safeguarding is a crucial area of good early years practice; please see Lindon (2012a) for a thorough coverage.

Does television make children aggressive?
A considerable number of studies, many undertaken in the USA, have shown a link between children's watching of violence on television with their own patterns of behaviour. There is not a simple causal link and David Buckingham (1996),

writing from the UK perspective, has emphasised how much children differ in their expressed responses to television programmes that adults are concerned may affect behaviour in a negative way. However, the overall implications of a review of the evidence (Bee and Boyd, 2004) are strong enough for adults to take children's viewing habits seriously.

Experiments with children show at least a short-term effect on children's behaviour of watching programmes with aggressive content. The themes of the programme can be observed in their later free play. Children in the USA who watch more television are almost always found to be more aggressive in their behaviour than their peers who watch television for fewer hours. Careful analysis explains this finding partly by the fact that children who are already more aggressive than the average child choose to watch more television and select the more violent programmes. However, the children who watched the most television within this more aggressive group emerged as the more violent and delinquent adolescents and adults. Another group of studies has looked at changes over time within societies, following the introduction of television or increased ownership of televisions. In small communities that previously did not have television, there have been patterns of an increase in children's aggressive behaviour in play. Levels of violent crime in several countries have been seen to rise dramatically some 15 years after television became widely available to children.

In contrast, Tony Charlton and his team (2002) tracked the introduction of television in 1995 to St Helena, a small island community in the southeast Atlantic. Children's behaviour was monitored before and after their exposure to television, by observation in the playground and survey of the views of parents, teachers and the children themselves. The children did not become more aggressive in their behaviour. If anything, the team observed less playground squabbling and teasing, which they suggest could be linked with the shared experience of the television programmes that fuelled conversations. This project highlights that television works within a sociocultural context. In St Helena, parents watched television with their children and the strong sense of community created an atmosphere in which children's behaviour was strongly influenced by the role models provided by parents and teachers.

Pause for reflection

- Over a period of several weeks, make notes in your setting of any children's games that include themes from television programmes.

- What themes are children using: phrases, characters, physical moves?

- Children's imitation will not always be negative. Identify some of the patterns that could be positive for children's development or behaviour.

- Are the children enjoying themselves? In what ways have you joined in the play?

Resources

- **Bandura, A.** (1986) *Social foundations of thought and action: a social cognitive theory*. Englewood Cliffs NJ: Prentice Hall.
- **Bee, H., Boyd, L.** (2004) *The developing child* (10th edn). Boston: Pearson Education.
- **Blurton Jones, N.** (1967) 'An ethological study of some aspects of social behaviour of children in nursery school', in Morris, D. (edn), *Primate ethology*. London: Weidenfeld and Nicolson.
- **Boulton, M.** (1994) 'Playful and aggressive fighting in the middle school playground', in Blatchford, P. and Sharp, S. (eds), *Breaktime and the school: understanding and changing playground behaviour*. London: Routledge.
- **Brown, D.** (1994) 'Play, the playground and the culture of childhood' in Moyles, J. (ed.), *The excellence of play*. Buckingham: Open University Press.
- **Buckingham, D.** (1996) *Moving images: understanding children's emotional responses to television*. Manchester: Manchester University Press.
- **Charlton, T., Gunter, B., Hannan, A.** (eds) (2002) *Broadcast television effects in a remote community*. New Jersey: Lawrence Erlbaum Associates.
- **Chess, S., Thomson, R.** (1996) *Temperament: theory and practice*. New York: Brunner/Mazel Inc.
- **Cousins, J.** (2003) *Listening to four year olds: how they can help us plan their education and care*. London: National Children's Bureau.
- **Dreikurs, R., Soltz, V.** (1995) *Happy children: a challenge to parents*. Melbourne: Australian Council for Educational Research.
- **Drummond, M.** (2000) 'Susan Isaacs: pioneering work in understanding children's lives', in Hilton, M., and Hirsch, P., *Practical visionaries: women, education and social progress 1790–1930*. London: Longman.
- **Dunn, J.** (1986) 'Children in a family world' in Richards, M., and Light, P., *Children of social worlds: development in a social context*. Cambridge: Polity Press.
- **Dunn, J.** (1993) *Young children's close relationships beyond attachment*. London: Sage.
- **Eisenberg, N.** (1992) *The caring child*. Cambridge M.A: Harvard University Press.
- **Gill, T.** (2007) *No fear: growing up in a risk-averse society*. London: Calouste Gulbenkian. Summary and full book on **www.gulbenkian.org.uk**
- **Graham, P.** (2009) *A biography of Susan Isaacs: a life freeing children's minds*. London: Karnac Books. (I accessed some chapters online with a search of Jean Piaget + Susan Isaacs.)
- **Holland, P.** (2003) *We don't play with guns here: war, weapons and superhero play in the early years*. Maidenhead: Open University Press.
- **Lindon, J.** (2007) *Understanding children and young people: development from 5–18 years*. London: Hodder Arnold.
- **Lindon, J.** (2011a) *Too safe for their own good? Helping children learn about risk and life skills*. London: National Children's Bureau.
- **Lindon, J.** (2011b) *Supporting children's social development*. London: Practical Pre-School Books.

- **Lindon, J.** (2012a) *Safeguarding and child protection 0–8 years* (4th edn). London: Hodder Education.
- **Lindon, J.** (2012d) *Understanding children's behaviour: play, development and learning* (2nd edn). London: Hodder Education.
- **Mynard, S.** (2008) *Making provision for how boys learn best*. **www.teachingexpertise.com/articles/making-provision-for-how-boys-learn-best-3130**
- **Nabuzoka, D., Smith, P.** (1999) 'Distinguishing serious and playful fighting by children with learning disabilities and non-disabled children', *Journal of Child Psychology and Psychiatry and Allied Disciplines*, vol 40, 833–90.
- **Newsom, E.** (1992) 'The barefoot play therapist: adapting skills for a time of need', in Lane, D., and Miller, A. (eds), *Child and adolescent therapy: a handbook*. Buckingham: Open University Press.
- **Paley, V.** (1984) *Boys and girls: superheroes in the doll corner*. Chicago: University of Chicago Press.
- **Paley, V.** (2004) *A child's work: the importance of fantasy play*. Chicago and London: Chicago University Press.
- **Rich, D.** (2003) 'Bang, bang! Gun play and why children need it', *Early Education*, Summer. **www.richlearningopportunities.co.uk**
- **Schafer, M., Smith, P.** (1996) 'Teachers' perceptions of play fighting and real fighting in primary school', *Educational Research* 38(2), 173–181.
- **Slaby, R., Roedell, W., Arezzo, D., Hendrix, K.** (1995) *Early violence prevention: tools for teachers of young children*. Washington DC: National Association for the Education of Young Children.

Children as part of a social and cultural community

Children's early life unfolds within a particular time, place and social context. The sociocultural framework has increasingly influenced the general theoretical approach within early childhood studies. It can, however, still be challenging for researchers, as well as practitioners within early years, to turn that awareness on to their own approach and practice. This chapter aims to offer readers plenty to think about, combining highlights from studies or key concepts with follow-up suggestions.

The main sections to this chapter are:
- Childhood experienced in a time and place
- Early years provision in context
- Children within families and a community.

Childhood experienced in a time and place

The details of childhood are shaped by the cultural traditions that children experience through family life and other settings that are influenced by the predominant culture, such as early years provision and schools. Sociocultural traditions are not fixed forever; they can and do change over time. Some knowledge of recent social history can help an understanding that there can be changes within a culture, as well as differences between cultures that coexist within a diverse society. This section offers a range of ways to step back and reflect on childhood in a time and place.

Raising children to fit society

Beatrice Whiting and Carolyn Edwards (1988) explored how young children start out with potentials that are shaped by adults. The older generation is not necessarily reflective about how they behave; it seems the right way. Whiting and Edwards suggested that cultural forces operate through:
- Adults' expectations of children
- What they give children most opportunity to practise, and
- Which behaviours adults make meaningful for children, in terms of the central cultural goals and values.

Whiting and Edwards concluded from observations in many societies that children were disposed to respond in a nurturant way to what they called 'lap children' (under-one-year-olds), in a dependent way towards adults and in a playful and challenging way to child companions. Young children are not noticeably different across the world; however, their familiar adults set them on a different path. Children may be allowed varied amounts of autonomy in daily life and, depending on whether they are a boy or girl, may be given a different pattern of responsibilities and limitations on the company they keep.

What does it mean?

Socialisation: the process by which children learn what is expected of them, in terms of behaviour and attitudes within their society, or social and cultural group.

Socialisation does not only operate within the family. Joseph Tobin et al. (1989) studied the pattern of interaction between teachers and children in pre-school settings in different countries. How teachers behaved and what they believed children should be doing varied between cultures. Teachers from Japan and the USA were shown a video of a pre-school day in the culture that was unfamiliar to them. Japanese teachers felt that the Americans intervened too much in children's behaviour and conflicts. On the other hand, American teachers thought the Japanese ignored behaviour that should have been tackled directly. The teachers in the USA were behaving so as to promote what they viewed as independence and self-reliance in the children. In contrast, the teachers in Japan stressed cooperation and a sense of interdependence in the group. Both professional groups judged they were active, in the best way, to promote the social learning they valued.

All children experience a process of socialisation and in some societies the intervention of the state is made very clear. Guido Knopp (2002) describes the explicit propaganda and methods used to socialise children in Germany in the 1930s and 40s. Jung Chang (1991) describes three generations of children growing up in China. However, children abandoned by adults still learn through their childhood. Melvin Konner (1991) describes studies of street children around the world forced to fend for themselves. The older children sometimes 'parent' the younger ones and socialise them into the behaviour, including stealing, that will ensure survival. Closer to home, Camila Batmanghelidjh (2006) describes the life experiences of children in the UK who are likely to be labelled as 'feral', bringing home the cost they pay in order to survive without positive socialisation by the adults who should have taken responsibility for their well being.

Like cultural tradition, socialisation is not something that only happens to other people. Until you reflect, it may be harder to spot the main themes within your own culture; it just seems like 'normal life'. Look back also at page 198 for the description of two societies given by Maybin and Woodhead (2003).

Any services for children will reflect in obvious, or more subtle, ways what it is that is valued by society. When several cultures coexist within a community then such differences become more apparent. For example:

- The behaviour valued in one culture as 'courtesy' (not pressing one's opinion, or disagreeing with a teacher) may be judged as 'passivity' and 'low self-confidence' within another culture.

- Ground rules about gesture and other forms of non-verbal communication can vary considerably. In some cultures, children are taught not to look an adult in the eye when being reprimanded. In a diverse community, children can meet an adult who interprets lack of eye contact as 'shifty' and requests, 'Look at me properly when I'm talking with you!'

In the best interests of children?

Margaret Humphreys (1994) documented the emigrations from UK residential children's homes to North America and Australia, which only finally stopped in 1967. This mass movement of children was purportedly to provide them with a better life and was viewed as in their best interests. Yet the children's welfare and emotional well being were strikingly ignored. There was no follow-up of the children, many of whom experienced harsh, sometimes abusive, conditions. Most of the children were given no information about themselves, such as their birth certificates. Some were told the blatant lie that their parent(s) had died, and spent much of their adult life believing they were orphans.

By 2009 the scandal of this child migration scheme had become more public, as surviving 'migrants', some of whom are now elderly, pressed for some type of compensation. Attitudes towards children and their well being have changed. But it would be an unwise practitioner who pronounced that children's well being would never be so ignored again.

Dan Kindlon and Michael Thompson (1999) describe their concern for the boys and male adolescents referred to them by parents or schools. They argue that young males are not helped towards emotional literacy in the USA, or Western culture in general. Kindlon and Thompson also express serious concern about families or schools that want to medicate ordinary boyish exuberance, because it is inconvenient for adults. Such concerns are expressed in the UK as part of the growing concern that a very sedentary, adult-dominated view of early learning risks labelling normal, lively play as 'behaviour problems'. This adult problem behaviour seems to have exerted an especially disruptive effect on boys.

Since the publication of the first edition of this book in 2005, there has been a significant development in reflective practice about boys and their experiences during early childhood. Changes are best summed up by saying that 'boy-friendly practice' is actually a return to good early years practice for all young children: generous time for self-chosen play, adult respect for outdoor learning and recognition that good early years practice is led by a positive home-like model (Lindon, 2012b). Good primary school practice finds ways to guide the more structured approach to learning and a thoughtful response to children's behaviour (Lindon, 2012d).

Pause for reflection

For a period of two weeks, cut out any news item or article about children in your regular newspaper. If you can do this activity with colleagues, you could cover several newspapers and magazines. Without ending up with a huge project, follow up a few stories online, for related features or any commentary.

- What range of images do you find?

- Are children portrayed as innocents in need of protection: 'No child is safe any more'? Are they described as instruments of 'pester power' to get their parents to buy a brand of snacks, clothing or a 'must-have' toy?

- What has made these children newsworthy? Do they have to be extraordinary: tragic 'little angels' battling illness, or 'terror tots', whose outrageous behaviour has led to exclusion from nursery?

- What do choice of material and language tell you about the images of children and childhood promoted within UK society?

- Imagine these reports were your only source of information about childhood. What beliefs could you develop about children in UK society today?

Never enough time?

It seems that time pressure is a feature of current childhood experience in the UK. The concept of 'quality time' underpins much of the advice of 'make the most of your time' in advice to parents. The original meaning was that mothers did not have to be constantly available to ensure their children's well being: a challenge to John Bowlby's influential views (page 83). The original idea envisaged generous amounts of attention. The reworking of quality time, in some material aimed at parents, has become that of 'fitting in' children for very short amounts of time.

What does it mean?

Quality time: the concept that children thrive with periods of full attention and do not require the continuous presence of their main parent/carer.

- Take a look at the range of childcare advice books for parents. How many titles imply that children have to be squeezed between other competing priorities?

- Make a brief survey of parenting magazines, or newspaper features written about family life. What are the messages, perhaps also amid sound advice?

- Another option is to dip into parent chatrooms on the internet and get a sense of how time constraints are felt to be a serious issue in these postings.

Undoubtedly, many families in the UK lead complex lives, in which management of priorities and limited family time are a serious issue. However, it does not help the well being of children if a social atmosphere develops that simply accepts that nowadays no parent has enough time. Sylvia Ann Hewlett (1993) described what I felt to be a chilling symbol of how a well-known publisher of greetings cards in the USA had published a range for absent parents, with messages that included 'I wish I were there to tuck you in.' I have not seen this type of card in the UK. Yet there are broad sources of concern, when children's best interests can seem to be much further down the list of priorities than a focus on what works well for adults.

Early years practitioners need to take a robust approach to managing time for the well being of children. A responsible outlook means dealing with inappropriate pressures to complete lists of adult-led activities within today, as well as child-unfriendly interpretations about 'getting children ready' for the next stage. Jacqui Cousins (2003) showed through her observations that many four-year-olds had recognised that life was a rush and that adults kept saying 'hurry up'. In some of the saddest examples, young children had stopped playing with favourite resources in nursery, because there was never enough time. Jacqui Cousins quotes one four-year-old's firm statement that, when you are enthused, 'time's as long as it takes'.

Jacqui Cousins made most of her observations during the 1990s. There are no grounds for complacency, but there is reason to be optimistic that a growing number of practitioners and teams have turned around their practice. There have been many sources supporting changes and one has been enthusiasm in the UK about the approach taken by the early years centres of Reggio Emilia, in northern Italy. Linda Thornton and Pat Brunton (2009) describe how the Reggio approach can constructively challenge early years practice and bring a more flexible approach to using time, as well as space(s) and following young children's interests.

Early years provision in context

Services exist within a social and cultural framework. Early years practitioners are familiar with the pattern within their own society and, without any comparison point, can assume that these services are the norm.

An artificial division between 'care' and 'education'

The four nations that make up the UK have increasingly determined the details of their own early years services. However, all share a common history of division between services known as 'childcare' and 'early education' (Lindon, 2006). Some other European countries, notably in Scandinavia, chose to create a coherent, publicly funded early years service, with a single early years profession. This approach takes the view that provision is a public service: a contribution to raising the next generation, needed by everyone in society. In contrast, in the UK a sequence of initiatives has been laid over the top of a continued artificial distinction between 'care' and 'education'. The different types of combined centres have often been very positive in their own context. However, centre managers continue to have to negotiate their way around the different qualification, pay structure and perceived status of the different professions involved with under-fives.

The issues raised about this point in the first edition of this book continue to be relevant now. Public statements from politicians still happily skip between the terminology of 'care' or 'early education'. Part-time early years provision is even claimed to operate as flexible childcare for working parents. There is no way that the hours in question cover an adult working day, without additional provision. On the other hand, sweeping claims are made about the significant impact of any type of 'early education' on young children's later achievements. Research studies, like the Effective Provision of Pre-School Education, focused on children who were at least two years of age and raised some serious issues about how practitioners behaved towards the children. Neither the EPPE study nor any other reputable study has given the green light to just any type of early years provision.

What about the children?

Peter Moss and Pat Petrie (2002) track how the prevailing view of childhood works to shape services for children and their families. One chapter sums up the link from adult attitudes to children's direct experience with the title of, 'Children – who do we think they are?' Peter Moss and Pat Petrie are based at the Thomas Coram Research Unit in London, where the team undertook a major rethink of approach in the late 1970s and early 80s. They challenged the predominant way of thinking about early years and childcare that the unit had shared up to that point. The team refocused on family, more than childcare or maternal employment as separate topics for study.

Over the first decade of the 21st century, initiatives for the development of early years provision have often been required to be flexible, linked explicitly with the perceived needs of parents and the great diversity of adult working hours. However, careful consideration of the needs of young children has raised awkward questions about the impact on young children. Variable and perhaps also unpredictable patterns of attendance at their early years provision are very likely to disrupt children's ability to settle, to make friends and to benefit from the opportunities in good-quality early years provision. Richard Reeves (2004) poses the awkward question of whether the 21st-century development of childcare in the UK has predominantly served a political agenda around employment. He suggests that, regardless of the official rhetoric, the result has been an attempt to create 'economy-friendly families', rather than a social atmosphere that is more friendly to parents and children.

Pause for reflection

Sue Miller and Kay Sambell (2003) share the experience of their Early Childhood Studies team working to put childhood and services in context. The team use a range of methods: visits, outside speakers, visual material (photos and videos) and students' own experience on which to reflect. Mel Gibson's chapter, entitled 'I'd no idea there was so much going on under the surface', sums up the need to step back from 'that's just normal life'.

Try this activity, modified from one used at the University of Northumbria.

- Collect a series of photographs of the entrance area for settings available for children: nurseries or pre-schools but also the local library and health clinic. Of course, ask permission before using your camera, even if there are no children in focus at the time.

- Consider the images, both on your own and with colleagues. What messages does each layout give to children as they come into this setting or part of the building? Is it 'We're pleased to welcome children' or 'We're a place for grown-ups'? Is it 'Be lively and please touch' or 'Quiet, ask before you take'?

- What messages could the environment give to parents and other carers who accompany the children?

I was provoked to think about the entrance area of a nursery, when I was consulting a few years ago with Community Playthings, as they developed their layout for furniture and storage that would provide a welcome entrance. The personal feel relates not only to the 'welcome' as families walk in; it is the 'goodbye' area as well. The entrance area can tell children, 'We're pleased to see you again, this is your nursery.' But it also gives the message of, 'See you again soon. We will keep you in mind while you are gone. You still have a place here.' **www.communityplaythings.co.uk**.

Partnership with parents

Good practice in early years, school and out-of-school services fully incorporates partnership with parents. However, this phrase does not carry the same meaning whenever it is used. The different working definitions make it difficult, probably impossible, to compare research studies because 'partnership' can mean very different activities, as well as underlying assumptions.

Figure 10.1 Raising children is a shared enterprise with families

This problem of definition and meaning is not new. Gillian Pugh et al. (1994) provide an overview of the tremendous variety of support programmes and underlying attitudes within that decade. In Lindon (2009) I offer an overview of the current diversity and good practice that sit under the very broad umbrella of 'partnership with parents'. A great deal is sometimes claimed for specific programmes designed to help parents. However, Helen Barrett's (2003) review shows how working definitions are so varied, and that it is a serious challenge to compare studies of parenting programmes and evaluate their effectiveness. The roots of different views of partnership lie partly in the social history of this development of professional practice.

It will be clear from this section that I value taking a perspective from social history. I have observed that reflective practice is supported by a willingness to consider 'How did we get here?'

- The concept of partnership has grown from several distinct strands. The divergence explains how open discussion about practice can become confused.

- Please reflect on each strand in turn and make the connections with your own practice. What does 'partnership' mean to you and your team?

- Can you recognise the strand of social history in partnership that has most affected the part of early years services familiar to you?

Parents need to be involved to help children

Successful early years intervention programmes, especially in the USA from the 1960s, involved parents in the programme directly through group work or regular communication about children's learning. These programmes were designed to counteract the effects of social disadvantage and parent involvement was crucial. Over a similar period, professionals in social work and social psychiatry concluded that problems experienced by children could not be understood or improved in isolation from their family.

This approach led to developments of family therapy and settings such as family centres, where parents and children attended together as a unit. The community focus developed significantly in the 1970s through centres that resolved the issues of a multi-disciplinary team and took a persistent line that relationships were forged with families. This type of centre has continued to grow, given different names depending on the current government initiative. National initiatives such as Sure Start have aimed to bring services together in a more integrated way through a substantial network of children's centres.

Pause for reflection

- The EPPE project found that the most effective early years settings shared their educational aims with parents. But in order to share the 'what and how' of good early years practice, you need to be clear and consistent within the team about your methods and the reasons why they are developmentally appropriate.

- Look back over page 152 about early literacy, or the importance of the positive disposition to learn, on page 101. How could you share those important aims and approaches with parents?

- Look at Dorothy Caddell (2001) whose practical ideas about communication with parents provide food for thought. Her approach is also a reminder of how the professional atmosphere about families has shifted to the assumption that, of course, you talk with parents about your early years approach in general and their children in particular.

Figure 10.2 The most effective early years settings shared their educational aims with parents

Sharing skills with parents to help children

Throughout the 1970s some professional teams rethought the medical model, in which it was usual for children to attend specialist sessions and their parent to have to wait outside the room. The Hester Adrian Centre in Manchester and the Wolfson Clinic in London provide two examples of teams that redesigned their programme and shared direct suggestions for parents of activities to do with their children between sessions. Schemes such as the Portage programme and Home-Start went one step further, by visiting families in their own home. The key assumption underlying this development was that parents were motivated and competent to help their own children. Local speech and language teams also moved towards giving direct advice to parents. The shift towards involving adults who spent significant time with the child also extended to sharing practical suggestions with early years practitioners.

Make the connection with… **The medical model of disability**

Prevailing attitudes can change over time. For instance, in the 1980s the dominant approach to disabled children and their families was to focus on disability in medical terms: diagnosis, treatment and management of the condition when, as often, no cure was possible. Challenge to the medical model came from disabled adults, who shared their childhood memories, and parents, who objected to an approach that treated their disabled sons and daughters as 'cases' rather than children.

An alternative social model of disability was promoted, which focused on children first, then disability. This model also highlights social conditions that can cause children to be disabled unnecessarily by circumstances. Examples would include difficult physical access to a play area, or a rule that no medicine can be given by school staff, when normal life for some children requires regular medication.

The social model approach does not deny the value of appropriate medical interventions, but stresses that children's life should not be driven by the disability label they are given, or by a regime of treatment. For more information see Lindon (2012b) or Dickins and Denziloe (2003).

Direct advice and leaflets for parents are so usual now that it is easy to forget that many professionals, not only in the medical sphere, resisted sharing skills or key ideas. A key argument was that 'just' parents would fail to understand and would disrupt the professional input out of ignorance. It is now normal life to see primary school children with their book folders. Yet innovations such as the Haringey Project in London, during the late 1970s, faced strong resistance from many teachers. They were convinced that parents would disturb the reading process as taught within school.

Many parents are already involved with their children

Barbara Tizard (1981) led a research project into parent involvement in the second half of the 1970s. The report offered constructive criticism that the nursery staff often held an implicit one-way model of parent involvement. They wished to influence parents' behaviour, because they believed some changes would benefit the children educationally. However, it was rare for staff to consider that their practice could, maybe should, change as the result of input from families.

The insights from this research continue to be equally relevant now (Lindon, 2009c). Barbara Tizard and her team reported that many parents of children in the 1970s nursery and infant classes were doing much more with their children at home than the teachers believed. The EPPE team, working nearly a quarter of a century later, concluded that, in some early years settings, parents engaged in as much, if not more, sustained shared thinking with their children at home as practitioners undertook within the setting. The EPPE team's findings confirmed that parents, who enjoyed activities such as reading books with their children at home, made a difference to their children's progress. Parents were already involved in these ways with their children; they did not need practitioners to tell them to do so.

There is further support for the proposal that some early years and school practitioners still underestimate how much is happening at home. Liz Brooker (2002) turned researcher, after her time as a reception class teacher, to track children through their reception year in a London school. Brooker documents that the reception team's open communication system did not enable all parents to access them in an equal way. The consequence was that the practitioners were unaware of how much some parents supported learning in their own way at home, and also the serious reservations about the extent of their children's learning in reception. A lack of shared fluent language was an additional factor for the team in communication with some of the local Bangladeshi families.

Make the connection with... **Your beliefs about partnership**

Barbara Tizard et al. (1981) reported that most parents were very interested in their own children and wanted to discuss their progress. However, practitioners sometimes decided parents were uninterested, because they chose not to participate in the form of involvement offered by the staff.

- Partnership in action is still sometimes defined from practitioners' perspective. I encounter teams who judge that parents as a whole are 'uninterested' because they have not turned up for an event. Or the judgement is made that 'partnership doesn't work' because not enough parents have agreed to the particular version of parent involvement that is on offer here.

Reflect on your own practice, even if you feel you avoid the extremes of one-way partnership.

Parents as people with rights and responsibilities

An alternative perspective emerged from growing pressure that parents had a right to be involved and consulted, since they were users of a public service, whether or not they actually paid for the provision. A parallel development unfolded about parents' right to information about their own children and easy access to their records. This theme of consumer, or service user, rights has continued against a social background of greater accountability in any service.

Parents with skills and experience to offer

A challenge has grown to the view that professionals, in early years or other children's services, were the people with expertise and parents had nothing special to offer; they were 'just parents'. The playgroup movement developed in the 1960s in response to insufficient sessional nursery provision. Leaders took what was then a radical approach in involving parents, mainly mothers, in the daily running and sometimes the management of the playgroup.

Schools had long acknowledged parents' skills through Parent Teacher Associations (PTA). But the traditional PTA role was restricted to fund-raising and did not offer direct involvement in educational decisions. By the 1980s some nurseries and primary schools had developed more of the playgroup approach to involvement, encouraging parents to help out, often with specific activities or hearing children read.

- Gather some different resources aimed at parents. Does the approach show respect for family life? Was it really a compliment for parents to be told 'You are your child's first teacher'? Now the more usual phrase is 'your child's first and continuing educator'. Is that an improvement?

- Be observant about the approach shown through features in early years magazines. Is partnership presented as a relationship of equals? When partnership runs through a tough period, which partner is seen to be the main problem?

Learning through play

Early years practice in the UK is very influenced by the perspective that children learn through play. Historical and cross-cultural data show that all children play unless they experience persistently restrictive, depriving or abusive circumstances (Lindon, 2001). However, the phrase 'learning through play' has come to have a particular meaning for early years provision.

The focus on the value of spontaneous play grew in Western Europe from the 1930s to become established by about the 1970s. The origins are often traced to the forms of early education pioneered by Frederich Froebel and Maria Montessori. But their approaches took a very broad view of playful activities and both placed a high value on children learning life skills through involvement in daily routines, not only by more recognisable play materials.

Peter Smith (1994) describes how spontaneous play came to be promoted as an essential support to children's early learning. The Plowden Report in 1967 was probably the first official statement, but Peter Smith suggests three main strands had supported the development of what he calls the 'play ethos':

Figure 10.3 The judgement for any experience is whether the children look engaged

- Theoretical perspectives from the psychoanalytic tradition (page 23) focused on play as vital for children to express their emotions and resolve what were seen to be inevitable conflicts of childhood.
- Studies from evolutionary biology (page 18) proposed that playing was an important part of how all young mammals learn skills during their years of immaturity.
- Socio-economic changes within Western Europe, along with smaller families, led to a separation of work from home life. Children largely ceased to contribute to the family income and a commercial toy industry promoted a focus on play with bought playthings.

What does it mean?

Play ethos: an approach that stresses the crucial importance of children's play within their development.

There is every reason to argue that young children can learn a great deal through relaxed play opportunities within an accessible learning environment. But the play ethos led to some adult-determined interpretations of learning through play. Professional discussion from the 1970s and 80s included ever-increasing use of phrases such as 'play with a purpose', 'well planned play' and 'structured play'. Reflective practitioners had to ask 'Whose purpose and whose structure?' In many cases the answer is not that of the children. The problem was exacerbated when practitioners accepted a working definition of 'planning' that directed them towards adult-planned and initiated activities, designed to deliver specific educational outcomes and products.

Elizabeth Wood and Jane Attfield (1996) focus on the situation that can be created when adults become invested in the value of play for their own professional purposes. The authors explain their goal of linking play closely to the task of teaching as a direct response to the concerns of some writers, who argued that children's play was sometimes limited or unchallenging in terms of learning. They raised the problems that follow, for children as well as adults, when inflated claims are made for play. Like Peter Smith (1994), Wood and Attfield are very positive about play, but they challenge the validity of some attempts to define 'quality' in play and the risks when adults seize control to make play 'educationally' worthwhile. I share the concern. When practitioners feel justified in evaluating the quality of play, without much reference to children's views, it is a short step to deciding that children's self-chosen play is irrelevant to the adult's agenda.

The potential problems highlighted by Wood and Attfield, and by Smith, have been accentuated since the mid-1990s. However, there is good reason for optimism about the ownership of play being given back to young children. The EPPE research emphasised child-initiated experiences and how practitioners need to come alongside, not take over, children's play and conversations. Observation-led planning, implemented with understanding, creates a flexible approach in which children's interests and play choices make a noticeable difference to what happens tomorrow and next week.

Play, as adults sometimes define it, is not the sum total of children's activity and they can be very interested and motivated to have an active role in how the domestic routines of their early years provision setting is run day by day (Lindon, 2011, 2006). They learn a great deal from helping out, a point made by Margaret Henry (1996) and supported by informal observations in home settings. Henry argued that the appropriate model for young children should be what works well in a family home and not a model from school, slightly adjusted. Children want and need relaxed time to spend with adults. An exclusive learning through play approach can reduce the opportunities for children to learn from direct coaching from adults; see, for example, the pleasure in the role of novice described by Margaret Donaldson (page 182) and apprenticeship in thinking from Barbara Rogoff (page 182).

The role of the early years practitioner

The innovatory work of pioneers like Margaret McMillan was a deliberate reaction against rigid school methods in the early 20th century. Difficulties have arisen throughout the last years of the 20th century and the early 21st century precisely because the job of early years provision has been seen increasingly to be that of preparing children for school. An exploration of the meaning for adults of 'learning through play' raises the important question of whether some approaches to early years practice become disrespectful towards children's play.

Take another **perspective**

- Much of the confusion about how best to support young learning arises from the whole framework created by 'pre-school'. Is primary school ever described as 'post-nursery'? What does that tell you?

- Children's experiences are further disrupted if there is no challenge to the erroneous assumption that 'proper learning' only starts with a structured approach, led by an adult in a school classroom.

A problem of words also arises because of the different professions involved in early years provision. It can be a challenge to find a term that everyone will accept. I am comfortable to use the term 'practitioner' to refer to all adults involved in supporting children's learning. However, some professionals with a teaching background object to the term. The overall term of 'educator' is more acceptable to some people. European countries that have established a coherent early years provision have often established a new term, to overcome the problems.

Whatever you call the early years workforce as a group of individuals, the words 'teach' and 'teaching' are often used to describe adults' behaviour. In the absence of more practical description, some early years practitioners assume they should behave close to their primary school memories of what a 'teacher' does. This classroom model includes greater adult direction of children's activities, including a balance towards sit-down, indoor activities, often with whole groups of children, regardless of their personal interests

What does it mean?

Pedagogy: a holistic approach to supporting children in learning, including the behaviour of practitioners and the learning environment they create.

However, good nursery-trained teachers do not behave like primary school teachers. In the Effective Provision of Pre-school Education research, the more effective early years settings were led by a nursery teacher who created a genuinely play-based experience of learning, following the threads of children's current interests. The research findings challenge the kind of top-down model that makes early years practitioners think they should copy school methods.

More detailed observations were made of 12 effective settings from the main EPPE study (Siraj-Blatchford et al., 2002). Early years practitioners who were trained nursery teachers were observed to undertake the most effective interactions with children, with greater amounts of sustained shared thinking. Non-teacher-trained practitioners were most effective when working under the guidance of trained teachers. The possible dynamic here, although not one described specifically in the report, is that the teacher-trained practitioners were able not only to show colleagues a supportive style of interaction, but also showed by example how good 'teachers' behave with younger children.

Janet Moyles et al. (2002) report on the SPEEL research (Study of Pedagogical Effectiveness in Early Learning), which is a project that also evolved from the EPPE research. This team explored the notion that teaching in the early years is qualitatively different from the rest of the educational system. Genuinely helpful adults need to share control with young children and avoid following an adult-determined plan. This approach can feel difficult if practitioners do not trust learning through open-ended play and at the child's pace. Practitioners can also feel they are 'not doing much' unless they are directive by words or action.

In the SPEEL project, early years practitioners were asked to produce a video showing what they believed to be effective adult behaviour to support the children's learning within their own practice. Despite their expressed commitment to learning through play, few practitioners chose to record play situations. Far more often, they selected literacy and numeracy sessions. The explanation seemed to be that, in these sessions, practitioners judged they were more active in advancing children's learning. A fair interpretation seems to be that they felt they were behaving like a teacher, and in England teams have felt under particular pressure to deliver literacy goals.

The focus on a suitable early years learning environment has been part of the shift away from a primary school model. Thoughtful practitioners look to provide opportunities, a range of possibilities offered by generous stores of play materials, with time for play to be developed by children themselves. Practitioners remain active and there are significant supports for young children but, in some ways, there is a return to the first traditions of UK nursery school practice, including a high value for the outdoors. Specific approaches to early learning, such as Montessori and High/Scope have always shown a strong commitment to thoughtful layout and resources that children can choose, organise and later return. The Steiner Waldorf approach has been very strong on the rhythm of the days and seasons, in supporting practical life skills and authentic experiences for children.

During the 1990s extensive interest in the Reggio Emilia early years centres in northern Italy (Thornton and Brunton, 2009) also encouraged serious thought about space, use of space and a focus on generous resources rather than adult-led, pre-planned activities. Early years support teams from some local authorities have produced well-illustrated support materials that show a welcoming learning environment especially for under-threes (Hope, 2007) and for three- to five-year-olds (LEARN, 2002).

Figure 10.4 What are young children enabled to learn?

Children within families and a community

This section covers key concepts around recognition that children are active learners within their own family or early years provision, and young citizens of their local community.

Children have a viewpoint and expertise

Berry Mayall (1994, 2002) challenged the regular statement that early years settings in the UK were 'child-centred'. She takes the thought-provoking view that even a firm statement about educational philosophy does not necessarily lead to practice that is genuinely attuned to children's needs. Mayall argued from her observations in early years settings that adult priorities were often most dominant. Yet the claim to be 'child-centred' meant that children whose behaviour was less than easy to handle could be labelled as 'problems'. Practitioners denied their actions could be responsible, because the setting was child-centred: a circular argument.

It is a respectful approach to recognise that the children have their own perspective on events. The narrative approach in study of children has been one way to document children's views and understanding. The work of Vivian Gussin Paley (2004) and of Jacqui Cousins (2003) has highlighted that children have considered opinions and are happy to express them to adults who show genuine interest.

The awareness shown by Jacqui Cousins's four-year-olds sharpens through their experience in primary school. Wendy Titman (1992, 1994) showed that children had valuable expertise about the quality of their school grounds and good ideas about resolving problems. She also demonstrated that children made sense of adult priorities through rules about activities such as keeping off the grass. Children concluded that protecting this part of the grounds was more important to the school than their play and well being. When the school grounds were poorly maintained, children assumed that the adults did not care much about them.

Consultation methods with children have been developed in recognition that even very young children have views, insights and preferences and that adults should listen. Alison Clark and Peter Moss (2001) describe the Mosaic method, which used practical techniques to welcome and hear children's views about their early years provision. Direct observation by adults enabled the gathering of 'nursery stories' that were then considered in an open-ended way. However, the technique of 'child conferencing' brought in short interviews with children, which could definitely happen on the move. Cameras were given to the children so they could take photos of anything that was 'important' to them in the centre. Individual children then led the adult on a tour of the nursery, both indoors and outside. Children were the experts in what was to be shown and why.

The Mosaic approach enabled a visual and very personal mapping of the nursery through all the material gathered, with the full involvement of the children. Some of the techniques have been used in other projects and the resulting food for adult thought has often been as important for improving practice as children's specific comments and personal observations. A significant point for practice is that consultation with children should not be seen as a one-off project. On the contrary, listening to children and genuine consultation should be part of daily life (Early Childhood Unit, 2004) and what children say should make a difference (Miller, 1996). Consultation with children is sometimes described as 'giving children a voice'. As Priscilla Alderson (2000) points out, children already have a voice; the problem is whether adults listen. She gives many examples of how children want to be involved and consulted and can, with information, partake in even complicated medical decisions that affect them

Several projects have shown the power of visual methods such as using happy and sad faces, or enabling children to take photos and then talk about why this image is important or special to them. Linda Kinney and Jerry McCabe (2000) show in their project at Stirling that young children make perceptive and possibly uncomfortable comments. For instance, a nursery team wanted to hear children's views about where they thought an adult was needed in the indoor and outdoor spaces. Children were given play figures and a paper diagram of the nursery. However, the children did not stop at placing the play figures; they named them and explained why individual practitioners would be better in one area than another. The report describes that the nursery team, although rather taken aback by constructive feedback about their strengths and personal weak spots from such young children, were prepared to learn. The comments were discussed in staff development sessions.

Make the connection with… **How would you feel if …**

It is important that consultation is genuine. How do you feel as an adult if you spend your time expressing your views (spoken or written) and then discover that the decision was already made, or nobody appears to have taken account of your preferences?

Young children may say, 'You could have asked us,' if you go ahead without having a conversation with them. But they are really cross if they say, 'We told you the bush was really important; it's a special place, where we play the Monster Game. So why did you cut it down?'

There has been an increased focus on consultation with children and adolescents (Lindon, 2007) and any setting with a community atmosphere takes this responsibility seriously. But teams are also clear that any involvement of the younger members of this community must be a genuine consultation. Responsible practitioners are honest about the nature of this current discussion and it helps to be straightforward about the difference between:

- This is an open decision for you to make and what you prefer is what will happen. The only practical issue in a group can be when children split into distinct sub-groups with different priorities.

- Within these limits, what you prefer is what will happen. Adults have to be honest at the outset about boundaries set by money, non-negotiable ground rules, time, and so on.
- The adults have had to make a shortlist because ... These are the options, now your choice will prevail.
- We have made this decision, for this reason. This conversation is for you to hear (maybe be the first to be told) and understand what and why.

Equality practice for early childhood

Early years services operate within society and good practice includes an active approach to equality: ensuring that all families are welcome and that issues are promptly addressed that could limit inclusion. A view of holistic equality practice, along with legislation, has encompassed social or cultural grouping, ethnic group and linguistic background, faith, gender, sexual orientation and disability. In some neighbourhoods, it may be especially important to address attitudes towards Gypsy/Traveller communities, refugee families or children who are distressed because a parent or other family member is currently in prison.

The challenge of reflective practice on equality is to balance active respect with resolving the dilemmas that can arise when a family's strongly felt belief or preference is not easily compatible with the core values of the provision (Lindon, 2012b). Partnership with parents does not override the need to address the situation, if children express family attitudes that are offensive to other children and parents, living locally or further away. Practitioner concern should be triggered, whatever the ethnic group or faith of the family whose views are disdainful of other people, solely on the basis of their group identity.

Young children are in the process of developing their attitudes, so early years practitioners are expected to be active in the following ways, within the realistic limits of their own early years provision.
- Promoting an active welcome for all children and families who are in contact with the service, and ensuring that resources and experiences reflect their family life, as well as extending understanding.
- Ensuring that none of your procedures or policies places any family at a disadvantage or work to exclude them, even if you are sure that was never your intention.
- Fostering respect and mutual understanding between children and families who see themselves as different from each other, helping them to find common ground. Such respect is a two-way process; it is not good practice to assume that offensive attitudes or action only emerge from one side.

Words matter, but it does not help good practice if early years practitioners get so anxious about using the 'wrong' words that useful actions are blocked by anxiety. All strands to anti-discriminatory practice need to find a balance between a rejection of persistent inequalities in UK society, and the strategies that are most likely to bring about change in attitudes and behaviour of individual adults.

Children are not born prejudiced or bigoted, but they are enthusiastic learners and they imitate the words and actions of familiar adults and other children. Adult divisions can then be reflected in what children say, as well as their beliefs about groups in society and their choice of play companions. Parents and early years practitioners may prefer to underestimate the extent that even three- and four-year-olds hear and imitate negative attitudes that are rife in their local neighbourhood. Research in the USA from the 1940s and in the UK from the 1960s established specifically that young children did notice ethnic group differences, drawn to their attention by skin colour (Milner, 1983). It was a separate step, although sometimes a swift one, to place social meaning on those differences.

It is important to realise that children do not need such apparently obvious group markers to learn social distinctions that adults judge to be significant. A significant part of anti-discriminatory practice in Northern Ireland involves anti-sectarianism. Similar issues also arise in some cities in Scotland, where the depth of sectarianism can shock outsiders. Paul Connolly et al. (2002) have shown that young children are aware of and begin to understand the importance of the different symbols that relate to Catholic and Protestant groups in Northern Ireland, such as flags, football teams and symbolic annual events like marches. They observed a few three-year-olds who were already aware of distinctions between the religious and social groups. But by five years of age there was a high awareness of the impact of sectarianism. Apart from children's likely increased understanding as a result of age, most children in Northern Ireland attend primary schools with a clear religious affiliation. There are few integrated schools in the province.

The traditions of anti-discriminatory practice for gender and disability have emerged along different paths from awareness of ethnic group or faith differences (Lindon, 2012b). Concern about gender equality was strongly shaped by feminist concerns about discrimination against women and girls. The cycle has turned towards more even-handedness with a concern about what can happen to boys, especially in a female-dominated environment such as early years. Disability awareness emerged through a challenge to the medical model (page 225) and an inclusive approach requires thinking of children as individuals, who live with their disability or chronic illness.

Young children start by finding differences of interest, or not, but they do not automatically believe that being different is wrong or less acceptable. Young children extend their general knowledge about people who seem to be different from them. But over the same period of time, they are also building their own sense of identity. Children younger than four or five years of age view the world from their personal perspective outwards into what they recognise as the broader social network for themselves and their family. All children need a positive sense of themselves, of personal identity and a secure sense of self-worth, before they can understand the sources of identity of others.

Make the connection with... **The zone of proximal development**

Each of the early years guidance documents across the UK sets out an aim that children are enabled to develop a positive outlook on their own cultural background, as well as begin to understand backgrounds other than their own. A sound understanding of child development leads to those realistic words 'begin to …'.

Anti-bias practice in the early years is in the process of sowing seeds, not harvesting the entire crop. You want to stretch children's understanding a bit beyond their own backyard, and always reflect on what a young child is likely to understand from any experiences or adult-led activities.

Children aged three, four and five years are at the beginning of a learning journey. It can be valuable for adults to reflect on: "How did I learn about my own culture?' and 'What confused me about unfamiliar faiths when I was a young child?'

Reflect on what and how much you are trying to do in this area of learning. In what ways can children connect with planned activities? Think about the zone of proximal development (page 174).

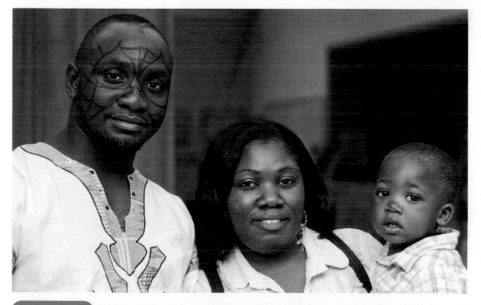

Figure 10.5 Shared family experiences matter a great deal to children

Vulnerability and resilience

Families live within a broader society and the pattern of their lives is affected by social and financial circumstances Children's behaviour and their development are not changed directly by social class or poverty. Children are affected by the attitudes, experiences and stresses that reach them through their parents, and other important adults in their lives. Urie Bronfenbrenner's ecological approach pointed to these complex patterns of cause and effect within the macrosystem (page 43).

- Mothers may have less easy access to prenatal care, which can increase the health risks to mother and child. Very poor families may live in areas that are realistically dangerous, so the children's play opportunities and experiences are restricted.
- Families with low financial resources are more likely to live in deprived areas with fewer services. When both parents have no option but to work, they may have to take poor-quality childcare, because that is the only local option.
- Financial and other stress in the family may mean that parents have less time to play and talk with their children. They may turn to more authoritarian methods of child rearing out of exhaustion. This feature of family life can, of course, arise in time-poor but money-rich families.

All these features combine to make for more negative outcomes for children's development. The Sure Start national programme in England was developed in recognition that alleviating the effects of poverty and social disadvantage on children required a network of initiatives.

After many studies of the impact of poverty and social deprivation, researchers in the 1980s became interested in those children who, against all the odds, emerged to do well in adulthood. Norman Garmezy and Michael Rutter (1883), and then Haggerty et al. (1994) developed the concept of resilience and relative vulnerability in children.

- Resilience in children seems to be developed when families are cohesive; they pull together and children feel confident of the support of their parents. Under tough social conditions, appropriate interventions, such as the well-funded early education programmes in the USA (page 72), promote feelings of competence in children, at least partly because their parents, too, feel confidence that education is worthwhile.
- The parent involvement part of the programmes appeared to strengthen family beliefs that challenges can be met. Resilient children tend to have loving parents but who also act in an authoritative way, providing boundaries for their children. The more resilient children felt a strong sense of attachment to their parents; they have an emotional grounding to protect against minor and more major disruptions throughout childhood.

Figure 10.6 Children deserve relaxed time and safe space for their childhood

Resilience is unlikely to be developed if parents protect themselves by believing their children are unaffected by distress or disruptive events within the family. Rosie Burrows and Bríd Keenan (2004) offer a good example of what can be done to support adults so that they are able, in turn, to support their children. They describe the Barnardo's project in Northern Ireland, which had strong community roots yet was equally committed to the welfare of children. The project was very supportive of adults, including parents, who coped with very stressful conditions, partly by hoping that their children were not seriously affected. Unfortunately, children are usually only too aware of serious problems in the neighbourhood that affect their family.

The concept of resilience has strong links with other outlooks, such as positive dispositions (page 101) and an outlook of mastery for learning (page 105). Research about children's experiences in hospital has highlighted that even young children can vary in their styles of coping with distressing experiences. Some children were more motivated to seek out information and this orientation can be encouraged. Health psychology and the importance of play in hospital have acknowledged much more that children's well being in hospital is shaped by opportunities for them to understand and influence, where possible, what is happening to them.

What does it mean?

Resilience: an outlook for children characterised by the willingness to confront challenges, with a sense of confidence that it is possible to deal with setbacks and a backdrop of emotional security that familiar adults will help.

Take another **perspective**

In the research about resilience, this concept is not used to mean that children can tolerate random change and adults who ignore their feelings and perspective.

Watch out for rather blasé use of a statement such as 'The children are so resilient'. Does more careful observation suggest that the children have given up expecting their lives to be predictable and have learned to tolerate that life is chaotic?

Robert Brooks and Sam Goldstein (2001, 2003) describe the concept of genuine resilience and the practical applications to families, but the ideas are equally relevant to practitioners.

Resources

- **Alderson, P.** (2000) *Young children's rights: exploring beliefs, principles and practice*. London: Jessica Kingsley.
- **Batmanghelidjh, C.** (2006) *Shattered lives: children who live with courage and dignity*. London: Jessica Kingsley.
- **Barrett, H.** (2003) *Parenting programmes for families at risk: a source book*. London: National Family and Parenting Institute.
- **Brooker, L.** (2002) *Starting school – young children learning cultures*. Buckingham: Open University Press.
- **Brooks, R., Goldstein, S.** (2003) *Nurturing resilience in our children*. New York: McGraw Hill.
- **Burrows, R., Keenan, B.** (2004) *We'll never be the same again*. Barnardo's Northern Ireland. **www.barnardos.org.uk/** and search by title.
- **Caddell, D.** (1998b) *Numeracy counts*. Dundee: Learning and Teaching Scotland.
- **Caddell D.** (2001) *Working with parents: a shared understanding of the curriculum 3–5*. Dundee: Learning and Teaching Scotland.
- **Chang, J.** (1991) *Wild swans*. London: Harper Collins.
- **Clark, A., Moss, P.** (2001) *Listening to young children: the Mosaic approach*. London: National Children's Bureau.
- **Connolly, P., Smith, A. Kelly, B.** (2002) *Too young to notice: the cultural and political awareness of 3–6 year olds in Northern Ireland*. Belfast: Community Relations Council.
- **Cousins, J.** (2003) *Listening to four year olds: how they can help us plan their education and care*. London: National Children's Bureau.

- **Dickins, M. with Denziloe, J.** (2003) *All together: how to create inclusive services for disabled children and their families*. London: National Children's Bureau.
- **Early Childhood Unit** (2004) *Listening as a way of life*. A series of papers available online at **www.earlychildhood.org.uk**
- **EPPE**: *Effective Provision of Pre-School Education Project*. **http://eppe.ioe.ac.uk/** The project is following the children through primary and into secondary school and you can access research papers on this site.
- **Garmezy, N., Rutter, M.** (1983) *Stress, coping and development in children*. New York: McGraw Hill.
- **Haggerty, R., Sherrod, L., Garmezy, N., Rutter, M.** (eds) (1994) *Stress, risk and resilience in children and adolescents: process, mechanisms and interventions*. Cambridge: Cambridge University Press.
- **Hewlett, S.** (1993) *Child neglect in rich nations*. New York: UNICEF.
- **Hope, S.** (2007) *A nurturing environment for children up to three*. London: Islington.
- **Humphreys, M.** (1994) *Empty cradles*. London: Doubleday.
- **Kindlon, D., Thompson, M.** (1999) *Raising Cain: protecting the emotional life of boys*. London: Penguin.
- **Kinney, L., McCabe, J.** (2000) *Children as partners: a guide to consulting with very young children*. Stirling: Stirling Council.
- **Knopp, G.** (2002) *Hitler's children*. Stroud: Sutton Publishing Ltd.
- **Konner, M.** (1991) *Childhood*. London: Little Brown and Co.
- LEARN (Lewisham Early Years Advice and Resource Network) (2002) *A place to learn: developing a stimulating environment*. London: LEARN.
- **Lindon, J.** (2001) *Understanding children's play*. Cheltenham: Nelson Thornes.
- **Lindon, J.** (2006) *Care and caring matter: young children learning through care*. London: Early Education.
- **Lindon, J.** (2007) *Understanding children and young people: development from 5–18 years*. London: Hodder Arnold.
- **Lindon, J.** (2009) *Parents as partners*. London: Practical Pre-School Books.
- **Lindon, J.** (2011a) *Too safe for their own good? Helping children learn about risk and Lifeskills*. London: National Children's Bureau.
- **Lindon, J.** (2012b) *Equality and inclusion in early childhood* (3rd edn). London: Hodder Education.
- **Mayall, B.** (ed.) (1994) *Children's childhoods: observed and experienced*. London: Falmer Press.
- **Mayall, B.** (2002) *Towards a sociology for childhood: thinking from children's lives*. Buckingham: Open University Press.
- **Miller, J.** (1996) *Never too young: how young children can take responsibility and make decisions*. London: Save the Children.
- **Miller, S., Sambell, K.** (eds) (2003) *Contemporary issues in childhood: approaches to teaching and learning*. Newcastle-upon-Tyne: Northumbria University Press.
- **Milner, D.** (1983) *Children and race: 10 years on*. London: Ward Lock.

- **Moss, P., Petrie, P.** (2002) *From children's services to children's spaces: public policy, children and childhood.* London: Routledge Falmer.
- **Moyles, J., Adams, S., Musgrove, A.** (2002) *Study of pedagogical effectiveness in early learning Brief No. 363.* www.education.gov.uk/publications/standard/publicationDetail/Page1/RR363
- **Paley, V.** (2004) *A child's work: the importance of fantasy play.* Chicago and London: Chicago University Press.
- **Siraj-Blatchford, I., Sylva, K., Muttock, S., Gilden, R., Bell, D.** (2002) *Researching Effective Pedagogy in Early Years: Brief No. 356.* www.education.gov.uk/publications/standard/publicationDetail/Page1/RR356
- **Smith, P.** (1994) 'Play and the uses of play', in Moyles, J. (ed.), *The excellence of play.* Buckingham: Open University Press.
- **Thornton, L., Brunton, P.** (2009) *Understanding the Reggio approach: early years education in practice.* London: Routledge.
- **Titman, W.** (1992) *Play, playtime and playgrounds.* Winchester: Learning Through Landscapes/WWF UK.
- **Titman, W.** (1994) *Special places, special people: the hidden curriculum of school grounds.* Winchester: Learning Through Landscapes/WWF UK.
- **Tizard, B., Mortimore, J., Burchell, B.** (1981) *Involving parents in nursery and infant schools.* London: Grant McIntyre.
- **Whiting, B., Edwards, C.** (1988) *Children of different worlds: the formation of social behaviour.* Cambridge MA: Harvard University.
- **Wood, E., Attfield, J.** (1996) *Play, learning and the early childhood curriculum.* London: Paul Chapman.

Using further resources

Finding books and authors

Sometimes you want to track specific books, or further publications by the same author. An internet search by name will bring up information about an author. If you know the publishing company then their website may help, so long as the book is still in print. Increasingly a search on www.amazon.com has become an effective way to track information as well as a means to purchase. A specialist mail order firm will home in on your interests. I use Books Education: **www.bookseducation.com** and Community Insight: **www.communityinsight.co.uk**.

It is wise to use the resources of a college library while you are registered as a student. Some local early years and childcare departments have developed their resource centre to support the growing numbers of practitioners studying for degrees and working towards Early Years Professional status. But do not overlook your local public library. Staff will often track a book around libraries in the same authority or further away. If library staff judge a book to be of general interest, they may buy the title you request.

Using the internet

Confidence on the internet is now an integral part of best early years practice, whether you are currently studying or not. Most organisations and government departments have websites and many have guidance and reports which you can download and print. Increasingly, a great deal of material is only available online. From bitter experience, I recommend you check the length of any document before printing. Longer reports often have a summary at the beginning, or are offered as a summary pdf, as well as the full-length version.

Again, from personal frustrations, I recommend you make a note (written or cut and paste into your working document) of the full address of reports or useful information summaries. You may want to find this item again and also you need full details for a website reference for any bibliography. Sometimes you need additionally to note the route you took within a substantial website. The quality of internal search facilities varies and, if you are getting nowhere, larger sites usually have an email address. I have experienced a good rate of reply to 'Where is it?' queries.

Any website reference within this book was correct when checked in summer 2011. However, websites are reorganised and materials do not stay online forever.

Useful general websites

The following sites are useful for tracking research or keeping up to date. All sites were accessed in August 2011. These are general sites, helpful in addition to the many specific website addresses given within chapters of this book.

Centre for Excellence and Outcomes in Children's and Young People's Services (C4EO) offers research reviews and practical implications. **www.c4eo.org.uk/**

Classics in the History of Psychology is an electronic resource developed by Christopher D. Green at York University, Toronto, Canada. The focus is on research studies and conceptual articles that have had a significant impact on the discipline of psychology. You can access journal articles which would be very hard to track otherwise. **http://psychclassics.yorku.ca/**

Current Education and Children's Services Research – search the database for projects in your area of interest. **www.ceruk.ac.uk/**

Educator's Reference Desk, home of the huge database known as ERIC (Educational Resources Information Center) which can be searched to find articles in educational journals and texts. **www.eduref.org**

Evidence for Policy and Practice Information – which aims to make it easier to access research, with information and research reviews online. **www.eppi.ioe. ac.uk/cms/**

Learning and Teaching Scotland with information about early years (and school) in Scotland, but valuable for anyone elsewhere in the UK. Online resources include the news magazine *Early Years Matters* and a range of practical booklets which have now been put online. **www.ltscotland.org.uk/earlyyears/index.asp**

National Educational Research Forum aimed to address links between research and practice but NERF has now ceased to exist. You can access their six bulletins *Evidence for Teaching and Learning* on this site. **www.eep.ac.uk/nerf/bulletin/index.html**

Scottish Centre for Research in Education – information and summaries of research undertaken in Scotland. The Spotlight section has downloadable research papers. **www.scre.ac.uk**

Skepdic – useful site that challenges some popular areas of research and 'everybody knows'. I found it when researching the 'Mozart Effect'. **www.skepdic.com**

Teaching and Learning Research Programme which offers a wide range of research briefings and commentaries. **www.tlrp.org/**

References

Acredolo, L., Goodwyn, S. (2000) *Baby signs: how to talk with your baby before your baby can talk*. London: Vermilion.

Alderson, P. (2000) *Young children's rights: exploring beliefs, principles and practice*. London: Jessica Kingsley.

Arnold, C. (1999) *Child development and learning 2–5 years: Georgia's story*. London: Paul Chapman.

Arnold, C. (2003) *Observing Harry: child development and learning 0–5*. Maidenhead: Open University Press.

Athey, C. (1990) *Extending thought in young children: a parent–teacher partnership*. London: Paul Chapman.

Attenborough, L., Fahey, R. (2005) *Why do many young children lack basic language skills?* **www.talktoyourbaby.org.uk**

Bain, A., Barnett, L. (1986) *The design of a day care system in a nursery setting for children under five*. London: The Tavistock Institute of Human Relations, Occasional Paper No. 8.

Bandura, A. (1986) *Social foundations of thought and action: a social cognitive theory*. Englewood Cliffs NJ: Prentice Hall.

Baron-Cohen, S. (2003) *The essential difference: men, women and the extreme male brain*. London: Allen Lane.

Barrett, H. (2003) *Parenting programmes for families at risk: a source book*. London: National Family and Parenting Institute.

Batmanghelidjh, C. (2006) *Shattered lives: children who live with courage and dignity*. London: Jessica Kingsley.

Bee, H., and Boyd, L. (2004) *The developing child* (10th edn). Boston: Pearson Education.

Belsky, J., Steinberg, L. (1978) 'The effects of day care – a critical review', *Child development*, vol 49, 929–49.

Belsky, J. (2001) 'Emanuel Miller Lecture – Developmental risks (still) associated with early child care', *Journal of Child Psychology and Psychiatry*, vol 42 , no. 7, 845–59. **http://cep.lse.ac.uk/seminarpapers/23-02-07-BEL.pdf**

Beyer, J., Gammeltoft, L. (2000) *Autism and play*. London: Jessica Kingsley.

Bilton, H. (2002) *Outdoor play in the early years: management and innovation*. London: David Fulton.

Bion, W.R. (1962) *Learning from experience*. London: Heinemann.

Blakemore, S., Frith, U. (2000) *The implications of recent developments in neuroscience for research on teaching and learning*. **www.tlrp.org/pub/acadpub/Blakemore2000.pdf**

Blurton Jones, N. (1967) 'An ethological study of some aspects of social behaviour of children in nursery school', in Morris, D. (ed.) *Primate ethology*. London: Weidenfeld and Nicolson.

Blythe, S. (2004) *The well balanced child: movement and early learning*. Stroud: Hawthorn Press.

Blythe, S. (2008) *What Babies and Children Really Need: how Mothers and Fathers Can Nurture Children's Growth for Health and Well Being*. Stroud: Hawthorn Press.

Boulton, M. (1994) 'Playful and aggressive fighting in the middle school playground' in Blatchford, P., and Sharp, S. (eds) *Breaktime and the school: understanding and changing playground behaviour*. London: Routledge.

Bowlby, J. (1965) *Child care and the growth of love*. Harmondsworth: Penguin.

Boxall, M. (2002) *Nurture groups in school: principles and practice.* London: Paul Chapman Publishing.

Brennan, C. (ed.) (2004) *The power of play: a play curriculum in action.* Dublin: IPPA.

Bridges, D. (2009) '"Evidence-based policy": What evidence? What basis? Whose policy?', *Teaching and Learning Research Briefing,* February no. 74. London: Teaching and Learning Research Programme. **www.tlrp.org/pub/documents/Bridges RB74 Final.pdf**

Bronfenbrenner, U. (1979) *The ecology of human development.* Cambridge MA: Harvard University Press.

Brooker, L. (2002) *Starting school – young children learning cultures.* Buckingham: Open University Press.

Brooks, R., Goldstein, S. (2001) *Raising resilient children.* New York: McGraw Hill.

Brooks, R., Goldstein, S. (2003) *Nurturing resilience in our children.* New York: McGraw Hill.

Brown, D. (1994) 'Play, the playground and the culture of childhood' in Moyles, J. (ed.) *The excellence of play.* Buckingham: Open University Press.

Bruner, J. (1990) *Acts of meaning.* Cambridge MA: Harvard University Press.

Buck, L., Nettleton, L. (2007) *Forest School in Greenwich: Principles into Practice October 2006–July 2007.* London: Greenwich Council.

Buckingham, D. (1996) *Moving images: understanding children's emotional responses to television.* Manchester: Manchester University Press.

Burrows, R., Keenan, B. (2004) *We'll never be the same again*. Barnardo's, Northern Ireland. **www.barnardos.org.uk** – search for 'We'll never be the same'

Byron, T. (2005) *The house of tiny tearaways*. London: BBC Worldwide Ltd.

Caddell, D. (1998a) *Numeracy in the early years: what the research tells us.* Dundee: Learning and Teaching Scotland.

Caddell, D. (1998b) *Numeracy counts.* Dundee: Learning and Teaching Scotland.

Caddell D. (2001) *Working with parents: a shared understanding of the curriculum 3–5.* Dundee: Learning and Teaching Scotland.

Call, N., Featherstone, S. (2003) *The Thinking Child: brain-based learning for the foundation stage.* Stafford: Network Educational Press.

Campbell, R. (1999) *Literacy from home to school: reading with Alice.* Stoke-on-Trent: Trentham Books.

Carr, M. (2001) *Assessment in early childhood settings.* London: Paul Chapman Publishing.

Chang, J. (1991) *Wild swans.* London: Harper Collins.

Charlton, T., Gunter, B., Hannan, A. (eds) (2002) *Broadcast television effects in a remote community.* New Jersey: Lawrence Erlbaum Associates.

Chess, S., Thomson, R. (1996) *Temperament: theory and practice.* New York: Brunner/Mazel Inc.

Christakis, D. (and a team of seven colleagues) (2009) 'Audible television and decreased adult words, infant vocalisations and conversational turns', *Archives of Pediatrics and Adolescent Medicine,* vol 163, no. 6. Summary on **http://archpedi.ama-assn.org/cgi/content/abstract/163/6/554**

Clark, A., Moss, P. (2001) *Listening to young children: the Mosaic approach.* London: National Children's Bureau.

Clarke, Ann, and Clarke, Alan (1998) 'Early experience and the life path', *The Psychologist,* September 1998, pages 433–6. **www.thepsychologist.org.uk/archive** (from this page go to the correct year and month and download this paper)

UNDERSTANDING CHILD DEVELOPMENT 0–8 YEARS

Close, R. (2004) *Television and language development in the early years: a review of the literature.* **www.literacytrust.org.uk/Research/TV.html**

Cole, M., Cole, S. (2000) *The development of children.* Worth Publishers: New York.

Connolly, P., Smith, A., Kelly, B. (2002) *Too young to notice: the cultural and political awareness of 3–6 year olds in Northern Ireland.* Belfast: Community Relations Council.

Cousins, J. (2003) *Listening to four year olds: how they can help us plan their education and care.* London: National Children's Bureau.

David, T., Goouch, S., Powell, S., Abbott, L. (2003) *Birth to three matters: a review of the literature compiled to inform the framework to support children in their earliest years,* London: DFES. **www.haringey.gov.uk/birth_to_three_matters.pdf**

Department for Children, Schools and Families (2007) *Confident, capable and creative: supporting boys' achievements.* **www.teachfind.com/national-strategies/confident-capable-and-creative-supporting-boys-achievements---guidance-practitio**

Devereux, J., Bridges, A. (2004) 'Knowledge and understanding of the world developed through a garden project', in Miller, L., and Devereux, J. (eds) *Supporting children's learning in the early years.* London: David Fulton.

Desforges, C. (2004) 'Talking point', *National Educational Research Forum Bulletin,* Issue 1, Summer. **www.eep.ac.uk/nerf/bulletin/index.html**

Desforges, C., Abouchaar, A. (2003) *The Impact of Parental Involvement, Parental Support and Family Education on Pupil Achievement and Adjustment: a Literature Review.* London: Department for Education and Skills. **www.education.gov.uk/publications/standard/publicationdetail/page1/RR433**

Dickins, M., with Denziloe, J. (2003) *All together: how to create inclusive services for disabled children and their families.* London: National Children's Bureau.

Donaldson, M. (1978) *Children's minds.* London: Fontana.

Donaldson, M. (1992) *Human minds: an exploration.* London: Penguin.

Donaldson, M., Grieve, R., Pratt, C. (eds) (1983) *Early childhood development and education: readings in Psychology.* Oxford: Blackwell.

Dowling, M. (2005) *Supporting young children's sustained shared thinking: an exploration.* DVD and booklets. London: Early Education. **www.early-education.org.uk**

Dowling, M. (2008) *Exploring young children's thinking through their self-chosen activities.* DVD and booklets. London: Early Education. **www.early-education.org.uk**

Dreikurs, R., Soltz, V. (1995) *Happy children: a challenge to parents.* Melbourne: Australian Council for Educational Research.

Drummond, M. (2000) 'Susan Isaacs: pioneering work in understanding children's lives', in Hilton, M., and Hirsch, P. *Practical visionaries: women, education and social progress 1790–1930.* London: Longman.

Dunn, J. (1984) *Sisters and brothers.* London: Fontana.

Dunn, J. (1986) 'Children in a family world' in Richards, M., and Light, P. *Children of social worlds: development in a social context.* Cambridge: Polity Press.

Dunn, J. (1993) *Young children's close relationships beyond attachment.* London: Sage.

Dweck, C.S., Leggett, E. (1988) 'A social-cognitive approach to motivation and personality', *Psychological Review,* 95 (2), 256–73.

Early Childhood Unit, *Everyday Stories.* Descriptive observations from the research undertaken of under-threes in day nurseries during the mid-1990s by Elfer, P., and Selleck, D. **www.everydaystories.org.uk**

Early Childhood Unit (2004) *Listening as a way of life*. A series of papers available online at **www.earlychildhood.org.uk**

Eckerman, C. (1993) 'Imitation and toddlers' achievement of co-ordinated actions with others', in Nadel, J., Camaioni, L. (eds) *New perspectives in early communicative development*. London: Routledge.

Edgington, M. (2002) *The great outdoors: developing children's learning through outdoor provision*. London: Early Education.

EPPE: *Effective Provision of Pre-School Education Project*, **http://eppe.ioe.ac.uk/** The project is following children through primary and into secondary school, and you can access research papers on this site.

Eisenberg, N. (1992) *The caring child*. Cambridge M.A: Harvard University Press.

Elfer, P. (2006) 'Exploring children's expressions of attachment in nursery', *European Early Childhood Education Journal*, vol 14, no. 2, 81–95.

Elfer, P. (2007) 'Babies and young children in nursery: using psychoanalytic ideas to explore tasks and interaction', *Children in Society*, vol 21, no. 2, 111–22.

Elfer, P., Goldschmied, E., Selleck, D. (2003) *Key persons in the nursery: building relationships for quality provision*. London: David Fulton.

Eliot, L. (2009) *Pink brain, blue brain: how small differences grow into troublesome gaps and what we can do about it*. New York: Houghton Mifflin Harcourt. Access presentation at **http://fora.tv/2009/09/29/Lise_Eliot_Pink_Brain_Blue_Brain**

Fabian, H. (2002) *Children starting school*. London: David Fulton.

Fajerman, L., Jarrett, M., Sutton, F. (2000) *Children as partners in planning: a training resource to support consultation with children*. London: Save the Children.

Featherstone, S. (ed.) (2008) *Again, Again: Understanding Schemas in Young Children*. London: A&C Black.

Garmezy, N., Rutter, M. (1983) *Stress, coping and development in children*. New York: McGraw Hill.

Gerhardt, S. (2004) *Why love matters: how affection shapes a baby's brain*. Hove: Routledge.

Gesell, A. (1954) *The first five years of life*. London: Methuen.

Gibbens, J. (1950) *Care of children from one to five* (4th edn). London: J&A Churchill Ltd.

Gill, T. (2007) *No fear: growing up in a risk-averse society*. London: Calouste Gulbenkian; summary and full book on **www.gulbenkian.org.uk**

Goldschmied, E. (1986) *Infants at Work: Babies of 6–9 Months Exploring Everyday Objects* (DVD). London: National Children's Bureau. **www.ncb.org.uk**

Goldschmied, E., Hughes, A. (1992) *Heuristic Play with Objects: Children of 12–20 Months Exploring Everyday Objects* (DVD). London: National Children's Bureau.

Goldschmied, E., Jackson, S. (2004) *People under three: young children in day care*. London: Routledge.

Goleman, D. (1996) *Emotional intelligence – why it can matter more than IQ*. London: Bloomsbury.

Gopnik, A. (2009) *The philosophical baby: what children's minds tell us about truth, love and the meaning of life*. London: Bodley Head. Also a conversational feature on **www.edge.org/3rd_culture/gopnik09/gopnik09_index.html**

Gopnik, A., Meltzoff, A., Kuhl, P. (2001) *How babies think: the science of childhood*. London: Phoenix.

Goswami, U. (2003) 'How to beat dyslexia', *The Psychologist,* volume 16, no. 9. **www.thepsychologist.org.uk/archive/archive_home.cfm?volumeID=16&editionID=98&ArticleID=598** (This is a useful general article about the task of reading.)

Gottman, J., Declaire, J. (1997) *The heart of parenting: how to raise an emotionally intelligent child.* London: Bloomsbury.

Graham, P. (2009) *A biography of Susan Isaacs: a life freeing children's minds.* London: Karnac Books. (I accessed some chapters online with a search of Jean Piaget + Susan Isaacs.)

Haggerty, R., Sherrod, L., Garmezy, N., Rutter, M. (eds) (1994) *Stress, risk and resilience in children and adolescents: process, mechanisms and interventions.* Cambridge: Cambridge University Press.

Hardyment, C. (1995) *Perfect parents: baby care advice past and present.* Oxford: Oxford Paperbacks.

Harris, A., Goodall, J. (2007) *Engaging parents in raising achievement – do parents know they matter?* Brief No DCSF – RBW004. London: Department for Children Schools and Families. **www.education.gov.uk/publications/standard/publicationdetail/page1/DCSF-RW004**

Healy, J. (2004) *Your child's growing mind: brain development and learning from birth to adolescence.* New York: Broadway Books.

Henry, M. (1996) *Young children, parents and professionals: enhancing the links in early childhood.* London: Routledge.

Hewlett, S. (1993) *Child neglect in rich nations.* New York: UNICEF.

Holland, P. (2003) *We don't play with guns here: war, weapons and superhero play in the early years.* Maidenhead: Open University Press.

Hope, S. (2007) *A nurturing environment for children up to three.* London: Islington.

Howard-Jones, P. (undated, *circa* 2008) *Neuroscience and Education: Issues and Opportunities.* London: Teaching and Learning Research Programme. **www.tlrp.org/pub/commentaries.html**

Hughes, A. (2006) *Developing play for the under 3s: the Treasure Basket and Heuristic Play.* London: David Fulton.

Hughes, A., Ellis, S. (1998) *Writing it right? Children writing 3–8.* Learning and Teaching Scotland: Dundee.

Hughes, M. (1983) 'What is difficult about learning arithmetic?', in Donaldson, M., Grieve, R., Pratt, C. (eds) *Early childhood development and education: readings in psychology.* Oxford: Blackwell.

Hughes, M. (1986) *Children and number.* Oxford: Blackwell.

Hughes, M., Grieve, R. (1983) 'On asking children bizarre questions', in Donaldson, M., Grieve, R., and Pratt, C. (eds) *Early childhood development and education: readings in psychology.* Oxford: Blackwell.

Humphreys, M. (1994) *Empty cradles.* London: Doubleday.

Isaacs, S. (1929) *The nursery years.* London: Routledge and Kegan Paul.

Jabadao (undated) *Developmental Movement Play.* Leeds: Jabadao. **www.jabadao.org/?p=developmental.movement.play**

Karmiloff-Smith, A. (1994) *Baby it's you: a unique insight into the first three years of the developing baby.* London: Ebury Press.

Kenner, C. (2000) *Home pages: literacy links for bilingual children.* Stoke-on-Trent: Trentham Books.

Kenner, C. (2004) *Becoming biliterate: young children learning different writing systems,* Stoke-on-Trent: Trentham.

Kindlon, D., Thompson, M. (1999) *Raising Cain: protecting the emotional life of boys.* London: Penguin.

Kinney, L., McCabe, J. (2000) *Children as partners: a guide to consulting with very young children.* Stirling: Stirling Council.

Knopp, G. (2002) *Hitler's children*. Stroud: Sutton Publishing Ltd.

Konner, M. (1991) *Childhood.* London: Little, Brown and Co.

Laishley, J. (1984) *'Taking responsibility for young children: Who? Where? When – a consideration of issue, evidence and implications.'* Discussion Paper 1 for the National Nursery Examination Board. London: NNEB.

LEARN (Lewisham Early Years Advice and Resource Network) (2002) *A place to learn: developing a stimulating environment.* London: LEARN.

Learning and Teaching Scotland (2010) *Pre-birth to Three: Positive Outcomes for Scotland's Children and Families.* www.ltscotland.org.uk/earlyyears/

Lindon, J. (2001) *Understanding children's play.* Cheltenham: Nelson Thornes.

Lindon, J. (2006) *Care and caring matter: young children learning through care.* London: Early Education.

Lindon, J. (2007) *Understanding children and young people: development from 5–18 years.* London: Hodder Arnold.

Lindon, J. (2008) *What does it means to be five? A practical guide to child development in the Early Years Foundation Stage.* London: Practical Pre-School Books.

Lindon, J. (2009) *Parents as partners: positive relationships in the early years.* London: Practical Pre-School Books.

Lindon, J. (2010a) *The key person approach.* London: Practical Pre-School Books.

Lindon, J. (2010b) *Child-initiated learning.* London: Practical Pre-School Books.

Lindon, J. (2011a) *Too safe for their own good? Helping children learn about risk and life skills.* London: National Children's Bureau.

Lindon, J. (2011b) *Supporting Children's Social Development.* London: Practical Pre-School Books.

Lindon, J. (2012a) *Safeguarding and child protection 0–8 years* (4th edn). London: Hodder Education.

Lindon, J. (2012b) *Equality and inclusion in early childhood* (3rd edn). London: Hodder Education.

Lindon, J. (2012c) *Reflective practice and early years professionalism* (2nd edn). London: Hodder Education.

Lindon, J. (2012d) *Understanding children's behaviour: play, development and learning* (2nd edn). London: Hodder Education.

Lindon, J. (2012e) *What does it mean to be one? A practical guide to child development in the Early Years Foundation Stage*. A set of four books, for each year of early childhood, so also *What does it mean to be two? (three?, four?).* London: Practical Pre-School Books.

Locke, A., Ginsborg, J. (2003) 'Spoken language in the early years: the cognitive and linguistic development of three- to five-year-old children from socio-economically deprived backgrounds', *Educational and Child Psychology,* 20 (4), 68–79.

Maclellan, E., Munn, P., Quinn, V. (2003) *Thinking about maths: a review of issues in teaching number from 5 to 14 years.* Glasgow: Learning and Teaching Scotland.

MacNaughton, G., Rolfe, S., Siraj-Blatchford, I. (2001) *Doing early childhood research: international perspectives on theory and practice.* Buckingham: Open University Press.

MacNaughton, G., Williams, G. (2004) *Teaching young children: choices in theory and practice.* Maidenhead: Open University Press.

Manning-Morton, J. (2006) 'The personal is professional: professionalism and the birth to three practitioner', *Contemporary issues in early childhood*, volume 7, no. 1.

Marsden, L., Woodbridge, J. (2005) *Looking closely at learning and teaching… a journey of development.* Outlane: Early Excellence. **www.earlyexcellence.com**

Mayall, B. (ed.) (1994) *Children's childhoods: observed and experienced.* London: Falmer Press.

Mayall, B. (2002) *Towards a sociology for childhood: thinking from children's lives.* Buckingham: Open University Press.

Maybin, J., Woodhead, M. (eds) (2003) *Childhoods in context.* Milton Keynes: Open University Press.

Meggitt, C., Sutherland, G. (2000) *Child development: an illustrated guide – birth to 8 years.* London: Heinemann.

Miller, J. (1996) *Never too young: how young children can take responsibility and make decisions.* London: Save the Children.

Miller, S., Sambell, K. (eds) (2003) *Contemporary issues in childhood: approaches to teaching and learning.* Newcastle-upon-Tyne: Northumbria University Press.

Milner, D. (1983) *Children and race: 10 years on.* London: Ward Lock.

Moore, S.C., Carter, L.M., van Goozen, S.H.M. (2009) 'Confectionary consumption in childhood and adult violence', *British Journal of Psychiatry*, no. 195, 366–7. You can find a summary on **www.rcpsych.ac.uk/pressparliament/pressreleases2009/confectionaryconsumption.aspx**

Morton, S. (2002) *Promoting number and mathematical development in nursery through staff development.* **www.pre-online.co.uk/feature pdfs/spotlight88.pdf**

Moss, P., Petrie, P. (2002) *From children's services to children's spaces: public policy, children and childhood.* London: Routledge Falmer.

Moyles, J., Adams, S., and Musgrove, A. (2002) *Study of pedagogical effectiveness in early learning Brief No. 363.* **www.education.gov.uk/publications/standard/publicationDetail/Page1/RR363**

Munn, P. (1997a) 'What do children know about reading before they go to school?' in Owen, P., Pumfrey, P. (eds) *Emergent and developing reading: messages for teachers.* London: Falmer Press.

Munn, P. (1997b) 'Children's beliefs about counting', in Thompson, I. (ed.) *Teaching and learning early number.* Buckingham: Open University Press.

Murray, L., Trevarthen, C. (1985) 'Emotional regulation of interactions between two-month-olds and their mothers', in Field, T.M., Fox, N.A. (eds) *Social perception in infants.* Norwood NJ: Ablex.

Murray, L., Andrews, L. (2000) *The social baby.* Richmond: The Children's Project.

Mynard, S. (2008) *Making provision for how boys learn best.* **www.teachingexpertise.com/articles/making-provision-for-how-boys-learn-best-3130**

Nabuzoka, D., Smith, P. (1999) 'Distinguishing serious and playful fighting by children with learning disabilities and nondisabled children', *Journal of Child Psychology and Psychiatry and Allied Disciplines*, vol 40, 833–90.

Newsom, E. (1992) 'The barefoot play therapist: adapting skills for a time of need', in Lane, D., Miller, A. (eds) *Child and adolescent therapy: a handbook.* Buckingham: Open University Press.

Nutbrown, C., Hannon, P., and Morgan, A. (2005) *Early literacy work with families: policy, practice and research.* London: Sage.

Oates, J. (ed.) (2007) *Attachment Relationships – Quality of Care for Young Children.* London: Bernard Van Leer Foundation. **www.bernardvanleer.org**

Ouvry, M. (2000) *Exercising muscles and minds: outdoor play and the early years curriculum.* London: National Children's Bureau.

Paley, V. (1984) *Boys and girls: superheroes in the doll corner.* Chicago: University of Chicago Press.

Paley, V. (1988) *Bad guys don't have birthdays: fantasy play at four.* Chicago: University of Chicago Press.

Paley, V. (2004) *A child's work: the importance of fantasy play.* Chicago and London: Chicago University Press.

Pascal, C., Bertram, T. (eds) (1997) *Effective early learning: case studies in improvement.* London: Hodder and Stoughton.

Pinker, S. (1994) *The language instinct: how the mind creates language.* New York: Morrow.

Pugh, G., De'Ath, E., Smith, C. (1994) *Confident parents, confident children: policy and practice in parent education and support.* London: National Children's Bureau.

Reeves, R. (2004) 'Economy-friendly families', in Diamond, P., Katwala, S., Munn, M. (eds) *Family fortunes: the new politics of childhood.* London: Fabian Society.

Reid, J. (1983) 'Into print: reading and language growth', in Donaldson, M., Grieve, R., Pratt, C. (eds) *Early childhood development and education: readings in psychology.* Oxford: Blackwell.

Rich, D. (2003) 'Bang, bang! Gun play and why children need it', *Early Education*, Summer. **www.richlearningopportunities.co.uk**

Rich, D., Casanova, D., Dixon, A., Drummond, M., Durrant, A., Myer, C. (2005) *First hand experiences: what matters to children.* Clopton: Rich Learning Opportunities (details on above website).

Rich, D., Drummond, M., Myer, C. (2008) *Learning: what matters to children.* Clopton: Rich Learning Opportunities.

Ridler, C. (2002) 'Teachers, children and number understanding', Conference paper, British Psychological Society Psychology of Education Conference, University College, Worcester.

Riley, D. (1993) *War in the nursery: theories of the child and mother.* London: Virago.

Roberts, J. (2000) 'The rhetoric must match the practice', *Early Years Educator,* 2(5), 26–27.

Robertson, J., Robertson, J. (1989) *Separation and the very young.* London: Free Association Books.

Robinson, E., Robinson, P. (1983) 'Ways of reacting to communication failure in relation to the development of the child's understanding about verbal communication', in Donaldson, M., Grieve, R., and Pratt, C. (eds) *Early childhood development and education: readings inn psychology.* Oxford: Basil Blackwell.

Rogoff, B. (1990) *Apprenticeship in thinking: cognitive development in social context.* Oxford: Oxford University Press.

Rutter, M. (1972) *Maternal Deprivation Re-assessed.* London: Penguin.

Rutter, M. (1999) 'English and Romanian Adoptees Study (ERA)', in Ceci, S., Williams, W. (eds) *The nature-nurture debate*. Blackwell: Malden Massachusetts.

Schafer, M., Smith, P. (1996) 'Teachers' perceptions of play fighting and real fighting in primary school', *Educational Research* 38(2), 173–81.

Schaffer, H. (1998) *Making decisions about children: psychological questions and answers*. Oxford: Blackwell Publishing.

Sheridan, M. (1960) *Children's developmental progress from birth to five years: the Stycar sequences*. Windsor: National Foundation for Educational Research.

Sheridan, M. (1977) *Spontaneous play in early childhood: from birth to six years*. Windsor: National Foundation for Educational Research.

Shore, R. (1997) *Rethinking the brain: new insights into early development*. New York: Families and Work Institute.

Siraj-Blatchford, I., Sylva, K., Muttock, S., Gilden, R., and Bell, D. (2002) *Researching Effective Pedagogy in Early Years: Brief No. 356*. **www.education.gov.uk/publications/standard/publicationDetail/Page1/RB356**

Siren Films Ltd (2006) *Exploratory play*. DVD and booklet. Newcastle-upon-Tyne: Siren Films Ltd. **www.sirenfilms.co.uk**

Siren Films Ltd (2008) *The Wonder Year*. DVD and booklet. Newcastle-upon-Tyne: Siren Films Ltd. **www.sirenfilms.co.uk**

Siren Films Ltd (2009) *Firm foundations for early literacy from 0 to 5 years*. DVD and booklet. Newcastle-upon-Tyne: Siren Films Ltd. **www.sirenfilms.co.uk**

Sightlines Initiative (2001) *Rising Sun Woodland Pre-school Project*. DVD. Newcastle-on-Tyne: Sightlines Initiative. **www.sightlines-initiative.com**

Skynner, R., Cleese, J. (1997) *Families and how to survive them*. London: Vermilion.

Slaby, R., Roedell, W., Arezzo, D., Hendrix, K. (1995) *Early violence prevention: tools for teachers of young children*. Washington DC: National Association for the Education of Young Children.

Smith, P. (1994) 'Play and the uses of play', in Moyles, J. (ed.) *The excellence of play*. Buckingham: Open University Press.

Sylva, K. (1994) 'The impact of early learning on children's later development', in Ball, C., *Start right: the importance of early learning*. London: Royal Society of the Arts.

Tayler, C. (2007) 'The brain, development and learning in early childhood', in Centre for Educational Research and Innovation, *Understanding the Brain: the Birth of a Learning Science*, Part II, 161–83. **www.oecd.org/dataoecd/39/53/40554190.pdf**

The Children's Project (2004) *The social baby*. DVD. Richmond: The Children's Project/NSPCC. **www.childrensproject.co.uk/**

Thomson, J., Tolmie, A., Foot, H., McLaren, B. (1996) *Child development and the aims of road safety education*. London: HMSO.

Thornton, L., Brunton, P. (2009) *Understanding the Reggio approach: early years education in practice*. London: Routledge.

Titman, W. (1992) *Play, playtime and playgrounds*. Winchester: Learning Through Landscapes/WWF UK.

Titman, W. (1994) *Special places, special people: the hidden curriculum of school grounds*. Winchester: Learning Through Landscapes/WWF UK.

Tizard, B., Mortimore, J., Burchell, B. (1981) *Involving parents in nursery and infant schools*. London: Grant McIntyre.

Tizard, B. (1986) *The care of young children: implications of recent research.* London: Thomas Coram Research Unit Occasional Papers, no. 1.

Tizard, B. (2009) 'The making and breaking of attachment theory', *The Psychologist* October, vol 22 no. 10. **www.bps.org.uk/thepsychologist**

Tizard, B., Hughes, M. (2002) *Young children learning: talking and thinking at home and at school.* Oxford: Blackwell.

Tobin, J., Wu, D., Davidson, D. (1989) *Preschool in three cultures.* Cambridge MA: Harvard University Press.

Togerson, C., Brooks, G., Hall, J. (2006) *A systematic review of the research literature on the use of phonics in the teaching of reading and spelling.* **www.education.gov.uk/publications/RSG/Developingreadingwritingandnumericalskills/Page1/RR711**

Tough, J. (1976) *Listening to children talking.* London: Ward Lock.

Trevarthen, C., Barr, I., Dunlop, A., Gjersoe, N., Marwick, H., Stephen, C. (2003) *Meeting the needs of children from birth to three years.* Edinburgh: Scottish Executive. Download the summary on **www.scotland.gov.uk/Publications/2003/06/17458/22696 or the full report on www.scotland.gov.uk/Resource/Doc/933/0007610.pdf**

Vygotsky, L. (1962) *Thought and language.* Cambridge MA: MIT Press.

Vygotsky, L. (1978) *Mind in society: the development of higher psychological processes.* Cambridge MA: Harvard University Press.

Ward, S. (2004) *Baby talk.* London: Arrow.

Warden, C. (2005) *The potential of a puddle.* Perthshire: Mindstretchers.

Warden, C. (2006) *Talking and Thinking Floorbooks: using 'Big Book Planners' to consult children.* Perthshire: Mindstretchers.

White, J. (2007) *Playing and learning outdoors.* London: Routledge Falmer.

Whiting, B., Edwards, C. (1988) *Children of different worlds: the formation of social behaviour.* Cambridge MA: Harvard University.

Waterman, A., Blades, M., Spencer, C. (2001) 'Is a jumper angrier than a tree?', *The Psychologist,* volume 14, no. 9. **www.bps.org.uk/publications/thepsychologist/search-the-psychologist-online.cfm**

Wood, E., Attfield, J. (1996) *Play, learning and the early childhood curriculum.* London: Paul Chapman.

Zeedyk, S. (2008) *Do Baby Buggies Affect Development?* **www.literacytrust.org.uk/talk_to_your_baby/news/1553_do_baby_buggies_affect_development**

Index